IMPETUOUS HEART

Impetuous heart be still, be still,
Your sorrowful love can never be told,
Cover it up with a lonely tune.
He who could bend all things to His will
Has covered the door of the infinite fold
With the pale stars and the wandering moon.
—from *The Countess Cathleen,*
W. B. Yeats

Impetuous Heart

The Story of Ethel Smyth

LOUISE COLLIS

WILLIAM KIMBER · LONDON

First published in 1984 by
WILLIAM KIMBER & CO. LIMITED
100 Jermyn Street, London, SW1Y 6EE

*Phototypesetting by Grove Graphics
and printed and bound in Great Britain by
The Garden City Press Limited,
Letchworth, Hertfordshire, SG6 1JS*

Contents

List of Illustrations

Acknowledgements

I am indebted to the Arts Council whose grant enabled me to write this book, and to the following persons for permission to quote and numerous kindnesses: Quentin Bell; the British Library; the late Sir Patrick Coghill; B. I. R. Davidson; D. R. Davidson; Miss N. M. Davidson; Mrs Angelica Garnett; the Humanities Research Center, University of Texas; Mrs R. D. Jeanes; H. C. E. Johnson and Lawrence Graham Middleton Lewis; Mrs Terence Johnston; Letcher and Son; the New York Public Library; Nigel Nicolson; Derek Parker; Miss Antonia Raeburn; Raleigh Trevelyan; the University of North Carolina, Greensboro; Miss Avril Wood; The Trustees of the Maurice Baring Will Trust; Shirley, Lady Beecham and Messrs Hutchinson for passages from *A Mingled Chime* by Sir Thomas Beecham; Rev Michael Hollings; Frank Magro for passages from Sir Osbert Sitwell's *Left Hand, Right Hand*; National Portrait Gallery, London; The Museum of London; The Royal College of Music; Queen's University, Belfast; Sir Stephen Spender; Virago Ltd for passages from *The Suffragette Movement* by Sylvia Pankhurst; The Literary Estate of Virginia Woolf and the Hogarth Press for passages from *The Letters of Virginia Woolf*, ed Nigel Nicolson; The estate of Christabel Pankhurst and Hutchinson Publishing Group Ltd; Michael B. Yeats and Macmillan London Ltd for some lines from *The Countess Cathleen* by W. B. Yeats; the four lines from *The Dance of Death* (copyright W. H. Auden) are quoted by permission of Curtis Brown Ltd.

CHAPTER ONE

Early Days

No one could have been conceived on a more appropriate date than Ethel Smyth, musician extraordinary. It happened in the year of the Indian Mutiny, 1857. Her parents were on leave from India – her father being in the army there – accompanied by their eldest girl and a boy, Alice and Johnny. Unfortunately, however, they had left little Mary, somewhat past her first birthday, with cousins in that country and it was quite a question as to what might have become of her. Under these agitating circumstances, the father hurriedly sailed east again, leaving his wife to bear Ethel on 23 April 1858 at Sidcup in Kent. The child turned out a lifelong mutineer.

Once Mary had been safely recovered and dispatched home, the household consisted, in addition to Mrs Smyth and the four children, of the in-laws. Grandfather Smyth was about ninety, of Irish extraction, once in the cavalry, veteran of many famous engagements, a great drinker, especially of port, and with a rough and ready military style of humour. In later life, Ethel felt she would have had much in common with him, but her memories were not altogether pleasant, chiefly because he had to be kissed goodnight and the feel of such enormous age against her lips revolted her. Grandmother Smyth was an indistinct shadow in the vicinity of the old reprobate.

The maternal grandmother lived in Paris and was regarded as not respectable, mainly, it seems, because she was separated from her second husband and had various male friends, though there was no hard evidence that any of them were her lovers. Her name was not mentioned before the children. Subsequently Ethel discovered that she had been in the habit of holding musical evenings which were frequented by eminent members of the profession, such as Chopin.

Mrs Smyth's early childhood had therefore been unconventional and she spoke perfect French. But at a certain stage, her relations removed her to England for what they considered a proper education. The girl was persuaded that her mother was an undesirable person, perhaps even that she had, as was alleged, enormous cupboards in her bedroom for the swift concealment of secret visitors. Nevertheless, there was an enduring bond between them. When Mrs Smyth was handed a telegram announcing her mother's death, she fainted dead away under an acacia tree.

In 1867 General Smyth was appointed to the command of the artillery at Aldershot and the family moved to Frimley nearby. England was an agreeable place for the middle classes in the victorian era. Never had they been so prosperous, or enjoyed such material comfort. These were the chief inheritors of the industrial revolution which had catapulted society from an essentially agricultural, and even feudal, world into one of proliferating cities connected by railways. Britannia ruled the waves. The British empire encircled the globe and still expanded: the interior of Africa, where Livingstone fitfully wandered, was as yet unclaimed. But perhaps the victorians' greatest gift was for peace, at home and abroad. There had been no major war since 1815. The Crimean adventure of 1854 was short and remote, as were the Mutiny, the Chinese opium wars, and the lesser skirmishes Lord Palmerston settled by the dispatch of a gunboat or two. The revolutionary movements which had erupted in Europe in 1848, bringing Garibaldi to Rome, tumbling Louis Philippe, passed England by. The condition of the poor was wretched, yet their efforts to obtain better wages, shorter hours, the suffrage and the formation of trade unions met with just enough success to obviate the need to do away with the existing social order by violence. There were riots and agitations, but not republicanism or sudden attempts at democracy on the continental model.

The Smyths lived according to the conventions of their class and position: plenty of servants indoors and out, governesses, dinner parties with local notabilities, dances, tea parties, picnics, hunting and other sports, visits to friends in different parts of the country and trips abroad. They were firm upholders of the Church of England, at the time much disturbed by Darwin's heretical work *On the Origin of Species by means of Natural Selection*, published in 1859, which plainly demolished the idea that God created heaven and earth and everything in them within the space of a week in 4004 BC. The parents were careful not to speak of anything that could remotely be called delicate in front of their eight children. If they thought the conversation at meals was getting dangerous, they continued in Hindustani. Although the general naturally considered discipline important, he was essentially a good-natured, easy-going man, always cheerful and popular with everyone. But he did have certain fixed ideas destined to cause friction between himself and Ethel. One was that all artists, like foreigners, were of low moral fibre.

His wife never openly disputed this dictum, though with her background and character she can hardly have believed it as staunchly as he did. She was in many ways an unhappy woman. Nothing could be more delightful than her good moods, but she suffered from depression at times and would frequently get up very early in the morning and make a pilgrimage round the children's bedrooms, accusing each in turn of having been spiteful to her, of having been unkind, of conspiring to humiliate her in public and similar imaginary crimes. She was also a vociferous complainer in the ordinary sense. Many furious quarrels arose out of small incidents. Ethel was her chief antagonist. This had a profound effect on the girl's emotional development.

She was, and always remained, devoted to her mother, the one member of the family fitted to understand her aspirations. She knew that her love was returned, but it was impossible to obtain from such a character the steady maternal support particularly necessary to one as volatile as Ethel, a child of strong will, given to tantrums. Perhaps they were too much alike. If Ethel had been calmer, less demanding of reassurance, her mother might have been able to manage better. But Mrs Smyth was herself an infant. She had no control over her moods. She might enchant her daughter, drown her with tenderness and then, unpredictably, reproach her, shun her, try to force the child to take the place of the mother and offer sympathy for grievances as desperate as they were unreal.

Looking back on her girlhood in later years, Ethel came to the conclusion that, in spite of all the gaiety and bustle of a large and energetic family, she had been basically unhappy. She could not withstand the violence of her emotions, did not know how to cope with them, had no one to turn to. Her life was punctuated by the search for a woman who would supply her mother's deficiencies.

It is remarkable that General Smyth retained his equilibrium against a tumultuous background that would have made mincemeat of many another old soldier. It was not so immediately bloody as the Mutiny, but was, in its own fashion, as lethal and there was no end to it. On retiring from the army, he decided to remain in Frimley, where he had many congenial acquaintances and friends who soon had him on the bench and in charge of other county work.

The district had the added advantage of an indefinite supply of presentable young officers which was a necessity for a father of six daughters. This was especially relevant after the Indian bank where he kept his capital failed. All at once, money became tight, a situation aggravated by Mrs Smyth's habit of suddenly taking a dislike to perfectly good carpets and curtains and ordering new ones. He did what he could to economize in those departments of domestic affairs that were more or less under his control. Horses were a case in point. He bought the cheapest he could find, that was to say ones not fully trained. When harnessed to the family carriage, these animals were hardly drivable, for they shied at everything, bolted at the slightest excuse and were quite likely to end up in the ditch, the adjacent Basingstoke canal, on the railway line, or any awkward place happening to be handy. Smyth accidents became a legend in the neighbourhood.

Luckily the education of daughters was not expensive. The general did not subscribe to the new-fangled idea that girls should study the same subjects as boys, even going to one of the modern boarding establishments and then to a university college. How could Latin, Greek, mathematics, science fit a woman for wife and motherhood? So much for the famous headmistresses Miss Buss and Miss Beale, the founders of Queen's and Bedford Colleges, and all their works. A smattering of French, German, sketching, sewing, music, and a good grounding in nice manners were enough to qualify girls for the task of inducing the presentable young men to assume the burden of their support.

In such a household as the Smyths' the governesses succeeded one another at a smart rate. The incumbent in 1870 when Ethel was twelve happened to be an ex-student of the Leipzig conservatorium. Instead of the usual drawing-room tinklings, she played Beethoven sonatas. It was the first time Ethel had heard classical music. She was overwhelmed. Suddenly, as in a conversion, she became aware that she was an artist and that music was her sphere. Her life was transformed. She determined to go to Leipzig and attend this conservatorium of which the Fräulein spoke, as soon as she was old enough.

It was a sensible ambition. For although literature, poetry, painting flourished in nineteenth-century England, music was very much the cinderella of the arts, Sterndale Bennett being almost sole luminary until the late 1870s when Stanford, Parry, Mackenzie and Sullivan heralded the renaissance. The Philharmonic and Hallé orchestras gave regular concerts, but these were almost invariably of foreign works, especially German, and by foreign artists.

Meanwhile Ethel and her next sister Mary were found too turbulent for the schoolroom and their father was obliged to send them to a classy establishment in Putney for a couple of years, in spite of the expense and his principles. There, it was hoped, they would learn discipline in addition to the other subjects on the curriculum. As they were not expelled, it is to be presumed that their behaviour moderated. Mary was, in any case, less wild than Ethel who had been in the habit of leading her into all sorts of tomboyish adventures that she would never otherwise have entertained.

Ethel was by this time fourteen – it was 1872 – and quite uneducated in a formal way, but, as in most victorian homes, the bookshelves contained a wide selection of the classics, and also contemporary authors such as Dickens, Thackeray, Trollope, Tennyson, perhaps even Ruskin, the Rossettis, Swinburne, Browning. Ethel had already acquired the habit of voracious reading without which a mind can never be properly cultivated. She wrote plays, stories and poems, although she had no literary ambitions, her attention being fixed on music: she was now studying all the great composers.

Her poems were often on the subject of unrequited love. For, as is usual with adolescent girls, especially when shut up in a boarding school, she had a series of heroines whom she worshipped, recording their names and attributes in a special book. Perhaps there was something keener, more poignant, in her feeling than was common since her nature was essentially passionate, volcanic and slightly hysterical.

'I set to music and dedicated to a latest "passion", a very religious woman whose name was Louisa Lady Sitwell, a long piece of sacred poetry,' she wrote of the year 1875.[1] It was a moment when she thought of becoming a nun, and doubtless of composing great masses in the manner of Beethoven. It crossed her mind, too, that it wouldn't be a bad idea to marry a rich man, a duke say, who would give her the background and the funds for a fine musical career. But mostly she reiterated that she must go to the Leipzig conservatorium.

The general found this exceedingly obstinate and tiresome. Whenever she mentioned the project, which was frequently, he would reply: 'Damned nonsense!' and apply himself to *The Times*. He did not believe in her musical abilities. It was just another of her crazes. Why should he have to pay for her to waste a couple of years, perhaps more, in Germany? She should get married immediately, like the two elder girls, Alice and Mary, who were to have a double wedding in a few months. Damned nonsense.

In the event, he had three children less on his hands by the end

[1] *Impressions That Remained*, Ethel Smyth, 1919.

of 1875. For his elder son Johnny, a most promising lad, had gradually declined into an invalid state after having what seemed a trivial riding accident. One evening at dinner he said, 'How queer, I can't read the letters on this biscuit', sank into a coma and died soon after.

Mrs Smyth never really got over her grief. Johnny was her favourite by a long way. Her moods became even more unpredictable, her quarrels more ferocious, especially with Ethel, her extravagances wilder. Her health also deteriorated. She was beginning to suffer from arthritis and deafness. When she could not hear all the conversation at table, she was apt to believe that people were whispering conspiracies against her. Her chief misfortune was, perhaps, that she had the artistic temperament to excess without any gifts to balance it. She was not interested enough in music, or books, or anything in particular, to apply her mind and discover the peace and happiness conferred by the practice of the arts. She was perpetually bored. The general, whose days were busy with the county court and various charitable organizations, took to lunching out rather frequently, with ladies on occasion.

The next event in Ethel's life was the arrival in Aldershot of Alexander Ewing, composer of the famous hymn 'Jerusalem the Golden'. He was in the Army Service Corps. There was much excitement in the Smyth household. Even the general was somewhat stirred. Though he didn't care for music, his dislike being aggravated by Ethel's continual playing, singing, and talk of it, he admired hymns. Mrs Ewing was literary, writing stories for children under the name of Aunt Judy.

Mrs Smyth called on Mrs Ewing. Ethel, the eternal schoolgirl, immediately became infatuated with the new friend, who accepted her devotion with good humour, only once protesting at the amount of gush to which she was subjected. It had the same effect on her, she said, as continual pious maxims. For the rest, she polished up the articles Ethel wrote for the parish magazine and declared that the girl had the makings of a writer. Mr Ewing requested her to play her compositions, whereupon he said she was a born musician who should have proper lessons. He himself was prepared to start her off with a course in harmony.

General Smyth took strong exception to these arrangements. Just when he had hopes that the stupid girl would settle down with one of the numerous young artillerymen he had provided for her choice, this interfering Ewing began encouraging her to think of herself as an infant genius. As if she wasn't already vain and difficult enough

16

Major-General John Smyth in India, 1852. (This and the photograph that follows it are reproduced from damaged originals)

Mrs Smyth and her eldest daughter Alice in India, 1852

without his help. The fellow was a cad. He was artistic. His hair was too long, his tie too loose, his shoes dingy. Besides, he was only in the Service Corps. After fulminating for some while, however, he succumbed to the combined assault of Ethel and his wife, who regularly changed sides and was, at the moment, against him. He agreed, with foreboding, that Ethel should take the pony trap twice a week to the Ewings' quarters in the camp.

Ethel felt herself moving in cultured circles at last. Mr Ewing introduced her to the splendours of Wagner, then still extant, singing all the parts and playing as much of the orchestration as he could on the piano. His pupil immediately decided to become a composer of operas. She would have one produced in Germany before she was forty, she swore. This actually came true at Weimar in 1898. There was naturally much talk of Leipzig, as her father had feared, which was considered the capital of the musical world, in Aldershot at least.

Mr Ewing produced scores by Berlioz and annotated them for her. He spoke of Brahms, the greatest living German composer, who was to be seen actually walking about in Leipzig. He gave her Schumann; and Liszt's newest work. She accompanied him and his wife to concerts in London. They discussed all manner of philosophical ideas. Ethel was at her best because she was happy. Mrs Ewing seemed a vision of beauty and other perfections. Mr Ewing was like an indulgent elder brother. On their side, the Ewings enjoyed her company. She was so vivid, so individual, gifted, downright and fundamentally goodhearted.

General Smyth regarded the proceedings with increasing suspicion. His house must have rung with the name and the doings of Ewing, since Ethel was not by nature self-effacing, tactful or reticent. He came on them in his drawing-room and garden, and was struck by Ewing's evident affection for his daughter. Mrs Ewing he liked, but took to gazing at the husband as if he were invisible and to snarling under his moustache in a forbidding manner. He declared the fellow's red nose pointed to whisky and not indigestion as Ethel tried to pretend.

It was not long before matters came to the boil. As he was browsing through her letters, which he evidently considered the right and duty of a careful father, he came on one from Ewing that caused him to explode in the most terrific fashion. It confirmed him in his belief that the man, like all artists, was totally undesirable. For it proved the two of them were, in the most friendly and intimate way, as if it were nothing extraordinary, in the habit of discussing atheistic ideas. This, in his view, could only lead on to other sorts of immorality.

Ewing found himself posted to Manchester.

Ethel never admitted that there might be some justification for her parents' fury and alarm. Mrs Smyth fully supported her husband and one can see why. Ewing wrote from his Manchester exile: 'Since I, so to speak, lost you, my music has languished and withered'. And: 'One thing is certain, there is not one, nor can I suppose there ever will be, who can ever oust you from your place. It would have to be a second you to do so and a second you does not exist'. Many a fond father of a wild young innocent might have presentiments on finding that his dear child was on these sort of terms with a married man. It could give rise to anxiety today. In 1877 it was catastrophe.

The storm was so terrible as to cause even Ethel to bow down for a while. Being still young enough to be slightly unsure whether she was always right, she made efforts to conform. It was not as if she were unattractive or unsociable. On the contrary. The trouble was that she had not developed emotionally beyond the normal school-girl stage of having crushes, passions, admirations, or however one likes to term the state, for other girls and women. Boys didn't interest her just because they were boys. The sillinesses of light flirtation did not excite her sufficiently to make her overlook the fact that her dancing partners were out of step, had never heard of Brahms and were not accustomed to philosophical discussion. In short, she was rather a horrid little snob.

The only proposal she actually received was from William Wilde, Oscar's brother, and that was rather equivocal. She met him while on a visit to friends of her father's in Ireland. They played the newly invented lawn tennis, which she liked and, even better, discussed poetry and the arts among the bushes. Returning on the same boat, they spoke of French literature until Ethel became seasick. On the train to London, quite recovered, she settled down to a further exploration of the whys and wherefores of the French classics with her new friend who at once began to profess the most passionate love, as if her sickness had provided him with the necessary elevation of spirits. She was carried away. They bought a ring in London. Yet he implored her to keep their engagement secret. This seemed to her pretty senseless, but she respected his scruples. He wrote many flattering letters in the ensuing three weeks, at which point she recovered her wits and broke it off. He did not repine, so far as can be ascertained. She lost the ring a couple of years later when obliged to separate some dogs who were fighting in deep snow.

Not that she had abandoned music during this interregnum. How could she? Every passing day convinced her that not only was she a composer, but a very good one. It was never her habit to underestimate her capabilities. She would slip away to afternoon concerts in London, borrowing the essential five shillings from shops where the general had an account. On one of these outings she heard Brahms sung by a certain Fräulein Redeker, for whom she felt an intense admiration, expressing it as well as she could in the artists' dressing room. It then transpired that this paragon frequented Leipzig and was acquainted with Brahms.

The poor general's defeat was upon him. The battle was tremendous. Military language of an unsuitable kind resounded. In skirmish after skirmish he reiterated that no respectable girl, let alone a daughter of his, could be allowed to live alone among foreigners, and artistic ones at that. She would go to the bad. He couldn't afford an allowance. It was out of the question. He absolutely and entirely forbade any further nonsense of the sort. Ethel did not give way before the barrage. She changed her tactics, refusing to go to church, go out riding, entertain guests with songs or even speak to them, retiring to her room instead and locking the door which, on one occasion, the general almost succeeded in kicking down.

This seems to have been the climax. He began to reflect on his strategic position: was it tenable? Was it possible, or sensible, to endure a family life reduced to permanent hysterics? Besides, decent people, nothing to do with art or foreigners, had told him that Leipzig university, to which the conservatorium was attached, was one of the best in Europe. They said Ethel had gifts beyond the charming singing of songs after dinner and these should be cultivated. Students came from everywhere to Leipzig, a protestant city with an English church. It was by no means a sink of iniquity and living was very cheap. Finally, we may take it that the general was sick of the whole subject. Whatever his exact reasons, he began to retreat and the atmosphere of the house returned to normal.

One of his conditions was, of course, that Ethel must fix herself up with a landlady who could be regarded as some sort of chaperone. Fräulein Redeker came to the rescue. Her friend Fräulein Friedlander, who had also been in London singing at Brahms concerts, had an aunt in Leipzig with the title of frau professor who would be willing to take Ethel as lodger and member of the family. It was only necessary to conceal the fact that the two young ladies had been discovered on a mid-morning visit reclining in deshabille in a frowsty room, the bed unmade, sipping port out of an egg cup. The frau professor, represented as the learned aunt of an international singer, passed muster. An allowance was settled, a brother-in-law summoned to accompany her on the journey and, in the summer of 1877, she set off on the great adventure.

CHAPTER TWO

Brahms in Leipzig

In 1877 Bismarck had only just succeeded in uniting under the leadership of Prussia the four kingdoms, six grand duchies, five duchies, seven principalities and three free towns into which Germany had been divided from medieval times. The kings, dukes and princes continued in their palaces as before with a considerable measure of autonomy, but were no longer fully sovereign. The existence of so many courts, each with a tradition of patronizing the arts, had had a beneficial effect on the intellectual life of the nation. There were many universities and schools of ancient foundation. The chief cities had concert halls, opera houses, bookshops, art collections in a profusion not found in the rest of Europe. England must have seemed quite barbaric in this respect to the educated nineteenth-century German. Dresden was the capital, but Leipzig was the largest and richest town in Saxony. It was the most important centre for publishing in Germany and the conservatorium, founded by Mendelssohn, had a high reputation in musical circles, though perhaps its best days were past.

To this city, bustling with authors, musicians and businessmen came eager little Ethel, flushed with victory over parental authority, bursting with herself, her ambitions, projects, genius; longing to be a success, to love and be loved; stuttering schoolgirl German. 'All ideas are flown,' she wrote ecstatically to her mother on the day of arrival, 'and I am mentally wallowing in one thought and one thought only, i.e. here I am and I have only just begun to realize the fact.' She had already rushed round the town to see the sights. The students looked rather stodgy, she thought, even those with duelling scars on their faces. But, '*Egmont* is to be played tonight at the theatre'.

She noticed other things too which, although they in no way lessened her excitement, she thought it best not to include in the home propaganda. There were certain smells, for instance, in the frau professor's house, due, no doubt, to unsophisticated drains. But what did that matter? The excellent public baths were round the corner. The meals were another experience: 'with the then North German ideas as to plenty of grease in the soup, very few beans in the coffee mill, meat baked in the oven with all its juice extracted

21

to make up something else'.[1] Some of the other lodgers were young men. As to the frau professor's title, it appeared she had inherited it from her deceased husband. It was not possible to discover, or to imagine, how he could have acquired it. Why bother with irrelevancies? She was such an amiable woman, so easy to get on with and never likely to push herself forward as unwanted chaperone.

In her haste to embark on the new life, and perhaps from a feeling that she had better go quickly in case her father had second thoughts, she arrived some weeks before term began at the conservatorium. This was most fortunate. Fräuleins Redeker and Friedlander and the latter's mother were just off for a holiday in the Thüringian forest. They were to be joined by George Henschel who had also been a soloist at the memorable Brahms concert in London.

'Shall I ever forget that fine August day in 1877,' he later wondered,[2] 'when our little circle was suddenly brightened by the meteor-like appearance among us of a young and most attractive girl who was staying in the neighbourhood, the daughter, we understood, of a British general? None of us knew what in her to admire most: her wonderful musical talent . . . or her astonishing prowess in athletic feats of agility and strength, showing us how to play lawn-tennis, then only just introduced into Germany, or, to the utter bewilderment of the German young ladies, and young men, too, for that matter, how to jump over fences, chairs and even tables . . . We were all agreed that we had among us an extraordinary, commanding personality that was sure to be famous some day.'

He was such a friend of Brahms that they had actually spent a summer holiday together in 1876 at a Baltic seaside resort. There the great man had taught him to swim under water with his eyes open and had regaled him with stories about girls. Henschel was making his way as a singer and accompanist as well as composing. He later settled in England, founded the London Symphony Orchestra and became a knight. None of his compositions has survived the test of time.

Ethel went mad with joy. How different this entertainment was from anything to be had in Frimley. They walked in the forest singing German folk songs until their throats were on fire, at which point they retired to the nearest beer house. Music was, indeed, continuous. If Fräulein Redeker was not drifting about in a divine pink dressing

---

[1] *Female Pipings in Eden,* Ethel Smyth, 1933.

[2] *Musings and memories of a Musician,* 1918.

22

gown filling the air with operatic snatches, Herr Henschel, that peer of Brahms, was seated at the piano, his beautiful voice floating out of the doors and windows.

Nor was she idle herself: 'I go up every day into the mountain and compose,' she informed her mother. 'The bliss of knowing that when I went on so about cultivating my talent I was not wrong! Henschel . . . thinks more of my music than ever I did and has written about me to Brahms . . . Don't think, mother darling, that this makes me lose my head,' she adds hastily, 'that I fancy I have only to put pen to paper and become famous. It's just this: men who have lived among musicians all their lives, who have been hand in glove with Schumann and Mendelssohn and who are so with Brahms and Rubinstein, say they seldom saw such talent, in a woman *never*.'

The future appeared altogether rosy as far as she could see, full of great triumphs and thunderous applause. She would never marry, naturally. The idea of a husband and children interrupting the glorious hours of inspiration revolted her. Even were Brahms himself to propose, she would refuse him. Nothing must be allowed to impede the flow of her genius. She was, in any case, much perplexed by the whole subject of love, knowing nothing of the mechanics of sex and being attracted to a whole series of girls without being able to understand what was happening. She treated boys in a rough and ready comradely fashion, but women could reduce her to a trembling suitor with a bunch of flowers in her hand. The emotions were more urgent and upsetting than they had been when she was a schoolgirl.

Now enrolled at the conservatorium, she was surprised to find that the teachers were by no means so impressed by her gifts as the Henschel circle. This she put down to their being a second-rate lot, trading on the reputation of the great Mendelssohn, an opinion which cannot be said to be wrong exactly, since the professors were not the equals of the illustrious composer and she did have unusual gifts. The students were disappointing, too. Instead of dreaming of concert halls ringing with their works, they expressed a plain ambition to obtain a teacher's certificate and so make their living. The romantic Ethel could only regard such a programme with contempt.

Although life was busy – she was forever at the theatre, in the concert hall, skating, dancing, singing, playing the piano – she began to be homesick as the months went by. 'I think, oh so often, of home and you all,' she wrote to her mother. 'I don't think you've been out of my thoughts one hour since the Xmas season came in and as

23

Xmas day draws near, I feel more and more the many miles there are between us.'

She was never more profoundly attached to anyone than to this mother in whose company she could hardly pass a single day without some ferocious quarrel. This home from which she had escaped with such difficulty haunted her dreams. There were mornings when she had to examine her room on waking to discover whether she was in Leipzig or Frimley. She longed to go hunting again. Her depression reached such a stage that she even doubted her genius slightly: would it last? She was stuck in the middle of a sonata. Suppose inspiration had permanently failed? She began to have certain symptoms: palpitations and faintness.

Early in 1878, however, the scene changed miraculously. She had been gradually meeting the musical worthies of Leipzig, some of whom had distinguished connections, Mendelssohn's daughter, for instance. When Brahms came to conduct a performance of his new symphony, Henschel introduced her to him. She was much overcome by his formidable appearance and very penetrating bright blue eyes. 'So this is the young lady who writes sonatas and doesn't know counter-point,' he remarked. At the time, she took it for a compliment, but later decided it must be sarcasm.

The composer was staying with the von Herzogenbergs as he always did when in Leipzig. He was particularly fond of Elizabeth von Herzogenberg, being a regular correspondent of hers on matters musical and social. People were continually telling Ethel what an altogether wonderful woman Elizabeth was. But, they added, she was very reserved and never saw anyone, except a few close friends. She was beautiful. She was clever. The extent of her musical knowledge had to be heard to be believed. Ethel wondered whether she would ever be privileged to make the acquaintance of this paragon.

At last it happened at some social gathering in February 1878. It was love at first sight for Ethel. Elizabeth, or Lisl as she was known to her intimates, was 'not really beautiful, but better than beautiful, at once dazzling and bewitching'. Golden hair waved over a 'very noble, rather low, forehead', suggestive to Ethel of immense brain power. 'I never saw a more beautiful neck and shoulders.'[1] There seemed to be no end to her attractions: an amusing conversationalist; high-minded and spiritual, yet homely; intellectual but not overburdened with reading to the point of didacticism; mature and

---

[1] *Impressions That Remained.*

also of a childlike simplicity; a reputed musical genius. Ethel simply worshipped from the very moment she laid eyes on this being whose detached manner seemed appropriate in a goddess.

Herr von Herzogenberg was more approachable. He occupied his time with a Bach society and in writing innumerable fugues, canons, piano duets and other pieces, generally uninspired although correctly composed according to the accepted rules of the day. He enquired after Ethel's studies, saying he had heard she was something special among young musicians. He said he would like to see her work. She took it round the next day.

Herzogenberg had a low opinion of the conservatorium and all the professors in it. He laughed heartily over the elementary mistakes they had neglected to correct. It was a shame that Ethel's gifts should remain uncultivated. They had never even introduced her to Bach. he would love to give her lessons. His wife could attend them too, thus obviating any cause for scandalous gossip. Lisl acquiesced, though distantly, as if obliged to humour her husband in his latest fancy.

Whether or not he meant to be taken seriously, his offer was immediately pounced on by Ethel. She left the conservatorium forthwith and devoted her considerable energies to pleasing the new teacher and especially his wife. But the adorable Lisl remained merely polite, to all appearance. The strains of unrequited love added to those of homesickness were too much. The Herzogenbergs were on the point of leaving for a holiday in Austria. Could they be relied on to continue, and improve on, the new friendship in the way Ethel found essential to her future happiness? In any case, she couldn't bear to part with them even for a day and collapsed dramatically at the birthday party of mutual friends.

This brought matters smartly to the crisis. Lisl took her home and the ensuing fortnight was a perfect dream of heavenly delights. Ethel remained in bed, very feeble with a high temperature which the doctor was rather at a loss to account for, saying vaguely that she must have been overdoing it. Lisl made it clear that she fully reciprocated Ethel's feeling for her. She arrived every morning at eight o'clock sharp and spent the entire day in the sickroom, washing the patient all over, writing letters at her dictation, cooking tempting little meals, reading aloud, playing suitable melodies on the piano.

There was also plenty of time for confidential talks. She explained to Ethel that though her marriage was superbly happy, yet a great sorrow oppressed her: she had no children. One doctor after another had declared her hopelessly barren. Oh, how she longed for a daughter such as Ethel, attractive, of strong character, gifted with music. She now felt that she had found one. For her part, Ethel confessed that the grief of her life was that her mother could never give her the steady, unfailing loyalty of love which she craved. 'It was settled that though my mother must never hear of it, I was really her child, that, as she put it, she must have "had" me without knowing it when she was eleven.'[1] This conceit gave them both infinite happiness.

As soon as Ethel began to mend, which was in a couple of weeks, Lisl was obliged to set off on her delayed holiday in Austria with her husband. Ethel cried herself to sleep every night; she couldn't help it. But these were voluptuous tears. She knew that a wonderful epoch had begun. Tradesmen deposited flowers, chocolates and books at the door every day. A stream of letters and postcards arrived. They were everything a passionate heart could desire: 'Really the last 14 days were such a delight, gave me so much pleasure, that I often feel quite dishonourable in calmly pocketing, as if I deserved them, the thanks that poured so generously from your mouth . . . I confess I do not look on it as a misfortune that you became so ill . . . because I doubt if we should ever have got where we are now but for those 14 days . . . Goodbye and my blessing to you, my darling.'

Within a week, on 9 June 1878, she was writing: 'My child, I wonder sometimes at the different way Fate spins the thread which binds people together – how it often takes years to enter into possession, and how in our case something has grown between us that tells me we belong together inseparably . . . To think how I hung back at first . . . and now, there you are, little tree, grown into my heart with such deep roots that nothing can ever tear them out!' These letters, all equally sentimental, are signed either Lisl, or else Your Mother.

Being now well enough to travel, Ethel started for home, as had been arranged long before. Notes and telegrams from Lisl were waiting at most of the stations. It was almost exactly a year since she left for Germany and the welcome to the returned prodigal was tumultuous. The general was especially delighted to find that she still loved dogs, horses, tennis and everything a healthy young woman should. She hadn't taken up with unsuitable men. She hadn't got into debt. As for the music nonsense, it had turned out pretty harmless. In short, he was exceedingly glad to see her.

---

[1] *Impressions That Remained.*

In spite of the fact that she had solemnly signed a document in Leipzig promising not to dance, ride or touch a tennis racquet, for fear of bringing on a relapse, Ethel soon began to feel so vigorous as to be unable to keep the promise, much as she wished to oblige her second mother. Mrs Smyth, somewhat jealous of the foreign influence, encouraged rebellious thoughts and suggested a visit to a proper English doctor who would confirm her complete recovery and absolve her from the oath she had taken. This was done.

The renegade immediately began on a strenuous round of sport and social entertainments of all kinds. She visited her married sisters and quantities of other friends, for some of whom she felt a revival of previous admirations. She sang in drawing-rooms and played her own compositions which were uniformly in the style of Brahms. She was also writing some unidentified piece of prose, presumably based on her German adventures.

Lisl's letters continued to arrive in torrents and cataracts. Only selected parts were read out to Mrs Smyth, for fear of adverse reactions. An hortatory note entered the correspondence. 'It seems to me you have a specific duty towards your gift for music and should not let yourself be drawn away in other directions . . . Talent is a Destiny that imposes definite responsibilities'. Excuses of youth and high spirits were not listened to. The anxious second mother, fearful of losing her child, continued to scold. 'How much time remains for music when you have got through your literary work, your riding, your social distractions, your dinner parties, your lying about in the fields with Goethe under your arm? I cannot imagine how you can get in any real work, even a little counterpoint . . . Besides that there is your piano practice to be done, your reading at sight, your studying, if possible, of scores and your Variations to be written'.

But the naughty girl was unrepentant, except for odd days and occasions. Deeply though she loved and needed Lisl, she had a wonderful feeling of having been let out of school, of having escaped from under a cloud of German solemnity and moral earnestness. Yet, 'as the summer went on, the old feeling of the staleness and pointlessness of home life came back and with it a furious longing for Leipzig and new friends'.[1] She had managed to finish the *Variations* which only they would properly appreciate. There were continual arguments in the house about money, the general declaring that they were living beyond their income and his wife refusing to

---

[1] *Impressions That Remained.*

agree to any sensible measures of economy. The old battles between mother and daughter revived, to the great regret of both.

So, one day in September 1878, just before breakfast, the door of the Herzogenberg flat flew open and there was Ethel, straight off the train, her *Variations* under her arm. Lisl turned completely white and nearly fainted. However, she immediately recovered and the welcome extended to her pseudo-daughter was as ecstatic as the most demanding of friends could wish. 'From now onwards I became, and remained for seven years, a semi-detached member of the Herzogenberg family; wherever they were bidden, I was bidden too.' If Herzogenberg himself had any repinings, he was obliged to keep them quiet.

Ethel was put to work at once copying out Brahms' latest composition, *Capriccio, Opus 76 No 2* which he had sent Lisl at her request because she adored it so. When she wrote to him, and it was frequently, she often sent him Ethel's regards. He sometimes returned polite messages in his replies. Her enthusiasm at his concerts knew no bounds. He posted his autograph to her, with compliments.

The great event of 1879 was his arrival in Leipzig to conduct his new violin concerto. The Herzogenbergs put him up as usual and Ethel was often of the party. Nothing could exceed her admiration for him as an artist, yet in other respects she found him wanting. 'I never could understand why the faithful had such an exalted opinion of his intellect.'[1] It was true that he said nothing stupid, but his pronouncements on politics, literature and even music, reverently repeated by his disciples, seemed to her perfectly unilluminating. She did give him credit, however, for persisting in his praise of Wagner, at the mention of whose name all the smart Leipzigers were accustomed to laugh heartily. And in addition to other shortcomings, he enjoyed his food to what she considered an excessive degree, though it was true that Lisl was a wonderful cook.

But the most fundamental objection Ethel had to him was his attitude to women. In particular cases, such as Lisl, Frau Wach (Mendelssohn's daughter) and Clara Schumann, his manner was everything the most exigent critic could wish. The trouble was that if a woman was boring, as tended to happen, he was rude to her; and if she attracted him he eyed her in a way Ethel thought disgustingly vulgar. It was evident that he much enjoyed sex, doubtful stories and the presence of pretty girls, whether or not he felt inclined to pursue an acquaintance.

[1] *Impressions That Remained.*

Nor had he inhibitions as to what was suitable in mixed company. George Henschel in his *Brahms Recollections* records: 'Our host began to ransack drawers and cupboards and shelves for things he thought might entertain us. Suddenly with that dear familiar twinkle in his eyes and a long-drawn "Ah-a-ah!" . . . he opened a large portfolio and showed and read to us with great gusto the famous letters of Richard Wagner to the milliner . . . chuckling with amusement as he went from one amazing letter to another.' Ethel was too new from Frimley, as yet, to approve such lack of inhibition. Though she thought herself, and indeed was, modern, unconventional, a rebel, a good deal of the victorian miss survived.

She had to admit that 'to me personally he was very kind and fatherly in his awkward way';[1] that he was profoundly modest about his own achievements; that he looked at one of her compositions and took the trouble to say appreciative things; that he was generous with money, supporting an uncongenial family and a crowd of poor musicians. She thought him a superb pianist, admiring the way his eyes became abstracted and the veins of his forehead stood out as he played.

All these virtues were not enough to balance the fact that he refused to take Ethel as seriously as, for instance, the Herzogenbergs and George Henschel. He relegated her, as it seemed, to the ranks of those fit only for the bed and the kitchen, with regular excursions to church by way of serious occupation and she felt very passionately that if she had been a young man, he would have esteemed her sonatas and other works as much as they deserved. It was a quarrel she was to have with men permanently.

He had no sense of humour, in her opinion, and a heavy hand with jokes. Certainly one perpetrated at her expense was rather school-boyish. Germans found it difficult to pronounce Smyth and it usually came out as Schmeiss, which word also indicated a dung fly. Brahms was unable to resist the temptation of nicknaming her the Dung Fly. She was continually flitting rapidly from place to place, he explained, and it always reminded him of a fly. Lisl was obliged to remonstrate with him, whereupon he good-naturedly gave it up and called her the Oboe instead.

'I never really liked Brahms,' Ethel said at intervals during the rest of her life.

---

[1] *Impressions That Remained.*

CHAPTER THREE

Harry Brewster

In 1882 Ethel took a decision that was to lead to a fundamental change in her life, to destroy her relationship with Lisl and to lay the foundation of the most important and fruitful connection she was ever to experience. The Leipzig routine had begun to bore her. There seemed to be no end to the repetitive exercises in counterpoint set by Herr von Herzogenberg. The atmosphere was so serious, as if the world began and ended in the musical parlours of this provincial German city.

Now twenty-four, she was a young woman of more varied tastes than could be accommodated by such an existence. She loved all forms of sport, for instance, which Lisl deplored as a waste of valuable energy. A discriminating reader, she was becoming educated in a wide sense. She wanted to see more of the world. She wanted change. She'd had enough of pure music for the time being. She was going to spend the winter in Italy, a country stuffed with beauties just as valid and as necessary to the soul as those she had devoted herself to with such assiduity for the last four years.

The Herzogenbergs were very much against the idea, feeling she would go off at a tangent to the detriment of her prospects as a composer. They believed in keeping one's eye fixed on the goal, in not allowing oneself to be distracted by inconvenient fancies, however attractive they might seem. She was actually proposing to give up her studies for a whole winter, and that was probably only the beginning of her journey downhill. In their view, dear Ethel could only be saved from herself if she remained under their controlling influence. It says much for Herzogenberg's opinion of her work and his sense of responsibility for what he considered her best interests, that he should express a vehement opposition to plans which would relieve the pressure on his marriage caused by her continual boisterous presence in his house and her claim on his wife's affections.

But since it had never been Ethel's practice to listen to advice conflicting with her own intentions, the Herzogenbergs were obliged to acquiesce. It was not as if she were proposing to bury herself in a musical wilderness, Frimley for instance. No, she was bound for

the home of opera and *bel canto,* where Verdi was still in full career
and, of the younger generation, Puccini and Leoncavallo, her exact
contemporaries to a year, gave signs of extraordinary promise. New
surroundings and excitements might adulterate the influence of the
hero Brahms, but that seemed to be the worst one could say of the
venture.

Besides, the Herzogenbergs themselves were well acquainted with
Italy and must often have described the delights of Venice, and
especially of Florence where Lisl's sister Julia lived with her husband
Harry Brewster. Ethel had already heard a great deal of Julia who
appeared to her younger sister to be a goddess. 'O, Ethel,' Lisl had
gushed in 1878, 'what a poor earthly dusty creature I feel near her,
yet this best of all women loves me and I feel as if this love could
prevent me from growing wicked and help me even to get better.'

It was true her attitude to her children seemed rather on the cool
side, 'but in other directions she has acquired a freedom in loving,
suffering and understanding before which I bow down in shame. And
what a heavenly absence of egotism!' Lisl continued with innocent
enthusiasm. 'You never hear her speak of herself.' This made her
difficult to know, particularly as, 'the expenditure of kindness and
sympathy fatigues her and she flies the company of others rather than
seeks it'. In fact, the admirable woman had no friends in a real sense,
only a few acquaintances. She was highly intellectual, occupying her
mind with metaphysical speculations of singular complexity and
receiving sustenance from the beauties of nature.

She was eleven years older than her husband who, to all appearance,
was perfectly happy in the midst of these austerities. He, too, was
of a philosophical turn of mind. American by origin, he had been
born and brought up in France, becoming so fluent in the language
as to be able, in later years, to write French poems which were admired
by people who knew what they were talking about.

He had fallen in love with Julia at the impressionable age of sixteen.
His feelings had not changed at twenty-one and so he married her.
They both had advanced views, declaring they went through the
ceremony merely to pacify their elders. Each was to remain perfectly
free to terminate the arrangement whenever it seemed the best and
most reasonable course of action. For the rest, they retired into a
domestic fastness and for ten years hardly spoke to outsiders. It was
the sort of dream world that only two very shy and uncertain people
could endure, let alone enjoy. But gradually Brewster began to stir
inside the chrysalis. His wife noticed it.

31

This was their situation in 1882 when Ethel arrived in Florence with an introduction from Lisl. Limping as a result of an encounter with a Swiss mountain where she had paused in her journey south, she demolished the delicate balance of the household with the force and despatch of a typhoon, a tidal wave, a volcanic eruption. She talked loudly, volubly, interestingly. She sang. She never sat still. She had no patience with metaphysics, much preferring tennis, swimming, cricket, riding, dancing. She was crazy about dogs. Yet she was not a philistine. What could be more different from the ethereal Julia? She was also very good-looking. Brewster was violently attracted.

Ethel was not aware of having made this impression, as her attention was entirely concentrated on Julia whom she thought beautiful, enigmatic and altogether someone she wanted to know better. Here was an exciting new friend. She would cultivate her, penetrate her extraordinary reserve and win her heart. It would not be easy as her visits to the house were rationed. None of the informal coming and going she enjoyed at the Herzogenberg establishment. Nevertheless, she was sure the impulsive warmth with which she had conquered so many would soon prevail. Had she not already a special position in the family as a pseudo-niece?

These preoccupations prevented her from attaching any significance to the fact that Brewster shortly left for a holiday in Algeria, explaining that he wanted to improve his rudimentary Arabic and to shoot lions. There was, in any case, something in his manner she did not care for, in particular the way he contradicted her on Shakespeare and Goethe. It never entered her head that the watchful Julia had suggested absence and a change of scene would cure what was obviously a silly little infatuation. But the mere fact that they should have considered such a step necessary shows what a threat they perceived in Ethel.

It was hardly surprising that she found it difficult to make progress with Julia, 'one step forward generally meaning two steps back . . . I also noticed that the simplest reactions of human nature seemed incomprehensible to her till she had stated them to herself in terms of metaphysics'.[1] However, she was very nice about a sonata Ethel was writing. Since she abhorred the social life, had really nothing in common with Ethel, and had been obliged to pack her husband off to Africa in order to cool him down, one wonders why she didn't get rid of the inconvenient young woman, either by freezing her out

---

[1] *Impressions That Remained.*

Ethel and her dog Marco, 1891

Ethel singing, by John Singer Sargent, 1901

or, should that be too subtle a method for the purpose, by slamming the door on her. Perhaps she felt this would be to exaggerate what was declared to be Harry's passing fancy, his mid-summer madness. And was she rather flattered by Ethel's attentions?

Harry returned a few weeks before she left in the spring of 1883. He assured his wife he no longer loved Ethel. It had all been an illusion, happily dissipated by Algerian scenes and desert airs. He got on more easily with her now and they had some interesting conversations about the French poets, of whom she was totally ignorant. On her side, she prevailed on him to take up the 'cello, on which he had once been somewhat proficient, and join her and a couple of friends in musical evenings. Julia was evidently certain that her husband had made a complete recovery, for she raised no objection when it became clear that Ethel was going to spend the next winter in Florence also, in order to see the sights she had been obliged to forego, on account of her knee which had not properly recovered from the mishap on the Swiss mountain.

So she set off on a round trip to England where she found her father speaking of retrenchment and her mother ordering new gowns by the dozen, clothes being her one interest in life. She visited her married sisters. She went to Germany, was reunited with Lisl and made the cordial acquaintance of Clara Schumann. She suffered a sharp fever of mysterious origin from which she perfectly recovered and reappeared in Florence in January 1884.

As soon as Brewster set eyes on her he knew that no matter how he might try to pretend to himself or his wife, he was madly in love with Ethel. This was no romantic fantasy. He had never felt more deeply, truly, imperatively. Had it not been understood from the beginning that his marriage could be abrogated the minute either partner desired so to do? He must and he would have Ethel as quickly as she could be persuaded to consent.

Julia was against rushed decisions. Of course she would stand by their pact and give him whatever freedom he required, but they must be quite certain that the new love would endure before taking steps they might all three regret. In spite of brave protestations, she was horrified and frightened by the turn of events. It seemed to her that the practical thing in the circumstances was to try the exact opposite of the previous treatment. If the lions of Africa had not been able to cure him, perhaps an undiluted course of Ethel would do the trick. He would soon find the philosophical calm in which he was accustomed to spend his hours and days shattered by this young woman with her perpetual restlessness, her sudden moods, her self-centredness, her singing, rampaging like an animal amongst the fragile flowers and dainty vistas of their enchanted garden. In addition, Julia's observation of Ethel may have led her to think that she was a complete lesbian.

'She became extremely friendly to me,' Ethel noted with some astonishment. She was encouraged to visit whenever she wished. 'I saw the Brewsters constantly and found them more and more delightful',[1] though Julia seemed fundamentally unresponsive, which was puzzling. 'I am carefully preventing myself from getting fond of her, as I don't think she would know what to do with my affection.'[2] Harry was by no means so difficult. 'What with comparing notes about mankind, morals, art, literature, anything and everything, what with the laughter and fighting and utter good comradeship, I have never had such a delightful relation with any man in my life.'[1] She remained, in fact, totally unaware of the domestic drama taking place under her nose. The attractive light thrown on her character by such openhearted innocence increased the danger to a marriage already tottering.

The unfortunate Julia was allowed certain breathers. Not only did Ethel thoroughly explore the sights of Rome and the towns of Umbria, but also announced that it was essential to march up the Appenines in order to have a simultaneous view of the Adriatic and the Mediterranean. She set off with a change of clothes in a knapsack and a revolver in her pocket, spending the nights at monasteries, if she happened to reach one by dusk, if not under a bush. This was courageous. Although Italy was unified and at peace as it had not been since the days of the Caesars, thanks to Garibaldi and Victor Emanuel II, it was not very safe for a handsome young woman to wander about alone. She treated all warnings with contempt, pointing out that she knew how to use the revolver.

In the course of her travels, she met an eccentric baron who suggested that they should together go to a place from where a far better view than she had seen was to be had. Although he struck her as raffish, she felt he was a gentleman and consented. Her confidence was not misplaced. An untimely mist obscured the Adriatic at the critical moment, but the extraordinary alfresco feasts he laid on complete with linen, silver and glass (rather dirty), the surprise musical evening he ended up with, made it a memorable adventure, as if she

[1] *Impressions That Remained.*
[2] Letter to Lisl.

had strayed into an opera. He gave her his card on parting. She subsequently lost it and couldn't even remember his name, fitting conclusion to a Cinderella story.

Julia and Harry endlessly discussed the situation during her absence. They could find no way out. When it came to the test, Julia was unable to give up her husband in accordance with her principles, her solemn promise made at marriage, the ideas of freedom and human dignity she thought she believed in. There had always been a contradiction: on the one hand they were supposed to be two kindred spirits come together in a sort of heavenly communion scarcely to be understood by ordinary mortals; on the other, nothing could be more possessive and restricting to the soul than the secluded fastness to which they had retreated, pulling up the drawbridge, letting down the portcullis and manning the guns on the battlements. Their dilemma was that she wished to remain in the fortress, while he had determined to flee.

So this man who had agreed to discipline for ten years, came to see the point of life where you went to parties and gave parties and had quantities of friends without bothering about their exact moral and philosophical significance in the scheme of things. He wanted to exchange the dominance of Julia for that of Ethel, reiterating his intention of persuading her into his bed. Julia replied that she doubted whether it would be as easy as he imagined. For all her wild unconventionality, Ethel was a general's daughter. To take a lover would be, in the opinion of her family and social circle, to cast herself into outer darkness. What evidence was there that she really loved Harry at all, let alone enough to make such a sacrifice for his sake? Was she the kind of person who ever sacrificed her own interests for another? But Harry was not to be dissuaded. Ethel had captured him entirely. He was a man of extremes.

For her part, Ethel continued to treat him as a comrade and brother: 'I never dreamed of caring for him until about 14 days before I left Florence',[1] in June 1884. She does not relate how Harry managed to precipitate matters. She who had sometimes flirted but never loved a man in her life, became aware that men could be as important to her as women, an idea she would not have entertained for a moment hitherto. She always felt herself to be profoundly different from other girls whose feminine outlook and submissive attitude to the opposite sex she despised.

It's all very well for two young people in love to say, 'You are

---

[1] Letter to Lisl, 1885.

absolutely free to leave me whenever you feel inclined and for whatever reason.' Such an eventuality seems remote and academic, as indeed it is at that moment in the history of an affair. Ten years later, they have perhaps become only too accustomed to each other. It's boring. Someone new and exciting turns up. But they have formed emotional bonds the breaking of which is pure agony for the party who is to be abandoned, and no less for him who wishes to make another start. Few misfortunes are more wretched than the crash of a marriage.

The last fourteen days of Ethel's stay in Florence were devoted to intense confabulations between the three of them. Julia clung to the idea that it was a simple case of infatuation. Harry should go to England for the hunting season with Ethel, joining in the hearty sports, the dances and other coarse amusements of military and county society. She was certain the experience would bring her husband back to his senses and to Florence quicker than anything.

Harry was mad about Ethel. He had never met a woman so original, so vital, such good company and so physically attractive. But his conscience wouldn't permit him to insist on his freedom when Julia was plainly unable to give it. He was a kind man and though he much desired his pound of flesh, he shrank from it.

Ethel had been often enough in love with women to recognize the nature of her feeling for Harry. Yet she had serious reservations. Firstly, she was hesitant about physical love, as was natural in a virgin, let alone one confused by the sudden revelation of her own bisexuality. Her ideas had been shifted into a different pattern. Secondly, the universally derided position of inamorata scarcely appealed to her passionate, headstrong independence of character. Above all, if she allied herself with this particular married man, she would lose Lisl who meant everything in the world to her. She said that the incident must be closed. She would clear out of the Brewsters' life and never communicate with them again.

In that firm resolution, she took the train to Germany where she immediately explained to Lisl what an awkward situation had arisen. She, Ethel, was perfectly innocent. The whole business had materialized out of nowhere. It had been like a thunderclap. The forces of nature had moved without prompting on her part. She'd had no reason to suspect the trend of Harry's thoughts, believing them to be merely the best of friends. Her own heart was equally deceptive. No one could be more amazed than she to discover love of Harry in it. But that was neither here nor there since she had very properly put a stop to the affair. The experience had lacerated her. Lisl accepted these explanations. The two friends parted with a sense of being 'more closely, if more tragically, knit than ever'.[1]

Ethel set out for England full of virtuous intentions. A few weeks later, Harry wrote and she replied. Soon a voluminous correspondence began with the object of deciding once and for all whether they had been right to cut off communication. Harry said, and declared Julia agreed, that it was impossible to know whether or not their love was an infatuation if they were unable to put it to the test by at least remaining friends. If she wouldn't see him, they ought to write regularly. This specious argument swayed her. He further said Julia was only waiting to know the truth of the matter and would give him his freedom gladly as soon as it was established beyond doubt that he really wanted it. Here was scope for endless discussion which was still in full swing when Ethel returned to Leipzig for the winter of 1884/5. She wrote to Julia as well, asking for guidance and received vague metaphysical replies. Harry twice turned up in Leipzig and they talked for hours at a time.

Lisl was greatly agitated by the new developments, directly contradicting solemn promises she had been given. It undermined her faith in Ethel's picture of herself as an unsuspecting young person caught unawares by a man's intemperance. The crisis came when she visited Julia. She found her half dead from misery. Any idea that she awaited the outcome between Ethel and Harry with the calm detachment either of a woman of the world or a stylite on a desert pillar was ludicrous. Ethel had irretrievably damaged the marriage.

Lisl was put in a difficult position. She still loved Ethel. But how could this be passed over? Or, if it could be done, how could she continue to fraternize with the destroyer? Was she to quarrel with her own family for Ethel's sake? The answer to all these questions being plainly no, she was obliged to end the relationship, though it cost her much pain.

Ethel could hardly believe it when her letters were not answered. 'I wrote to her bewildered, appealingly, in despair!'[1] Her second mother, the one she loved as much as her true one, had failed. What for? All over nothing. Of course she was giving Harry back to his wife and they would make it up. The previous equilibrium would be restored, just as if she had never visited Florence. Lisl would see. It was perfectly simple. She wrote to mutual friends in Leipzig, hoping

[1] *Impressions That Remained*, Ethel Smyth, 1919.

37

their intercession would bring her strayed mother back. It did not.

Harry's position was ambivalent. He wanted Ethel and Julia. He loved both in different ways. It would be very hard on Julia, he argued, if Ethel insisted on breaking with him. 'If I have to give you up,' he wrote in 1885, 'I shall give her up too. What will you have gained then? You will have made us all three miserable and brought everything to a complete smash. Please believe that I am honest when I tell you that I will not and cannot love either of you alone and against the other.' 'Are you going to tell her that it is quite in her interests that you should love another woman?' Ethel retorted with devastating common sense: 'Do you expect her to say that she has no objection to our meeting and corresponding?'

She determined once more to cut off all communication with Harry. They did not see each other again for five years, although their correspondence continued intermittently. But Julia and Harry were as unable to return to their former state as they were to part. Nothing happened to conciliate Lisl, or even to convince her that Ethel was not still actively undermining the marriage.

Harry tried his best, even to the extent of refusing Ethel's suggestion, in a moment of weakness, that they meet in 1887. He filled the vacuum as well as he could by writing his first book, *The Theories of Anarchy and of Law*, which he published in 1887, sending her a copy. It is a philosophical essay, cast in the form of a Socratic dialogue. The fundamentals of life and thought are passed in review by a company of friends who are spending a serious evening together at an inn. Every so often the calm progression of the argument is punctuated by such statements as: 'I cannot live on subtle ideas and exquisite states of mind; I need some coarser food; I should starve on your abstract speculations and psychological niceties. I want thought that will rouse my passions and throw me as a combatant among men . . . Being a world of myself, I stand alone. And this solitude is poverty. Something is dead in me that lives in those who are not only psychical but also social beings', Ethel, for instance, one might relevantly add.

Not everyone is suited by conventional morality. 'The entire system of ideas under which we live is a lie to them,' he says of the rebels. 'Their truest, happiest, most self-forgetting instincts they are taught to be ashamed of. Duties are set before them, and ideals held up for their admiration which they can only conform to at the cost of sincerity, and if they attempt to lay aside hypocrisy and step forward free and ingenuous as God made them, such a storm of opprobrium greets them that their light-hearted innocence is gone and they recognize themselves no more.' He returns to the theme again and again: 'Practical sense is far closer akin to wisdom than morality,' he expounds. (Hear, hear, wrote Ethel in the margin of her copy.) 'The enjoyment [a man] finds in the exercise of the senses he is endowed with traces his course to him. His guide is wisdom, not morality.'

He was not able to draw his long cogitation to any very firm conclusion, except that a thorough scepticism was probably the most useful habit for one who hoped to win his struggle with the problems of the world. It seemed as impossible to espouse the tenets of anarchy, represented by Ethel, as those of law, laid down by Julia. He could only put his book in front of them both and await the outcome. He was a patient man, unaggressive yet persistent.

CHAPTER FOUR

Converted

For Ethel the crisis was worse since she had lost a friend who meant more to her than Harry yet did. She grieved as one would at the death of a beloved and could do no work. Her hope that Lisl might relent grew fainter as time passed and still no letter came. The thought of Germany was insupportable. She decided to live at home, her parents now being old, the last unmarried sister engaged, and the brother on the point of joining the Indian army. Mrs Smyth had become fearfully deaf and arthritic and pathologically quarrelsome, which underlined the absolute necessity to Ethel of a surrogate mother. No amount of rushing round friends and relations could assuage her.

She thought she had discovered what she so urgently required in Mrs Benson, wife of the Archbishop of Canterbury, to whom she had an easy introduction since her eldest sister, Alice, had married the primate's chaplain. Benson was at the height of his reputation. Having thoroughly organized the recently founded Wellington school during his headmastership, he passed to the new bishopric of Truro, supervised the building of the cathedral and finally, in 1882, Gladstone translated him to Canterbury. He was renowned for his diligence, integrity and careful attention to moral questions. His sense of humour was undeveloped.

'From 1886 onwards,' writes Ethel, 'the mainstay of my life [was] Mrs Benson and . . . no one could have striven harder than she did against the long cold night of the spirit that fell upon me when all hope of a reconciliation with my friend had to be abandoned.'[1] She had a great reputation as a counsellor. Her mission in life was the healing and directing of sick souls, either by conversation, or through the medium of small sheets of notepaper inscribed with some pithy advice, or thought for the day. Ethel immediately poured all her troubles, hopes and aspirations into these ready ears.

They had a good deal in common. 'My mother, throughout her life, like all very intellectual women,' her son E. F. Benson rather strangely remarked,[2] 'formed strong emotional attachments to those

[1] *Impressions That Remained.*

[2] *Mother*, E. F. Benson, 1925.

of her own sex.' She was also amusing. But there were fundamental differences of outlook and character. Mrs Benson had a masochistic side which coloured her strong religious views and her relationship with her formidable husband. She was distantly connected to the future archbishop (he had determined on that eminence since infancy) who fell in love with her when she was eleven. He was twenty-three and just finishing at Cambridge. 'As I have always been very fond of her and she of me with the love of a little sister,' he noted in his diary, '. . . it is not strange that I should have thought first of the possibility that some day dear little Minnie might become my wife.'

It appeared to him that she reciprocated his feelings and he asked her mother whether he might speak to her on the subject of marriage. The good lady was somewhat doubtful, the child being still only twelve. However, she consented. 'So at last the day came and I spoke to her,' he later recalled, 'and asked her if she thought it would ever come to pass that we should be married.' The precocious little thing made no reply, simply bursting into tears, seizing his handkerchief and tying it in a lover's knot.

Married at eighteen, young Mrs Benson found the realities of life somewhat alarming after such a long romantic courtship. Her husband continued to treat her as a child, correcting her faults in public, ignoring her wishes and tastes and generally behaving as an unregenerate victorian *pater familias*. Yet, he became strangely dependent on her. 'He thinks more of little remarks, is more sensitive, more easily wounded than I am. Therefore I must not think of being at ease, but of suiting my ways to his feelings,' the saintly woman wrote in her diary.

Thus she learned patience and charity, how to love fellow human beings enough to listen to their troubles unendingly, to bear gladly with their egotism, muddleheadedness, lack of grip, emotional self-indulgence. It was a lonely training. At a certain point she lost her faith. Such a catastrophe could not be confided to her husband. It would have been the end of the world. Luckily she met 'a woman with whom she instantly made one of those intimate and noble friendships, not knowing, as she records, that she was the messenger. "I played with the human love I had for her and she for me and all the time Thou hadst sent her" '.[1] After this she felt she understood at last the meaning of love and of religion. When Ethel bustled into her life, she was a well-qualified mother figure.

[1] *Mother.*

There were, of course, problems. One was that the demands of her other protégées interrupted the exclusive attention Ethel expected, and sometimes gave an unfortunate impression of queues at a psychiatric clinic. Ethel often reproached her quite severely on this score. Mrs Benson bore it with good humour. She was over seventy, immensely busy with every sort of works and social duties as a primate's wife must be, yet always had time for one more labouring soul, no matter how exigent. Though her understanding and kindness were of a high order, Ethel felt she had small grasp of the special qualities that constituted the artistic personality. It touched her pride to be treated as another patient looking for a cure.

She became an habituée of Lambeth Palace where the presence of the gifted Benson sons and daughters ensured interesting and sprightly conversation, despite the ecclesiastical background. The archbishop could be very forbidding. He did not look on Ethel with favour, thinking her an unnecessary addition to his household. 'The sight of his majestic form approaching the tea table scattered my wits as an advancing elephant might scatter a flock of sheep,' wrote Ethel sadly,[1] for she admired both his good looks and his brains. 'I never did quite such stupid things with other people.'

She related a funny story about General Booth and the hymn 'Rock of Ages', for instance. This situation was only just saved by Mrs Benson's at once enquiring after the Bishop of Rochester who had made a speech that morning. On another occasion, he asked her to explain her reported opinion that Handel's music resembled a mothers' meeting. 'After listening in silence till a halting explanation had died away on his interlocutor's lips, he remarked: "Are you aware that you have used the words *that sort of thing* seven times running?" '[1]

Here she rallied: 'I was quite civil but firmly stuck to my point in spite of his continually exclaiming, "That is bosh". Finally he declared peremptorily that he would discuss music no longer.'[1] And he looked at her as if she were a toad. 'We all realize,' Mrs Benson sighed later, 'that you and the Head of the Church are *not* two dewdrops destined to roll into one.'

'Eventually I got so terribly on his nerves, that it was found expedient to smuggle me into Lambeth by back entrances and hastily herd me into side rooms.'[1] Even the sight of her through a window ruined his day. Ethel was deeply insulted, as well she might be, saying Mrs Benson had much to answer for: 'If the men of the family are

---

[1] *Impressions That Remained.*

insupportable, it is generally the fault of the women for not standing up to them.'[1] 'I don't want to drop Ethel,' the beleaguered Mrs Benson confided in a friend, 'but I must stop her coming to see me when the Archbishop is at home.'

Luckily, her attentions were not unremitting. Any emotional upheaval is death to an artist as far as his work is concerned. The current inability to pursue her vocation, added to her natural restlessness, greatly exacerbated the quarrels she always had with her mother when they saw too much of each other. She began to feel she must revisit Germany, especially as the Herzogenbergs had settled in Berlin for the time being, leaving the coast clear at Leipzig where she still had a large number of lesser friends, all of whom advised her that she could not expect to resume her intimacy with Lisl after what had happened, though it might be possible to renew the acquaintance to some degree when a decent interval had passed. Besides, she had been unable entirely to break with Harry Brewster. Not only were they again in correspondence, but she arranged to stay with his sister who lived in the south of France and was a notable huntress of stag and wild boar, as well as an excellent shot, all of which pastimes Ethel greatly enjoyed, except for the actual death of the stag.

One of her objects in Germany was, naturally, to promote her career by getting some of her compositions played at concerts. To this end, she had sent Joseph Joachim, the famous violinist, her violin sonata and also a trio. But, on 22 March 1888, he replied: 'Honoured Miss Smyth . . . In spite of talent here and there, and many a clever turn and a certain facility, candour compels me to say that both works seem to me failures – unnatural, far-fetched, overwrought and not good as to sound.'

To this Ethel retorted that 'I much wondered if he considered Mr So and So a genuine talent . . . a youth never heard of before or since whose deadly dull Opus I he had recently produced in London and whose mama was a giver of smart musical parties at which the Joachim Quartet performed about once a fortnight for fabulous fees, throughout the season'.[1] Joachim evidently felt further contact would be unprofitable, for silence supervened.

During 1888, she became acquainted with Grieg who was staying in Leipzig, and Mahler, at that point resident conductor of the municipal orchestra. 'But of all the composers I have known the most delightful as a personality was Tchaikovsky.'[1] The feeling was reciprocated. 'While we were all sitting round the tea table,'

[1] *Impressions That Remained.*

Tchaikovsky related[1] of a Christmas party at which Grieg was also present, 'a beautiful dog of the setter breed[2] came bounding into the room and began to frisk round the host and his little nephew who welcomed his arrival. "This means that Miss Smyth will appear directly", everybody exclaimed at once, and in a few minutes a tall Englishwoman, not handsome, but having what people call an "expressive" or "intelligent" face, walked into the room and I was introduced to her at once as a fellow composer. Miss Smyth is one of the comparatively few women composers who may be seriously reckoned among the workers in this sphere of music . . . She had composed several interesting works, the best of which, a violin sonata, I heard excellently played by the composer herself.' So much for Joachim.

'She gave promise in the future of a serious and talented career. Since no Englishwoman is without her originalities and eccentricities, Miss Smyth had hers, which were: the beautiful dog which was quite inseparable from this lonely woman and invariably announced her arrival; . . . a passion for hunting, on account of which Miss Smyth occasionally returned to England for a time; and finally an incomprehensible and almost passionate worship for the intangible musical genius of Brahms. From her point of view, Brahms stood on the supreme pinnacle of all music and all that had gone before him served merely as a preparation for the incarnation of absolute musical beauty in the creations of the Viennese master. And in this case, as invariably when I come into contact with rabid Brahmsites, I tormented myself with the question: Are they all wrong and imagine what does not exist, or have I so offended God and nature that the "revelation" will never condescend to bless me?'[1]

They had many conversations. 'He would argue with me about Brahms by the hour, strum passages on the piano and ask if they were not hideous.'[3] His charm was such, she relates, that he was able to abuse her hero without giving offence. She might have reservations about Brahms as a person, but his music was another matter. All her early compositions are heavily under his influence. But now, in the absence of the Herzogenberg phalanx, and at the most severe crisis she had ever had in her private life, she was ready to change direction in her music, to entertain ideas of orchestration which would have seemed heretical before.

[1] See *Tchaikovsky*, Rosa Newmarch, 1908.
[2] Actually a cur St Bernard.
[3] *Impressions That Remained.*

Tchaikovsky urged her to strike out on her own, to listen to the world about her without any preconceptions. 'What happens in ordinary conversation?' he asked her. 'If you have to do with really alive people listen to the inflections in the voices. There's instrumentation for you!' Her ears were opened. 'I followed his advice on the spot, went to concerts with the sole object of studying orchestral effects, filled notebook upon notebook with impressions and ever since have been at least as much interested in sounds as in sense, considering the two things indivisible.'[1] She began to write a serenade for orchestra in four movements shortly afterwards, and also an overture, *Antony and Cleopatra*, finishing them the next year, 1889, in Munich where she had paused in her travels to visit old friends and badger local conductors for a place in their repertoire. Tchaikovsky and the passage of time had mended her heart.

Here, one evening while listening to *Lohengrin*, she suddenly saw amongst the audience Sir Alfred and Lady Trevelyan and two of their daughters, Pauline and Beatrice, all of whom she had met once or twice in London at entertainments given by her sister Mary, now become a fashionable hostess, thanks to her husband's coalfield. Sir Alfred was a fine example of the leisured class: cultivated, even learned, responsive to the arts, just a little eccentric, a trait brought out in him and emphasized by his Irish wife. Both the girls were musical. All were devout catholics. Ethel found her attention strongly focused on Pauline.

The whole family suffered from aches and pains of various sorts and were consequently on their way to a village in the Bavarian mountains where lived a celebrated healer called Kneipp of magnetic character, expressed in manners of great simplicity and a wonderful old face. Many persons far gone with gangrene and cancer had been cured by him. Ethel determined to join the Trevelyans in their excursion. She tended to have rheumatic twinges.

The lodgings were rough and the food horrible, but that was nothing to the point. The medical side of the establishment comprised various sheds, some for men, some for women. The treatment was the same for every disease: the patient stripped and got down on all fours when buckets of cold water were poured over selected parts. 'You then got, dripping wet, into your clothes, the thermometer being well below zero, and walked about briskly for a quarter of an hour, by which time your clothes were dry and you yourself in a wonderful glow.'[1]

[1] *Impressions That Remained.*

Strolling around barefoot in the snow was also recommended, together with draughts of certain herbal mixtures boiled up in a nearby convent whose inmates were careful never to complain of their health. The saintly Kneipp spent his days wandering through these extraordinary scenes, clad in a linen garment. Deaths were not unknown, but that was God's will. Other cases progressed well: 'a man who has been in agony daily for ten years from a railway accident' for instance, and, 'a blind man who is beginning to see'.[1]

During the course of the ablutions, which the ladies took together, and the conversations that must have filled the rest of the day since there can hardly have been any other amusements available, Ethel found herself in love not only with Pauline, but with the whole family.

'Do you know, there is a curious element of passion in my affection for Lady Trevelyan,' she wrote to Mrs Benson. 'I am always feeling I could kiss the hem of her garment and also (if I ever confessed to amateurs) confess to her. I think some day for the fun of the thing I must tell her . . . I think she would turn white and flee from the room and mutter prayers (for me and herself) all the way upstairs.' But this was a pale state compared with her adoration of Pauline.

They all went back to Munich in the middle of December 1889. Two days later the Trevelyans left for Cannes. Despite the good Kneipp's ministrations, Ethel had an appalling cold and was seriously troubled with rheumatism. 'Possibly the cure was *not* a happy thought,' she wrote to Nelly, the Benson daughter with whom she was most in sympathy. 'But all the same I'm glad and thankful I went there for that stay has revealed to me certain things about myself.' These revelations left her in a great state of agitation.

'O, Nelly,' she cried on 19 December 1889, 'love is a misery-bringing thing. I have never felt so absolutely miserable as now . . . This is partly the reaction of such *storms* of love in me as have been going on in the silent watches of the night of late.' Sometimes she thought she would go mad. Sometimes that she might kill herself but for her dog. She lay on a sofa for hours on end, quite supine.

The strain was caused, in part, by uncertainty as to whether her feelings were reciprocated. There was something distant and other-worldly about Pauline, an impenetrable serenity. 'She is a most difficult person to understand . . . decidedly gushing at first – too much so to please me. Afterwards she is, as all the family are, very affectionate.' But this was nothing like enough for Ethel. 'She *kisses*

---

[1] *Impressions That Remained.*

46

. . . as if she could feel and one thing, her religion, undoubtedly goes very deep. I'm not sure how much she likes me. Not so much I think as the second one, Beatrice, but I *don't know* . . . I know few people who impassion me more than she does. There's something in her face (I did not feel it at first) that fills me with infinite longing and love and I never felt so bitterly my incapacity to believe religious truths as with these people. They, those girls, live with God and you feel how they would be nothing without him.' Mrs Benson seemed merely pious in comparison.

One encouraging aspect was that though very attractive to men, Pauline seemed indifferent, treating her suitors in a way her mother and sister found rather cold-blooded. They said she would come back after the most harrowing scenes and begin to play her scales as if nothing had occurred. At least she was not likely suddenly to get married. This gave hope of eventual progress. 'If I care for a person like that, I can almost make passion grow under my hands as the Indian jugglers make a cactus grow under a cloth', even if it frequently happened that 'by and by I find out the glow is but a reflection, not an independent fire'. How best to rouse her from friendship and admiration of Ethel as a composer to an apprehension of the real thing? 'I can't tell you what these days have been.'

The crisis came when Pauline wrote to say she had left her *Imitation of Christ* in the hotel and would Ethel collect and keep it until they next met? Ethel's cold had now become feverish, but she hurried off and discovered the book under a cushion, 'but struggling against the awful wind and snow from the mountains it must have got jerked out of my pocket and when I got home it was gone . . . Well, I advertised and O, Nelly, last night it came back almost like a message from him whom the book is about.'

Her cold became a particularly virulent 'flu as she lay on the sofa reading the *Imitation*. Time was in abeyance. She only vaguely remembered it was Christmas eve. She read day and night with a rising temperature. Finally the illumination came: 'I had always thought of myself and of nothing else, of what I had to achieve in life, of what my duty to myself was, always myself. No wonder I had failed; no wonder all I had touched, no matter with what excellent intentions, had turned to dust and ashes . . . There was only one road to happiness, renunciation.'[1]

She must go home and look after her aged parents, even though it

---

[1] *Impressions That Remained.*

should mean the ruin of her musical career. She staggered out to the English church and knelt in a corner weeping throughout the communion service. The next day she brought a ticket to London, some brandy and a large fillet of raw beef to share with her dog on the journey.

CHAPTER FIVE

Harry Resurgent

General and Mrs Smyth were astonished, not so much by their daughter's unexpected religious turn as by the extraordinary effect it had on her conduct. She was reasonable, patient, forgiving far beyond anything they had previously experienced. And this mood lasted, not just for a day, but in seeming perpetuity. The utter chaos which overcomes a household where the members are too aged or otherwise feeble to maintain control had reached an advanced stage. Ethel inspected the bills, deleting those rendered for goods never delivered. She dismissed hangers-on who drew wages and had no occupation except eating and drinking at the general's expense. She promoted schemes of economy, such as a reduction in the number of horses and the amount of new carpets and furniture ordered by Mrs Smyth on the grounds that the old ones were boring. She did it all with such sympathy that there were no rows.

Her conversion had not been to the catholic persuasion, as she had rather hoped might be the case on account of Pauline, but to the anglican high church. Mrs Benson was not too pleased at the development, being herself low church, almost evangelical. The high church smacked of popery, a very great wickedness, most dangerous to the soul both here and hereafter. This quaint attitude can best be observed today among the Ulster protestants. Mrs Benson could not help deprecating her friend's spiritual progress, admirable though it might be in some respects. It is easier to bring an unbeliever into the fold than to deflect the recent convert. Also, she regretted the loss of influence over one of her dependents. However, the shade between them was slight as yet.

In due course, the Trevelyans returned from their continental jaunt and Ethel was able to renew direct contact with Pauline. The relationship prospered. Ethel felt she had never been so perfectly understood. They visited each other constantly, growing more and more devoted. But the real significance of this friendship was that it inspired Ethel to write a *Mass in D*, her first important work. It is dedicated to Pauline. Her conversion and the unnatural behaviour that went with it did not survive the composition of the mass, departing as strangely as it had come. Nevertheless, it was a genuine experience while it lasted.

Eighteen ninety was an eventful year altogether. The serenade she had written after meeting Tchaikovsky was included in a concert at the Crystal Palace, the first public performance of any of her music in England. There was a great flurry in the Smyth family. The general had never been to a concert before in his life and was much terrified as well as proud and excited to an extraordinary degree. Before leaving the house he wrote out and put in his pocket a telegram to his absent son. It said: 'Great success'.

The serenade was warmly received by the audience and when Ethel was called on to the platform to take a bow, she naturally looked towards the row where her parents, sisters and friends, including Pauline, were installed. Harry Brewster was sitting immediately behind her mother. For a moment she doubted her eyes. He had grown a large beard. However, the fluffy hair she had always so much admired was still intact, as was the beautiful, calm brow. He looked like a certain portrait of a Venetian nobleman by Titian, she thought.

They at once adjourned to a nearby café and settled their future over a momentous cup of tea. Harry was en route for Liverpool and the boat to America, where he had business to attend to. It was quite plain to both of them that they were not going to end their relationship. They were not even going to try any more. Harry said they should start meeting again as well as keeping up a regular correspondence. He had just finished his second book, *The Prison*, another philosophical dialogue on first principles, religion, ethics, the nature of the self and its relation to eternity and death. The prisoner is imprisoned in himself by himself. Only metamorphosis or death can free him.

After these prolonged meditations, Harry was clear in his mind as to what he wanted. It was Ethel. She attracted him more strongly than any woman since he fell in love with his wife, Julia. Nobody else had had the least effect on his marriage. Ethel had precipitated his metamorphosis. Instead of the rigorous delights of seclusion, he wanted a cheerful life with plenty of friends and conviviality. He had not been able to induce the metamorphosis in Julia. At the same time, he did not feel it possible to abandon one whose world he had ruined.

He explained all this to Ethel as they drank their tea in the vicinity of the Crystal Palace. Now that he had become a published author, he further said, he intended to cultivate the English literary scene, making frequent visits for the purpose. Surely it would be ridiculous for them to avoid each other when it could do Julia no harm as she wouldn't know of it? It was not as if they had quarrelled, or cooled off. Far from it.

Ethel prevaricated, saying it would be dishonourable to deceive Julia like that. Who could object to an innocent friendship? Julia should be informed and her consent asked. Ethel appeared not to see anything unrealistic in the proposal. She still cherished a dream of reconciliation with Lisl which would be entirely extinguished if she took up with Harry again secretly. In any case, her need for him was less than his for her as she was still deeply attached to Pauline Trevelyan, though the latter's marriage the following year fundamentally altered their connection. Ethel was now thirty-two and as yet a virgin. She did not guess how much pleasure and how much happiness Harry could give her through sex. When she eventually did find out, some while later, it surprised her greatly.

There were other psychological impediments. Her independence and love of personal freedom made the position of wife unattractive. She was not one to stay modestly in the background, preferring a husband's interests to her own, occupying herself with his comforts and bringing up children. She had a contempt for babies with their endless demands for attention and solace. Dogs were a better proposition, for they worshipped you uncomplainingly, without qualification. To be sure, in this case there was no question of marriage since Harry was not prepared to leave Julia unless she positively wished it. But he naturally wanted to make Ethel his mistress, to give her second place in his life, the object of furtive meetings which would have to be concealed from everybody, particularly his wife, as a shameful thing. Such a prospect affronted Ethel, much though she esteemed him. Her religious feelings, currently being expressed in her uncompleted *Mass*, had also to be taken into account; and her continual homosexual affairs.

Harry was not a person to try and compel a woman to a course of action against her own judgement. It was contrary to his principles and his nature, which tended to the passive. But he knew how to wait. It was agreed that he should ask Julia whether she would mind his meeting Ethel on his visits to London, it being strictly understood that there would be nothing reprehensible in the friendship. He put down his teacup and left for America.

When Mrs Benson heard all this, she was most upset. Ethel had assured her that the unfortunate involvement with a married man had ended. As an orthodox victorian, as an archbishop's wife, it was impossible for her to be other than profoundly shocked by the unexpected development. To be a single woman was to be sufficiently despised. As the particular friend of someone else's husband, one could only be execrated by all decent people. Nobody believed in innocent connections where the woman was unattached. Besides, the indiscreet Ethel was at pains to explain that Harry was in love with her and she with him; that this love which she had thought evaporated had blazed up over the tea table in a manner not to be denied.

Not only were the social consequences deplorable – who could doubt that the news would spread – but there was the danger to her soul. Mrs Benson was horrified by the thought of Ethel going straight to hell. Death was ubiquitous in nineteenth-century families. At this very time, Nelly Benson was suddenly carried off by diphtheria. Ethel might find herself confronted by eternal damnation before she had time to repent.

Though full of religion, Ethel did not allow her convictions to stand in her way. She disputed the idea that an intimate correspondence with Harry could have the result Mrs Benson believed and presented her with a copy of *The Prison*, just published, urging her to call on Harry at Aix when she passed through in the summer. He would be staying with his sister there. Mrs Benson actually did so and declared him a charming man, but did not consider his agreeable personality altered the facts of the case.

A certain coolness began to invade the relationship between the two women. Ethel said Mrs Benson was constitutionally incapable of understanding the artistic temperament. She was too rigid in her attachment to principles, whereas, 'love and what it entails is the gospel of my life'. She irritatingly objected to Ethel's hearty enjoyment of doubtful jokes. Perhaps Mrs Benson had never really wanted her except as 'an outside patient . . . It is always I who take the initiative. I daresay you would never have made one step in my direction if I had not made 20 in yours . . . I was sure I would love you enough to please a more greedy person than yourself but . . . this was not to be'.[1] It was never easy being Ethel's friend, especially if there were others in your life towards whom you had obligations.

They remained on reasonably good terms until the next crisis which was the unexpected death of Lisl from heart failure in January 1892. Ethel was thrown into a great state of emotion. 'I am trying to keep in my senses,' she wrote to Mrs Benson, three days after hearing the news. 'It is not that I am wild with grief. I go on as usual. But for the first time in my life I feel how near madness lies, how certain

[1] Letter to Mrs Benson.

52

blows entirely rob you of the sense of your own identity.'

Mrs Benson offered comfort, as did Harry and Pauline Trevelyan. The shock was magnified by the fact that it followed on the death of Mrs Smyth whose last days had been so difficult as almost to obscure a sense of loss; yet the natural relief at deliverance from an impossible home life was shadowed by a grief and remorse the more profound for being the result of a love inextricably mixed with hate and the sheer weariness of daily struggle with unreason. On the other hand, a well-known conductor in Vienna was very complimentary about the *Mass* and there seemed good grounds for hope that he would give it at least one performance. There is nothing like success in the professional field for settling the artistic soul.

The main practical consequence of Lisl's death was that Ethel agreed to meet Harry at regular intervals in London, Paris, and other convenient spots, despite Julia's objections. Ethel thought her opposition evidence of a nasty character, especially since it was plainly understood that the friendship was to remain innocent. Can one blame Julia if she took a sceptical view? She was steadily losing her husband to a younger woman whose personality was the exact opposite of her own. Now it had come to this that she was expected to encourage her rival to close with him.

Mrs Benson's reaction was equally predictable. Ethel was taking another large step towards the eternal fires. Correspondence had led to meetings which must result in sin sooner or later, no matter what virtuous intentions the parties expressed. They would be accounted lovers in any case. These thoughts led to such sharp passages between her and Ethel that relations were suspended.

Mrs Benson's son Arthur, at the time a master at Eton, tried to mediate without much success: 'You must take them as *they* are: in certain matters they have an instinct (I do not say true necessarily) absolutely ingrained which makes one view of life impossible to them . . . You complain of their wanting to alter you, and yet you want to alter them.' 'I wrote to tell him,' says Ethel in an indignant note to this letter, 'I did not want to alter them, but only to stop their endeavours to alter me.' 'I think the thing best let alone at present,' the diplomatic Arthur concludes. 'My mother is not happy about it, I know: she is puzzled and distressed: but I do not think she will change her attitude – and indeed it would not be natural: I think you had better give them up altogether for a while and see if you miss them out of your life', a piece of advice one imagines his father, the archbishop, heartily endorsed.

Ethel was still too fond of Mrs Benson completely to break with her. 'I see you as I have always seen you,' she wrote on 22 October 1892, 'and love you as I have always loved you. True, the thing has not grown into what I expected; as a rule, if you love much and imagine you are loved, much intercourse ensues, but in our case this could not be.' 'We are in a mess, Ethel,' Mrs Benson replied on 24 October, 'but light will dawn.' It was a pious hope.

She now moved into the background of Ethel's life, as is the way when friends discover that they have outgrown each other. The front rank was occupied by Harry. Arthur Benson met him at a party in this year and gave her his impressions. 'It is a curious face. He looks as if he had seen and hoped and thought much, and was a little weary of things in general – of the stupidities and banalities at all events: he came and sat next to me and I had an indefinable wish of wanting to interest him . . . Of course we talked about you: I said frankly again what I have said to you, that I do not know anyone whose personality is so potent, whom I would rather see in a room that I entered than yourself, and I think to be candid we went on talking about you till he went away . . . I suppose him to have a very subtle and analytical mind; and to have much virility and independence . . . with a delicate exterior both of form and manner . . . There is a certain negative air about him. I do not suppose he has any illusions, but I should like to know whether anything has taken their place. Seeing him was like peeping into a pleasant room and then having the door shut in your face.'

Thus this shy and melancholy man lived his ruined marriage, dreaming of fascinating Ethel. 'There are things in these letters of yours,' he wrote from Rome on 8 February 1892, 'so vibrating and so good that you seem quite near to me, in the room; and I would like to take them one by one and talk with you as by the fireside.'

We can eavesdrop on these conversations. 'No one is, or can be all we want,' he remarked on 23 September 1892. 'Everybody agrees about this and no one, I suppose, expects one person to be all in all to another except newly married German girls.'

'I have pondered much on matrimony lately and on my absolute want of talent for it,' said Ethel on 26 September. 'Such gift as I may have had has perished of atrophy (this is very pathetic). But do you know when I realized all this so keenly? In re-reading *Anna Karénine*.' 'To think that the man who wrote that book now wants us to live on vegetables,' replied he on 3 October.

'I wonder why it is so much easier for me, and I believe for a great many Englishwomen to love my own sex passionately rather than yours?' she enquires on 6 October. 'Even my love for my mother had an intense quality you can only call passion. How do you account for it? I can't make it out for I think I am a very healthy-minded person and it is an everlasting puzzle.'

He considered until 29 October, answering then: 'You wonder why so many women prefer friends of their own sex, to the degree of being able to work up a much greater amount of excitement about them. Probably there are several reasons; among others this one, that these affections entail no duties, no sacrifice of liberty or of tastes, no partial loss of individuality; whereas friendships of equal warmth with men have that danger (and others) in the background . . . As regards the morbidity of these feelings, I don't see it. You are the healthiest person I have ever met. Nervous and twangy sometimes, which is the fault of social conventions, but structurally health-in-person made woman for my delight.'

Sometimes they had tiffs. Ethel on 26 November 1892: 'Wait a thousand years and you will never see a shadow of huff in me. Whenever such a wretched growth shows its head through the soil it is uprooted as an alien weed.'

'I recollect your being much affronted when told by the Bensons that you had no love of nature,' returned Harry on 30 November, 'though the same reproach would not have ruffled me in the least.'

'I was not *huffy* at the Bensons,' said she on 13 December. 'That was merely the finishing touch to a long series of misconceptions. . . . As for you and me, we can be angry with each other, but huffiness between close friends is inadmissible.'

'Tomorrow morning,' Harry continued serenely on 22 December 1892, 'I am going out riding with an Italian officer, young Cini, who I fancy would rather like to be my son-in-law, having great illusions concerning my fortune . . . I have mused over your amusing letter. You seem determined to prove to me that I have a horrid character . . . As for the kind of hatred you allude to as cherishing sometimes against me, I know it well and return it heartily and have not the slightest objection to it; nor you either, if the truth were known. Don't stint yourself in that direction on my account.'

Thus these two friends conversed with an ease increased by distance: their love grew the stronger for not being exposed to the wear and tear of daily contact. In spite of the long period of courtship, it had not the hectic, claustrophobic tone that so many of her affairs with women display. She always regarded it as her most successful and

55

fruitful love. There was a saving balance and sanity about it.

She introduced him to her sisters who were happy to invite them both to their houses, though the husbands were somewhat scandalized to begin with. She did not think it expedient to reveal his existence to General Smyth as yet. She felt altogether as if she had entered on a renaissance and it was reflected in her music. Whereas Pauline Trevelyan had been celebrated in a mass, Harry inspired her to opera. They were collaborating over the libretto of the first one, *Fantasio*, based on de Musset's comedy of the same name.

CHAPTER SIX

The Empress Eugénie and The Mass

Ethel had an almost pathological need for the reassurance and comfort of loving relationships with women, in addition to Harry's attentions. Scarcely a day passed, it seems, without her being drawn towards some new star appearing, in the distance, as the perfect, the longed-for friend who would combine intelligence, physical beauty, instant understanding and a ready ear for Ethel's music. Much patience was also required. This hunger was not assuaged even when she had what anyone else would have considered a plethora of current enthusiasms, her passionettes as Harry called them. There were many disappointments, naturally, since few were able to conform to the ideal. But with some who fell short she remained on cordial terms for life. The Empress Eugénie was such a one.

This proud and melancholy figure, the relict of Napoleon III, had settled at Farnborough, a few miles from the Smyth family home in the 1870's and been accustomed to invite the general, his wife, and as time went on, Ethel, to her soirées. A Spaniard by origin, she was very beautiful, temperamental, intelligent, prejudiced and kind. Many adventures had befallen her, the last being the fall of Napoleon III after his defeat by the Prussians at Sedan in 1870.

In the ensuing confusion, the *communards* took over Paris suddenly, rushing the Tuileries with a roar of, *'A bas l'Espagnole!'* The empress and her lady-in-waiting managed to jump into a cab at the back door and make their way to an American dentist of their acquaintance. That good man conveyed them to a boat at Deauville, representing himself as a doctor, Eugénie as a lunatic and the lady-in-waiting as a nurse-keeper. They arrived safely at the Marine Hotel in Brighton.

Ethel did not become an accepted member of the empress's circle until 1890, on taking charge of the parental household. She would bicycle the few miles from Frimley to Farnborough, change into formal dress in the bushes and so present herself. Eugénie did not discover this for some while, perhaps on a wet evening. A room was then put at Ethel's disposal in the house.

It was a moment when she was searching for the mother figure she needed at the time. There was Harry and there was Pauline Trevelyan,

57

but the third person of the trinity, Mrs Benson, was proving unsatisfactory. Eugénie offered a beauty which age had not diminished; a wide knowledge of politics and the interest this gave to her conversation; a practical goodness toward friends that could not but be advantageous to a struggling composer.

What about her attitude to, and capacity for, love? In some ways she was passionate. 'I think no one can ever have had greater violence of temperament . . . Notwithstanding this unquenchable fire within, you felt instinctively that love can never have played a great part in her life. People have said that her skill, as Caesar's wife, in avoiding the breath of scandal is a great proof of her "cleverness", but I suspect it was still more a case of absence of temptation from within. She was not tender, for one thing, nor imaginative; and imagination plays a great part, I think, in women's love affairs. Above all, not to beat about the bush, there was no sensuality in her composition. Age has nothing to do with it.'[1]

In spite of this fundamental coolness which prevented anything of the emotional, let alone the motherly, invading the atmosphere, Eugénie took to Ethel whom she found an asset to her drawing-room, especially after dinner when the entertainment tended to collapse in cards, yawns, silences. For then Ethel could be asked to perform and it was always a success. She had any number of songs in her repertoire, some with her own settings. She would also play bits of new compositions, the *Mass*, for instance, rendering the different orchestral instruments on the piano and singing all the voice parts simultaneously at tremendous volume.

Eugénie's virtues were many, but Ethel was obliged to admit that she had certain limitations. A sense of humour, though present, was of the rudimentary, or banana skin, variety: 'obviously funny situations appealed to her much as they do to children'.[1] She had a fund of amusing stories of that kind and would tell them very well once, and then, pleased with success, immediately 'a second and perhaps a third time with regrettable amplifications and explanations'[1]. Art was not her subject either. 'One of the difficult moments at Farnborough Hill was being called upon to admire works of certain famous painters of the Second Empire which were unhesitatingly accepted by her as masterpieces.'[1] And the furniture seemed hideous to Ethel who liked the plain, straightforward style.

A similar lack of judgement often invaded her choice of friends.

---

[1] *Streaks of Life,* Ethel Smyth, 1921.

'One could not help marvelling at some of the specimens she delighted to honour . . . Though herself compact of integrity, she was fairly easy to take in.'[1] During the days of her power, this characteristic had been an important element in her downfall. So, too, had her shaky political sense. Though her 'knowledge was unlimited, her judgement on past events sound and even brilliant', yet 'listening to her comments on current English politics, I reluctantly came to the conclusion that seldom was anyone more pertinaciously wrongheaded'.[1] Even the most cursory glance through Eugénie's previous history shows how true and how penetrating are all these observations made by Ethel; and what a shrewd and humane judge of character she was when not blinded by love or rage.

Eugénie could not help responding to Ethel's warmth and enthusiasm. In the summer of 1891, she appointed her temporary *demoiselle d'honneur* and took her to Cap Martin where she was planning to build a villa. They were afterwards to cruise the Dalmatian coast in her new yacht, *Thistle*. It was a most successful excursion. 'Lord, how happy I was at Cap Martin!' cried Ethel.[2] She had the uncompleted *Mass* with her and wrote immensely long letters about God to Harry, which he found uninteresting on the whole, in spite of his philosophical leanings. He wanted the correspondence to come round to sex: the desirability of it between people fond of each other; its absolute necessity if the full meaning of love was to be experienced. He was obliged to be patient for another couple of years.

The two ladies had many confidential talks. She 'told me what I already knew,' Ethel wrote to her brother, 'that she cannot really care about anything or anybody. She touched me so horribly . . . I feel all the time as if I were reading *Antigone* or *King Lear*'. On these sympathetic terms, they paused in Venice on their way to pick up the yacht. 'It was amusing and at the same time embarrassing to look at pictures in her company, so anxious was she to believe and prove that she was enjoying it, yet so obviously at sea; also secretly bored to death.'[1] Her comments on portraits were banal in the extreme. 'But if it were the case of an historical picture, the battle of Lepanto, for instance, you could listen to her by the hour, such was her grasp of the interests at stake and of what would have happened had the issue been the other way.'[1]

Eugénie's appreciation of music was on the same level. She was

[1] *Streaks of Life.*
[2] *As Time Went On.*

perfectly ready to believe, however, that Ethel was a fine composer, destined to become famous in her profession and that the *Mass* was a first decisive step in that direction. Neither of these propositions was untrue, even though Ethel eventually turned out not to be a reincarnation of Brahms or Bach. That she was highly gifted no one could dispute. Eugénie therefore set herself to promote her friend's prospects in every possible way.

On hearing that Ethel was having the usual difficulties all artists face in their efforts to persuade someone that their work is worth money and should be supported, staged, published and generally regarded as a superb investment, she paid the printers of the score and announced that she would grace the first performance of the *Mass* in person. Business at once became smoother. Realistic negotiations began. Not content with this, she proposed to bring her to the notice of Queen Victoria, a matter which could be very conveniently arranged as she was allowed the use of a house on the Balmoral estate whenever she wished.

The great day came one afternoon in October 1891. Everybody except the empress and a lady-in-waiting was hidden, for the queen had as great a horror of coming across stray people as she had of driving in a closed carriage. Rain drove in sheets before a furious north-easter. 'Will the Queen have the carriage shut?' Ethel enquired. 'Oh dear no, I think not,' was the reply, shouted against the noise of the elements. It proved to be the case, in spite of the sciatica from which Her Majesty was then suffering.

When the royal visitor had negotiated the waterlogged red carpet and was seated in the drawing room, Ethel was summoned. 'I went in and saw a little old lady with a straw hat tied with a black ribbon under her chin . . . She is not half so red and coarse looking as one would imagine from her photos and has the very sweetest smile you ever saw and less accent, I think, than the princesses. She is very stiff now . . . but won't have a hand to help her out of her chair, even when it's an armless chair, but does a sort of little one, two, three and away business and gets up all right . . . The princesses are awfully frightened of her.'[1]

Eugénie was braver, chatting her way through formidable silences and rather giving the impression of 'a small child with its grandmother'.[1] In due course, she suggested that Ethel might sing to the assembled company, which was accepted. A number of German

---

[1] Letter to her brother Bob, 24 October 1891.

songs went down so well that the faithful Eugénie said, 'You ought to hear her sing her Mass.' The queen was graciously inclined. Whereupon Ethel launched into her star performance, playing the orchestral parts, singing all the voices and solo instruments and occasionally drumming on the floor with her feet for extra effect. The volume of sound was unbelievable as the sanctus, the benedictus, the gloria rang through that Scottish drawingroom in the middle of the tempest. Her Majesty was charmed with the novelty of it and asked for a repeat performance at Balmoral in a few days' time. She lingered on and on, which must have pleased her suite as the rain was now a perfect waterfall and it was eight miles in the open carriage before they got home. 'In fact, she never made a move to go until a gillie came banging at the door and said: "Your Majesty *must* go. The horses can't stand this" '.[1]

Eugénie was naturally delighted by her protégée's success and took much trouble with Ethel's toilette, arranging a special headgear in the form of a black serpent in her hair. Though insecure, it somehow remained in place, only becoming 'uncoiled and hanging in festoons over my face' on the way home, a remarkable piece of luck considering the athletics it was put through during the evening at the keyboard. 'Balmoral I think ugly,' Ethel reported to her brother. 'Inside, the word is too mild for applicability. It is *ghastly*. Imagine furniture draped (or rather tightly covered over) with *tartan*!' But 'the dinner was beautiful and the champagne ditto' and she was not put off her stride. The queen sat close to the piano – was she a bit deaf? – and seemed as delighted as before. Several of the princesses declared they would attend the concert to be held, it was hoped, at the Albert Hall quite soon.

'I think you are sometimes disproportionately ambitious,' Harry ventured after receiving a letter full of royalty, titles and social highlights. 'I don't mean above your abilities,' he hastened to add. 'I mean at the cost of your entire self. Is that so?' In the vehemence of her disagreement, she sent him a diatribe with special reference to his beard of which he was, in her opinion, inordinately vain. The difference between them lasted no more than a few days.

In spite of all Eugénie could do, it was January 1893 before the great day came. After many an up and down, Sir Joseph Barnby, conductor of the Royal Choral Society was persuaded to include it in one of his programmes, together with Haydn's *Creation*. Though

[1] Ibid.

he had reservations, he did his best to secure a good performance. He had also to cope with Ethel who was naturally in a great state of nerves and excitement. Luckily for everyone, she was supported and calmed by her old friend from Leipzig times, George Henschel, now become a settled figure in the London musical world. The greatest crisis concerned the rescoring of certain passages which when let off in the huge spaces of the Albert Hall sounded to the distracted Ethel like husky mosquitoes. All in all, however, she had high hopes of this *Mass*, inspired as it was by Pauline Trevelyan and the spiritual awakening which had resulted from their love. Fortunately Pauline's subsequent marriage had not had a deleterious effect on the music.

On the evening before the concert, Henschel gave a cosy little family dinner, the guests being Ethel's five sisters, their husbands, her father and Harry. It was the general's first introduction to Harry, though given Ethel's habit of talking about everything to everybody, it seems unlikely that he had not heard a good deal of him. He didn't care for the look of this artistic fellow with a beard. 'A nasty face,' he said later. He must also have realized, for such things are impossible to conceal, that this unprepossessing man, already married, was on very close terms with his daughter. But that victorian soul, who had abolished Mr Ewing, Ethel's first music teacher, fourteen years before, had learnt some wisdom in the interval. He behaved impeccably, snarling under his moustache to such a very small extent that only his relatives were aware of it.

He knew, besides, that these were great days for an old man, even if he could not altogether approve of the details. The queen had allowed her name to be used in the advertisements. The empress had promised to fill the royal box and to attend in person, although she never now appeared in public. Crowds of fashionable people had taken tickets. And this audience had not come to listen once more to Haydn's *Creation*, but to Ethel's *Mass in D*.

Military and hunting men were in attendance, too, one of whom was heard to remark at a certain point: 'I say, this is slashing stuff, what?' He referred to the Credo, loudly applauded, of which the *Daily News* critic remarked: 'Miss Smyth seems fond of strong contrasts'. Whereas the Hosanna 'fairly brought down the house',[1] with its trumpet solo, the Sanctus had 'a curious and beautiful effect'.[2] The Benedictus was also thought 'very melodious', though the Agnus Dei seemed 'not quite so grateful'.[3] The gloria, however, was terrific.

[1] *The World.*
[2] *The Times.*
[3] *Daily Chronicle.*

Bernard Shaw, present in his capacity of music critic, was reminded 'not of anything so vulgar as the Salvation Army, but of a crack cavalry band'. He was unable to detect any religious feeling, 'consequently her Mass belongs to the light literature of church music'. She ought to write a comic opera, he thought. And this, of course, was exactly what she and Harry were engaged in with *Fantasio*.

Archbishop Benson was equally doubtful. 'In the Mass,' he complained, 'God was not implored, but commanded to have mercy.' On its being explained that the intention was to convey an impression of terror, he remarked: 'Indeed? I can only repeat that to me it sounded like orders issued in an extremely peremptory manner.' The main part of the audience had no reservations. They demanded her appearance on the platform and cheered and clapped with gratifying enthusiasm.

Festivities continued some days. Ethel's sister Mary gave a splendid dinner. 'To the part she played so well,' Osbert Sitwell observed,[1] 'she brought a massive and gilded beauty like that of the Italian and Spanish furniture with which she filled her houses, a power of imagination . . . and above all a capacity for organizing that was to make her the Kitchener of hostesses . . . In the highest degree she was lavish, and if her house was a little over exuberant, the curves and gilding of table and chair a little over-emphasized, the velvets a little too complicated in pattern, these were faults of taste indicative of her epoch.'

One of her guests at the sumptuous entertainment was Maurice Baring, then in the infancy of a distinguished literary career. 'There I met Mr Brewster,' he recorded.[2] 'His appearance was striking; he had a fair beard and the eyes of a seer . . . He looked like a Rembrandt. His manner was suave, and at first sight one thought him inscrutable – a person whom one could never know, surrounded as it were by a hedge of roses. When I got to know him better I found the whole secret of Brewster was this: he was absolutely himself. He said quite simply and calmly what he thought.' An unusual trait in any man.

But the insatiable Ethel was still unsatisfied. Among the press compliments were remarks she considered anti-feminist. 'It is but seldom,' said the *Morning Post*, that a lady composer attempts to soar in the loftier regions of musical art.' The *Star* was equally backhanded.

[1] *Great Morning*, 1948.

[2] *The Puppet Show of Memory*.

'Is a great female composer possible? No, says your psychologist.
. . . With women, however, it is just the impossible that is sure to
happen:' 'If you take an average mundane young lady,' laughed
Bernard Shaw, 'and ask her what service to religion she most enjoys
rendering, she will probably, if she is a reasonably truthful person,
instance the decoration of a church at Christmas.' Though *The Times*
said, 'The Mass is distinctly original in conception and most
unconventional in treatment', nobody echoed George Henschel: 'The
most remarkable and original woman composer in the history of
music'. In short, she was not hailed as the new Brahms, and took
a dim view of that.

There were also suggestions that she owed her position more to
royal influence than to merit. The *Daily News* referred pointedly to
'the preference shown to this gifted young English lady when numerous
compositions by prominent musicians still await a hearing by our
premier choral society'. The *Musical Times* felt she was 'revealed in
the character of a very fortunate person'.

'What have they not said of Brahms and Wagner,' wrote Harry
soothingly on receiving these complaints. 'Original work generally
seems strained . . . I am sure your Mass has its faults; and so have
you; but it is strong and sweet as yourself.'

With this she had to be content, and was sufficiently encouraged
to start out almost at once on a grand public relations tour of the
continent with the object of persuading all possible orchestras and
choral societies that they should perform first of all her *Mass*, graced
and promoted as it had been by the top ranks of royalty, and next
her light opera, *Fantasio*, still in the process of composition. She began
operations at Amsterdam, receiving much politeness and what
appeared to be firm promises of inclusion in the next season's
programme. The same thing happened in Cologne, Heidelberg,
Munich, Leipzig. But, in spite of queen and empress, *Fantasio* was
only produced in 1898 at Weimar. The second performance of the
Mass had to wait until 1924 when Adrian Boult conducted it in
Birmingham and London. This time the press was exemplary.

CHAPTER SEVEN

Lovers

The Empress Eugénie may not have been an emotional friend, yet she was pre-eminently steadfast and true, always ready to do what she could to improve Ethel's prospects, even thinking up ingenious ways of relieving the poverty of a general's daughter unfitted for any employment except writing and promoting her own music. There was an occasion when, realizing her invitation to Cap Martin and a yacht trip had been refused for lack of funds, she declared she detested a certain antique piano and urged Ethel to take it away and sell it for what she could get.

Perhaps the most memorable thing she did, from Ethel's point of view, was to introduce her to Lady Ponsonby, wife of Sir Henry Ponsonby, Queen Victoria's private secretary. She had always lived in the court atmosphere, having been appointed a maid of honour at the age of twenty-one. Her interests were, however, a good deal wider than such a genteel occupation might suggest. A voracious reader, she had friends amongst the literati, such as George Eliot and Vernon Lee, already the author of thirteen various books and becoming internationally known. Maurice Baring was her nephew. She was active in the founding of Girton, in movements to alleviate the exploitation of working women and to widen the opportunities for these of the middle classes. Her opinion on all subjects was valued by her husband.

Her headquarters was at Norman Tower in Windsor Castle. She restored the medieval part to its original appearance, complete with graffiti scratched by forgotten prisoners. These rooms took her fancy particularly and she made them her own, filling them with books and the accoutrements of her various hobbies which were chiefly painting, carpentry and silver repoussé work. She was also fond of music. Some found her formidable: her keen intelligence and ready wit prevented her from suffering fools gladly and she had a way of speaking that was a little intimidating to the nervous. But her temperament was essentially warm and generous. She was sixty-one in 1893 when her relationship with Ethel changed from an agreeable acquaintance to 'that most magical of springtimes the beginning of a friendship which

I well knew would change the whole colour of my life. At last I found what had been lacking ever since Lisl broke the link between us – a woman a good deal older than myself who drew out every ounce of what seemed the natural compliment to such creative power as I possessed – the devotion it was in me to give'.[1]

Ethel's devotion was no light matter, but Mary Ponsonby was a better manager than Mrs Benson had been. If Sir Henry sometimes groaned at the sound of the well-known voice as he entered his front door, his wife was able to make amends and he never was driven to the archbishop's pitch of exasperation. His manner was only slightly alarming, although he was a man accustomed to speak his mind: Queen Victoria had once had occasion to send a message ordering him to stop muttering, 'That is absurd', at certain of her remarks.

There were times also when the sons and, especially, the daughters of the house complained that their mother allowed herself to be dominated by the intrusive Ethel, and that they felt obliged to dine out rather too frequently with the Ranee of Sarawak, a near neighbour. Mary Ponsonby pacified them and continued to receive Ethel with unabated zest. Their conversations lasted hours and were reputed to cover every subject in the universe.

The questions of women's education, rights to their own property, to a vote, to practise the professions, to receive the same wages as men whether in the factory or the office must have been included in these discussions, one would suppose, since Lady Ponsonby was interested in them all. Ethel, however, had neither time nor inclination for good works. The days and years were filled with the struggle to compose and to persuade conductors and producers, inevitably men, to stage the results of her labours. If she carried on the fight in her own limited sphere, it was as much as she could do. Her outlook was essentially emotional. Wide experience of the world and voluminous reading in four languages never gave her an intellectual's detachment. Problems were always personal. Not for her the patient devotion to a cause of those members of the women's suffrage societies who from 1870 onwards organized a private member's bill for the enfranchisement of women every year without result. How could a vote get her music into the concert hall? She must have admired the spectacular career of Florence Nightingale, but such self-discipline in the interests of humanity was totally beyond her capacity, even her comprehension of any woman's place in the scheme of things,

[1] *As Time Went On.*

let alone Ethel's. It was to take her eighteen years to see the light and join the suffragettes under Mrs Pankhurst.

Lady Ponsonby had none of the sentimentality of the revered Lisl, nor the censoriousness of Mrs Benson. But she was a passionate woman which was her main attraction for Ethel who never had any use for frigidity. This led to their having differences of an intensity Ethel had not experienced since the demise of Mrs Smyth. While Ethel shouted and stamped, her friend's eyes, normally blue-grey, turned black, as insults and accusations flew through the air. 'When I got back,' one of the daughters reported to the rest of the family, 'Ethel had been gone half an hour and the house was still rocking.' The reconciliations were sometimes so sweet that they felt tempted to quarrel again. Every explosion blew them closer together. It was 'the happiest, the most satisfying and for that reason the most restful of all my many friendships with women'[1]. This was how she viewed the situation in 1936 as she wrote her autobiography.

In 1893, however, restful seems not the word one would use in the context. 'Do you know how much I love you? Can you guess?' she demands. 'When . . . I rush up the stairs and open your door and see you are really there in the Prisons, I find I have feared goodness knows what. It is as if a new lease of life that I had hardly expected has been granted me . . . Yesterday you said you didn't know if you love me . . . What will become of me if you don't? . . . Goodnight, take me into your arms and shut me up in your soul and keep me there always.'[2] In September of the same year, she is writing: 'It is most profoundly true that voices mean to me more than anything almost and that your voice sums you up to such an extent that for me it stands for you . . . [It] is always with me, but when in moments of intense craning for sight, sound, touch of you I say, "Let me at least hear her voice", I can't hear it. I remember that in the illicit "Encyclopedia" readings I used to indulge in in years gone by . . . there was a long jaw upon impotence as resulting from over-desire.'

Lady Ponsonby took these wild declarations with a certain calm. 'Ethel Smyth has just left us and was in a charming and very companionable mood while she was here,' she wrote to Vernon Lee. 'I am glad you have discovered the kind gentle vein in her . . . The gentle tenderness E.S. shows in her relations with me is the thing I like best in her. This sounds very egotistical, but I mean I like for her sake as well as for mine, the pleasure her affection

[1] *As Time Went On.*

[2] Letter to Lady Ponsonby 16 March 1893.

gives me in spite of her rather hectoring manner; for to be thoughtful and gentle to one much older than herself proves that she is not all steel. Her singing is very beautiful and there is a vibration in it which does not suggest the cling clang of engines and the hammering out of metal on an anvil, but something much more intense and tender . . . But I find it very difficult to make up my mind as to the amount of capacity and force there is . . . My interest in her career is unbounded and I should like to leave off groping and I cannot . . . There is a splendid vigour about the way she does what she has in hand as if it were the one thing in the world worth doing. There is something in her Mass very near genius, but not quite. It is because of the demon of restlessness which seems to take the force out of it. Again, her strong belief in herself, her assertion, positive and deliberate that she knows her work is very good, is very convincing.'[1]

She tried to moderate Ethel's ardour which, fond though she was and remained of her, she could not fully return. 'You want to know what hurts me?' Ethel wrote. 'Well, just that you won't kiss me. Love and longing to see you accumulates in me in these long absences and when I see you . . . I want to say nothing but hold you close to me. This you won't have and I can't resign myself.' Letter after letter reiterates the theme: 'If I were to die, would it make you happy to know you had kept me at arms length, under the notion that my way of caring for you is ''exaggerated'', and really made that love for you more like something gnawing at a nerve than the beautiful thing it might be?'

Finally she did resign herself, writing in July 1895: 'I feel that with my anxiety to see you I am becoming a bore perhaps and that I may have overdone that note. In a way you must feel flattered. Everyone does at being desired above all things by someone they are fond of at all. But I also feel as if I were a little importunate and that you had, as it were, to fence yourself in against my importunities and that gives me rather a *serrement de coeur*. It shan't be so in future . . . My presence can't be as much to you as yours is to me . . . You have your family and your life to be fitted in and are not just an atom floating in space. And that makes a difference, of course, a difference I am over-slow to allow for.'

At this point, Sir Henry Ponsonby was mortally ill and it seems quite likely that, charming though he was, he made it plain that Ethel put a strain on him in his present condition. Whatever extra motive

[1] See *Mary Ponsonby*, ed. Magdalen Ponsonby, 1927.

she may have had to strengthen her resolution, his wife had determined that the relationship with Ethel must be continued on a reasonable level of emotion: that of dearest friends and nothing more.

Ethel always felt something more. She could not help it. But they settled into a *modus vivendi* and lived happily ever after until Lady Ponsonby's death in 1916 with only the kind of temporary estrangements one would expect between people of pronounced character. The connection was wholly beneficial for Ethel. In order to win Mary Ponsonby's affection, she had had from the beginning to cultivate self-discipline, endeavouring to control her irritability, impatience and emotional extravagance. Everybody noticed it. One of her nieces was staggered and said so.

Mrs Benson was quite jealous writing as early as 7 August 1893: 'Well, Ethel, and how do things stand between us now? I scarcely know, but I am acutely conscious of one thing – the alteration in you since you have known Lady Ponsonby. It interests me most deeply. I am and always have been very, very glad you have her. Though like many other most pardonable pangs, I may be forgiven . . . for feeling that I would rather have produced the alteration than come under its operation.'

Harry felt a slight draught: 'I think you can leave me in the cloakroom for more weeks at a stretch than I can leave you for hours. It goes with your proneness to new passions and grand discoveries of the right person, which is a beautiful gift with a touch of tipsiness in it.'

He was at this time writing *The Statuette and The Background*, a dialogue on the nature of art and of the artist. 'Certainly you will understand every line of my Statuette at first glance,' he assured Ethel. In the event, she didn't find it all that easy to follow. Her copy is annotated with such remarks as, 'This is beyond me', and, 'O, I understand but it is difficult'. Some passages she marked with approval. 'Do least what you do worst', for example; and, 'The acceptable sacrifice is that of the instincts we have not got but think we would like to have.'

Whereas Mrs Benson had been unable to take a broad view of the Harry question, Lady Ponsonby was more worldly. The whole history of the affair was related to her at length with sympathetic result. 'You say such warm endearing things to me,' he wrote on 8 March 1893, 'that I wonder who is buying my shares to make the stock rise in that manner; it is not difficult to discover the "bull" . . . he is Lady Ponsonby. Of course I am very glad of her favourable opinion.

But what rejoices me most therein is the effect it has on you.'

One of the perennial subjects, whether of conversation or correspondence, was, should they become full lovers or not? Ethel continued to resist this, though not quite so adamantly as heretofore. She had both a longing for and a shrinking from the act and put forward all sorts of excuses. Since the last thing she wanted was a baby, 'I'd rather be shot first', fear of pregnancy may have added to natural hesitations. She was also disinclined openly to flout conventional morality both for the effect it might have on her career and because of her father, to whom she had come very close since her mother's death. Although he had accepted her incomprehensible music and other vagaries with easy good nature, it was doubtful if his tolerance would stretch to her living in sin. On being asked for advice, Mary Ponsonby gave it as her considered opinion that it was a perfect miracle Harry hadn't abandoned the siege years ago and found someone more accommodating.

He persisted steadily. 'If for conversational purpose we allow that it would be "tragic unreason" in your case to give in to our (mutual) natural instincts, I want you to understand that I feel "tragic unreason" in privation. Well, at least love me in some unreasonable way, if not that one which seems most natural. But also, please, very reasonably. How wearisome is the thought of passion (for more than twenty minutes) without all the rest – the activity, the general expar;ion, the fun. And how flat all this is without the passion.'

Still she replied that she'd rather they waited a while longer, adding some remarks about the necessity of freedom for an artist.

'My ambition would be not to fold you around with my love,' he protested, 'because I think you don't want to be folded up in anything; you would complain of stuffiness in three weeks, or three minutes.' Though not seduced, she said: 'I love you with all my heart and soul'.

It was not until April 1895 that she succumbed. Her father had died in 1894. She had reached a convenient point for a break in the composition of the new opera, *Fantasio,* They could meet in Paris for a few days before she joined Eugénie at Cap Martin for their usual holiday at the villa and on the yacht. In this practical mood, she set out for the long adjourned appointment in bed with the man who, displaying the patience of Jacob for his Rachel, had been waiting, enchanted, for eleven years.

'I shan't attempt to try to influence your opinion about my last step,' she wrote to Mary Ponsonby on 21 May 1895, 'but I can at least try to explain why I acted as I did and do . . . I have always disliked the idea of not living out to the full as much of a woman's possibilities as would square with my active life. I disliked the idea of dying an old maid and also the idea of parting with my virginity (a sort of superstition, wholly fleshly, not moral on my part). I promised Harry years ago that if ever the moment came, I would say "when" . . . I started for Paris with a fixed determination and had I seen you ere I started should probably have told you what I meant to do . . . There is a mystery in this actual belonging to the best being you know, to the one who knows you best, which has come upon me, with all my 37 years, as a surprise, a new force in life. I can understand your saying once you were more in love with your husband after marriage than before. No wonder . . . If you knew what it is to be loved with his sort of love. Nothing but the strength and depth of it would redeem it from its almost unnatural absence of selfishness. When I see his intense happiness and gratitude since Paris, which I can only compare to one thing (i.e. my own) . . . it begets in me a sort of feeling of wonder at having such a thing in one's life as such love.'

Lady Ponsonby could not help being somewhat disconcerted by these confidences. 'One can understand a *surprise des sens*,' she said, 'but I don't like that sort of cold-blooded scheming.' However, she came round later, remarking, 'The best thing you ever did was to annex Mr Brewster.' Other friends refused to take the great news seriously. One who habitually spoke in telegraphese laughed heartily, saying: 'Ethel not like idea old maid so trumped up little affair.'

Hardly had the lovers accustomed themselves to the new era when Harry's wife, Julia, had a heart attack and the doctors said she might fall down dead any time. 'I am not at all muddled morally,' Harry wrote. 'The gist of my meditations is simply that our monogamic system is not suited to all natures. If we were Mohammedans, nobody and none of us, the concerned ones, would find it at all strange that I should take tender care of one wife and sit soothingly at her bedside all night as I have just done, and at the same time love another one. Yet because of our marriage laws and the artificial psychology in vogue, I must be supposed to wish evil to one woman and forget a past for which I am deeply grateful, because I wish well to another woman and the present is richer with her.'

In September 1895 she died. 'I want to tell you this once how I feel towards her now that she is gone,' he said. 'Think of a beautiful villa with a garden of unsurpassed dignity in a malarious desolate country. It is ague and almost death to linger there and yet almost impossible to tear oneself away. I have loved her and hated her deeply; not successively, but simultaneously.' These were the daily agonies he had concealed under an exterior of imperturbable urbanity and calm.

Ethel could pretend truly to regret Julia's passing, but it did mean that Harry now expected her to marry him, as seemed the right and proper next step. 'Oh, for the happy days when no such odious idea could possibly poison our correspondence!' she exclaimed. Her position was that if they married it must be only in order to meet openly. In all other respects their life should go on exactly as before. By this she meant her life. His had been fundamentally altered by widowerhood.

'I see endless rocks ahead if we *don't* marry,' she wrote in a long, confused letter on 18 October 1895. 'As yet few people know about you. You have been but as a bird of passage.' But should he come to live in England, as he thought he might, 'I should not be able to see you without explanation and to go about London with a man who has many friends would be impossible'. There would be 'kind warning words from sisters (who up to now, alas, think the best and ask no questions), gossip in the village, anxious enquiries from the Empress, none of which would affect *you*'.

On the other hand, she 'doesn't want a home, or more money, or a social position, or whatever women marry for', and certainly not children. 'No marriage, no ties, I must be free,' she had written to Lady Ponsonby in 1894. 'I love my own loves, my own life. I thank God for teaching me to know my own mind in some few things that matter.'

Harry wanted their marriage chiefly because, under present arrangements, he saw her only infrequently and for short periods. They always had to waste some of the precious time in getting used to each other again. He was sure she would come to enjoy sex as much as he did if they made love regularly in a relaxed home atmosphere.

'If I could have these things naturally,' she replied, 'I think I could get the greatest delight in them. Though mind you, that side of life which you say gives you wings is not a necessity to me and my feeling about you, the most important I can have about anyone, is nothing to do with sensations of that order, but with something that to me *is* the chief thing. Still, I know the flesh is a power.'

What she really sought in her continual romances was highly charged friendship supplemented by the preliminaries of sex: kisses, hugs, being arm in arm, or hand in hand. For all her talk of love,

Lovers

her constant pursuit of new objects, it could be said that she was a chaste woman and also emotionally immature. This is not to say she never consummated an affair with a woman, but it was rare in proportion to the number of times she declared herself, and indeed was, head over heels, hopelessly, helplessly, in love.

Any woman who has pursued her own career alone until the age of thirty-seven would have difficulty in accommodating herself to the constraints and duties of marriage: the loss of personal freedom; the regularity of the days; the problem of the beloved's friends and connections; above all, his constant presence. How much more Ethel who was either shut up with her piano, or out on some jaunt of business or pleasure. 'See what you ask?' she cries, 'My life is too full as it is.' She could sometimes just conceive of marrying a man, 'but not his children or his relations'.

Having considered the matter from every angle, with a good many *non sequiturs* and flat contradictions, she came to the firm, correct, conclusion: 'I know marriage is not for me and no one but a madman would think it would be.' Harry resigned himself to the fact that his matrimonial ideas, natural though they might seem in the circumstances, were too cosy for Ethel. 'What prompted me to ask you to marry me was the wish to complete and perfect the work of many years,' he wrote, 'but very fairly and wisely you showed me that it would be the wrong way; a conventional conclusion tacked on for the satisfaction of the upper gallery.'

It was finally settled that he should live in Rome. They met at intervals in Italy, Germany, France, England, sometimes spending several weeks together on bicycling or mountaineering expeditions. They further agreed that if either wished to end the association for any reason, it should be done without recrimination. The impracticability of such an arrangement had been fully demonstrated in his marriage, but this made no difference to the optimistic Harry. 'I think generally speaking,' Ethel remarked, 'that you, like all seers, like all people who walk with their head in the stars, are apt to neglect very terrestrial matters.'

In other ways, they were quite sensible. Harry said he needed more sex than Ethel intended to provide. Had she any objection to a certain woman of Rome? Ethel had not; firstly on the grounds that the young person was not a lady; and secondly because he promised never to go near her during Ethel's visits. He said she, of course, would be equally free to indulge in a subsidiary affair in his absence, not that there was much danger of such a thing, as he very well knew. Her

73

perpetual entanglements with women, he didn't count.

This understanding saw them through the rest of their life together which lasted until 1908 when Harry died of cancer. They remained deeply in love. As is often the case, the intermittent character of the affair heightened their passion. Quarrels were terrific, but short. 'I cannot understand why you and Mr Brewster don't marry and have done with it, 'Mary Ponsonby said at a certain point. 'Simply because we don't want to have done with it,' Harry replied.

CHAPTER EIGHT

Operatic Adventures

These momentous questions were not the only subjects of discussion. There was the genesis of *Der Wald* (*The Forest*), Ethel's idea for a new short opera. A melodramatic story, it concerns two simple peasant lovers destroyed by the evil machinations and jealousies of the local noble lady. The subject had some relevance to her own history, for she had always hated, and even feared, the mother of Lisl and Julia, the redoubtable Baroness von Stockhausen, who had represented her as a common adventuress and done her best to expel Ethel and all her works from the family.

Der Wald was to be entirely in German because all her most useful musical connections were continental. Besides, English opera did not exist, except in the form of Gilbert and Sullivan whose successful career, begun in the 1870's, might indeed be the envy of any aspirant. But Ethel's plan was to become a *grande dame* of international opera, a female Wagner. She felt a certain affinity for him, being violently romantic and much attracted by the vague grandeurs of myth and symbol expressed in stories of doomed love, primeval forces and music recalling the tempests of the soul in torment, in spite of a saving sense of humour which sometimes conflicted with serious intentions. Her ambitions were too high, as often happens in such cases, yet they could not be dismissed as altogether wrong. Her future operas were to be performed on the international stage. She was the most distinguished English operatic composer of the 1890's and early 1900's.

First, there was the business of placing *Fantasio*, a much lighter work. Perhaps the conductors, orchestras and musical authorities of the numerous German states felt a tremor at the approach, yet again, of Ethel in her tweeds, with her dog, her music under her arm, a sheaf of introductions to the local royalty in her hand, her emphatic voice ringing through clouds of cigarette smoke. At Dresden they thought the text too colloquial. Wiesbaden tended to agree. She polished up the diction in Leipzig without positive result. Munich suggested that the people at Carlsruhe would find it perfectly to their taste. If not, then Weimar should prove a certainty.

Meanwhile, Eugénie had had a wonderful idea. Since neither

Covent Garden nor the Carl Rosa company cared for new opera, particularly of the light variety, why not turn it into a sort of musical play with spoken dialogue, songs, interludes and so on? She had found an interested theatre and would herself put up the money. Ethel was not keen to have her masterpiece presented as 'a series of music-hall turns sandwiched between words calculated to get a good laugh every three minutes . . . Eventually my wonderful Empress saw that Weimar would be better.'[1]

'Darling,' she wrote to Harry when everything seemed to be fixed, 'I am slowly and surely going mad with joy. After so much hope and so much despair, it has taken days for the truth to dawn upon me and make me the indescribably happy being I am.'

After several more alarums and excursions, (the leading singer lost his voice at the last moment), *Fantasio* was actually produced on 20 May 1898 at Weimar. A large contingent of Smyth family arrived, a good number of friends, and, of course, the faithful Harry. Splendid parties were given by the grand duke and others. The audience seemed to enjoy itself on the great night, but the press was cool.

She did not put this down entirely to prejudice against women. 'I think there is a discrepancy between the music and the libretto. Far too much passion and violence for such a subject . . . If, as I believe, the Gilbert and Sullivan output is immortal, it is partly because of the absolute identity of texture between subject and music.'[1]

Ethel and Harry had chosen this improbable story of princes disguised as court fools, young ladies pursued by rich men hiding their baldness under wigs, in the unreal tradition of opera. It expressed the lighthearted side of their relationship. But the music came from altogether different levels. 'You think I purposely don't talk about my musical affairs,' she wrote to Lady Ponsonby in 1894 during the gestation of *Fantasio*, 'and I have always told you I talk freely when I have something to say. But those moments are few and far between . . . My talkative moments are like moleheaps which mark here and there the line of the underground work, but between each moleheap there is silence.' At such times the stress of creation was best alleviated, she found, 'by the society of golfers and readers and those I am fond of, but not (then) of musicians'.

The diggings and tunnellings were into a mind at that time reverberating with two of the most profound and successful love affairs Ethel ever had: Mary Ponsonby on the one hand; Harry Brewster

---

[1] *What Happened Next,* Ethel Smyth, 1940.

76

on the other. What wonder that the music came crashing and rolling in a manner suggesting 'you really might be assisting at the peak moment of an opera entitled *Death of King Charles, Martyre!*' as she herself remarked,[1] rather than the snatching off of a wig and the discomfiture of an elderly lover.

It was not all sound and fury, however. 'The opera contains some lovely songs . . . and some of the most delicate music Ethel Smyth ever composed,' Maurice Baring wrote of the only other performance, which was at Carlsruhe in 1901, 'but the libretto is undramatic and there are not enough bones in the framework to support the musical structure.'

Although they had worked long and hard on *Fantasio*, with constant arguments, consultations, rehashings, neither Ethel nor Harry had had previous experience of writing for the stage. His published work in 1898 consisted of three books of philosophical dialogues and some poems and articles, none showing the least propensity to drama. Theatricals strike one as alien to his ruminative mind, his quiet, mysterious manner, his tendency to shrink from the world which kept him at his wife's side even after he had been captured by the robust Ethel and shown that he had led an impoverished life hitherto.

His habits were now totally changed. He became almost a *bon viveur*, giving much-appreciated lunch and dinner parties in Rome and cultivating an army of friends and acquaintances. He tried to see Ethel as often as possible. They had, after all, to get on with the new opera, *Der Wald*. 'Please don't stay a month in Scotland,' he implored, 'I want so much to see you . . . That you should be away when I arrive has a certain socially aesthetic look about it that I appreciate, but enough is as good as a feast and too little almost as bad as starvation.'

One revolution he would not consent to was that he should take up golf. Ethel had become perfectly mad on the game and remained so for the rest of her life. Hunting had been her passion for many years, but she had gradually felt a revulsion at the idea of chasing a defenceless animal to its death for fun. Harry was at least spared efforts to get him into the field. He was ready to join in certain of her other recreations, such as climbing mountains and bicycling. He also enjoyed visiting Eugénie, whom he had previously dismissed as superficial, frivolous and not worth bothering about.

'We often dined together at Farnborough Hill – just he and I and the house party; and the presence of a man who had passed his youth

[1] *What Happened Next.*

in France and spoke French like a Frenchman brought her out and made the rather dreaded hour and a half between dinner and bed-time pass like a dream.'[1] This was the interval during which Ethel usually got to work on the piano in the hope of mitigating the general boredom, or distracting attention from some such scene as the following, described in a letter to Lady Ponsonby: 'Prince Victor [Bonaparte] is such a great oaf. He never opens his lips unless to make remarks of an amorous and risky character. Nothing but the subject of la femme can rouse him from his torpor and he and "the beauty" Mme Chevreau[2] sit and murmur in corners, crammed up against each other in a way that makes me rather sick – so very vulgar. This sort of thing by the hour (in whispers). Prince: Madame, je vous conjure, nô montez pas votre pied comme ca. Mme: Et pourquoi pas, Monseigneur? Vous deplâit-il? Mon pauvre pied? Prince (d'un voix étouffée): Parce que je ne peux pas répondre de ce qui arrivera . . . il y a des choses qui me troublent d'un façon que . . .! And so on by the hour. I could kick him. I admire the Empress who has the supreme gift of ignoring what she wishes not to see – and don't I know how she abhors such a thing.' It seems that even spirited renderings of *Der Wald* were insufficient to deter him.

Ethel declared herself intoxicated with the new opera, comparing her sensations to those of a mother with a newborn child. She tried it on Covent Garden, now venturing on modern works, and had a satisfactory reception. But as she had been given too many false promises in her time to be easily convinced of their coming true, she set off on another tour of Germany. Even if a London production should materialize, it would be silly to neglect the country where she had just begun to make real progress with *Fantasio* played in Weimar and Carlsruhe. It was true these two cities declined to repeat the experiment, but Dresden seemed keen enough. Advanced arrangements were made and then, at the last moment, evaporated as in a repetitive dream.

The furious Ethel took a train to Berlin where the wife of the chancellor, von Bülow, happened to be an Italian lady for whose mother she had conceived an admiration when in Rome. She was therefore in a good strategic position for an assault on opposing forces. The enemy was strong. Some said, as usual, that a woman composer was a contradiction of terms. Others that she was nothing like famous enough to be considered: had this *Fantasio* she was always talking

---

[1] *What Happened Next.*
[2] Another relict of the Empire.

about been such a roaring success? Others simply that she was English, perhaps the greatest disadvantage for it was now 1901 and the Boer war was in full swing. The Germans were fanatically pro-Boer, believing every sort of atrocity story. The newspapers were full of them, often supported by photographs of doubtful authenticity. A particular favourite showed a British soldier holding his bayonet straight up in the air with a baby on it. The streets were not pleasant. 'We English abstained from gazing into shop windows lest our turned backs should present too convenient a target for the patriotic, but cautious, spitter.'[1] More to the point, the distinguished Muck, who was to conduct *Der Wald*, turned purple and swelled alarmingly in the veins at the mere mention of Englishmen or Boers. Only a belief in his sacred duty to art and in Ethel as a composer enabled him to subdue his feelings to a certain extent.

He was probably helped in this supreme effort of self-control by a consideration of Ethel's social position in Berlin. She was frequently invited to dine by the chancellor, with whose wife she was now on the most cordial terms. The kaiser was in the habit of spending informal evenings there, on occasion. He chose the guests, generally all men, and ordered them to treat him as an ordinary human being. He felt the better for these escapes from protocol, artificial though they were. The faithful Eugénie had recently written to him about Ethel, of whom he had naturally also heard from the von Bülows. His curiosity aroused, he commanded that she be produced and placed next to him at table.

Ethel admired the deft way he managed an implement combining the properties of a knife and fork, necessitated by his withered arm. She thought he looked like an overgrown schoolboy and was agreeably surprised by his good manners and kind air. His conversation was another matter. 'He said such incredibly stupid . . . things about art to a horrible man, a certain court painter, that I wheeled round and talked to my other neighbour, feeling I should say something too awful if I listened.'[2] This was after she had heard him propound: 'One man is capable of painting a tree. Good! Another can paint a human figure. Better still! But the real problem is to combine man and tree on one canvas', and the court painter murmur in a swoon of delight, 'An amazing pronouncement! The whole function of art in a nutshell!'

He greatly improved after dinner when he took her aside and became absorbed in conversation with her for an hour and three

---

[1] *Streaks of Life.*
[2] Letter to her sister Alice, 11 March 1902.

79

quarters, standing all the time, as was his custom. He never sat if he could help it. They spoke of Eugénie and the events leading to the downfall of Napoleon III; of the Boer war, on which he expressed moderate and tactful opinions; of his scheme for the complete reorganization of the English army. Ethel lectured him on English history and the English character in order to give a proper perspective of the war. He stared rather, but said, 'I daresay you are right.' 'I *know* I am,' replied Ethel.

But in spite of her connections, she still encountered obstacles of all sorts at rehearsals. There were catcalls and other demonstrations on the first night of *Der Wald*, 21 April 1902. The press was terribly sarcastic. Yet in the end, four performances were given and members of the orchestra went out of their way to praise her music.

The kaiser, naturally enough, had not been informed of these activities by his subordinates. A few days later, he found it convenient to while away a couple of hours at the von Bülows' before catching a train. 'Miss Smyth,' he said at once, 'I am delighted to see you again.' And he asked her how things had gone in his opera house, certain that he would receive an enthusiastic reply. His host was in some trepidation as to what Ethel might say. But she made the expected remarks, for once, and the conversation veered to the safer ground of politics, shipping trusts and the kaiser's hope of making Berlin a cultural centre like Paris, or London. He seemed to regard Ethel as a sort of court fool. She found it easy to make him laugh uproariously. He nearly fell off a chair, on to which he had been skilfully manoeuvred, in one of his paroxysms. Whatever she said had much the same effect, even when she crashed her fist down on a rickety table in vehement disagreement with his views on England.

He did not forget the mad Englishwoman. Some years later she happened to be bicycling in the Campagna near Rome. A carriage approached swiftly. Seeing the imperial eagles, she scrambled up on the bank and curtseyed as well as she could with a bicycle in one hand. The kaiser stared. He stood up. He waved and disappeared in a cloud of dust.

Berlin was a famous victory, to be followed almost immediately by another. Covent Garden sent a contract and expressed a desire to put on *Der Wald* within three months. Perhaps they were spurred by reports of her exploits in Berlin. Perhaps the Empress Eugénie, or Lady Ponsonby, or others of her superior friends, had a hand in it. She tore back to London.

The stage director at Covent garden in 1902 was Francis Neilson.

(Above) Harry Brewster

(Right) Ethel in 1913
(The Museum of London)

Ethel supports Emmeline Pankhurst as she is arrested at Ethel's garden gate, May 1913. The militant Nurse Pine looks on with indignation. *(The Museum of London)*

He had previously heard her play *Fantasio* at the house of a mutual friend without being impressed. 'Ethel herself was far more interesting than her opera. She played it while smoking cigarettes incessantly. She would even stop in the middle of a scene to light another.' The voice parts were evidently not included in this rendition, or else they were sung by somebody else. On being offered a cigar, 'she took it and said that she would smoke it after dinner, that it was a pity to ruin a good cigar by letting it go out every now and then'.

He was not very surprised, therefore, when she arrived at ten o'clock at night with *Der Wald* under her arm, announcing that the Royal Opera Syndicate had offered her a production and she wanted him to direct it, personally. She was 'just the same Ethel Smyth, but this time wearing a tam o'shanter . . . She wanted to know when I thought rehearsals would begin . . . I took the score home with me and worked on it over a weekend. It was a strange and beautiful thing and my estimate of Ethel Smyth went one thousand percent'.[1]

Everything seemed to be going smoothly when the management announced that it would be necessary to put off *Der Wald* until next year in order to make way for two new French works. 'I made up my mind then and there that *Der Wald* should not be dropped,' writes Neilson stoutly, 'but paragraphs appeared in the newspapers stating that it had been postponed. Ethel Smyth was upset, to put it mildly.' She did not waste time in useless fulminations. Turning to the old girl network so carefully built up over the years, she arranged that a message be received at Covent Garden requesting the date of the first night as the king intended to send a representative. The reply was, 18 July 1902.

'I more or less trained all the principals myself,' the indefatigable Ethel relates, 'and of course the chorus, a job I always love. Anything like the keenness and fiery enthusiasm of the whole company I never saw.'[2] At the same time, she was circularizing her wide acquaintance, ordering them to buy tickets. And she was organizing a tremendous dinner to follow the performance with her sister Mary, ever generous in money matters. The famous Melba lightly said she wouldn't come unless three duchesses were of the party. 'The redoubtable composer started work at once to find the three duchesses. She found them: one was lame, and the other two were quite deaf.'[1]

In addition to all this, she was sending long letters to Harry who was on holiday in Greece; and sometimes as many as five notes

[1] *My Life in Two Worlds,* Francis Neilson, 1952.
[2] *What Happened Next.*

a day to Neilson. 'These were sent from the oddest places – a restaurant, a telegraph office, a place where she was staying for the weekend. Some were written in railway trains and posted at wayside stations,' says Neilson. In the course of three years, he received about five hundred. He sometimes wondered how she managed to carry the huge quantities of notepaper, envelopes and stamps she needed for the day.

'That Covent Garden *Wald* was the only real blazing theatre triumph I have ever had,' Ethel wrote in happy recollection. The royal box was full of royalty. People like Henry James and Sargent were dotted about the stalls and other boxes. The critics were in a good mood, in marked contrast to the curmudgeons of Berlin. 'Miss Ethel Smyth's one act German opera is more serious and infinitely less fantastic than the same clever musician's *Fantasio*,' the *Times* critic pronounced. 'She has furnished herself with a libretto so intelligent and well constructed as to prove her literary and poetical gifts to be equal to her musical ability.' Nevertheless, he felt it dragged in places and could do with a bit of pruning.

The audience had no such reservations. The applause was terrific. There were innumerable curtain calls. The pandemonium lasted almost ten minutes. 'Who is the little woman with Neilson?' asked Lady Ponsonby of her neighbour in a voice audible on the stage where Ethel stood, clad in a heliotrope evening gown produced by Mary at Neilson's instigation. On being informed that the little woman was Ethel, Lady Ponsonby shouted indignantly: 'I can't believe it. Ethel never looked like that.'

Exciting prospects began to manifest themselves. Covent Garden promised another performance the next season, 1903. A contract was made with Strasbourg, though Ethel hadn't much opinion of that city as an operatic centre. But what really thrilled her was an offer from the Metropolitan Opera House in New York. By a coincidence Mary was on the point of going to America to visit Sargent with whom she was so friendly that he 'inclined to see in every woman he painted the reflection – which he himself projected – of Mrs Charles Hunter [Mary] – of whom he made so many portraits. Upon all his female sitters he liked to bestow a little of her massive, embalmed and enamelled beauty'.[1] He was at that moment frescoing the Boston Library. She was ready to pay Ethel's expenses. Harry was against her going on the grounds that she would find it exhausting, vulgar

---

[1] *Left Hand, Right Hand, Osbert Sitwell, 1945.*

and perhaps detrimental to her reputation as a serious artist. 'See here!' she retorted. 'If it catches on in America I shall make money . . . But for it to catch on it must be produced properly, and as Neilson can't go I *must.*'

Inspired by these high hopes, she embarked for New York with her sister in the spring of 1903. The first misfortune was that the impresario who had negotiated the contract and intended to produce the opera was suddenly struck down by a mortal illness. His successor had a girlfriend, 'a music hall type', and insisted that she be given the leading part. Ethel defeated him in a sharp fight. He remained sulky and uncooperative thereafter. Then she got tonsilitis and lost most of her voice. She didn't like the Americans, finding them boastful, pushing and uneducated. They were not able to understand how she could be a famous composer when it was obvious, not least from her clothes, that she had no money at all. Mary was much more their idea of a successful woman: rich, beautiful, perfectly dressed, friend – some said mistress – of the renowned Sargent, charming, knowledgeable about literature and the arts. Ethel became irritated by a general tendency to treat her simply as a poor relation, and even more by what she regarded as Mary's sham culture. It was her conviction that her sister had no artistic feeling and merely repeated third-hand opinions picked up in smart drawing-rooms. 'She belonged essentially to the world that in the words of Walter Sickert "dined out for Art".'[1]

Nor did Ethel make any cash worth speaking of from two indifferent performances in New York and one, even worse, in Boston. 'Though the press, except for certain rather unfriendly German-owned papers, was excellent, I felt in my bones that *Der Wald* was as out of place in America as one of the Muses would be at a football match.'[2]

---

[1] *Great Morning,* Osbert Sitwell, 1948.
[2] *What Happened Next.*

CHAPTER NINE

Wrecked

There was not much time for regrets or repinings, for she was already engaged in the composition of her next, and most successful, opera, *The Wreckers*. It was an idea she had had vaguely in mind since a Cornish holiday eighteen years before, when she had explored the smugglers' caves, especially Piper's Hole in the Scilly Isles, entered by a narrow passage which runs under the sea and ends in a strange subterranean lake, at that time stocked with blind goldfish. She had listened with avidity to the guide's stories of ships lured on to rocks by false lights; of looting, rapine and murder; of a people who considered this a perfectly legitimate way of life. It was not for them to question God's wisdom in thus providing for their greater comfort in a hard world.

She was never quite sure how she conceived the plot of two young lovers who lit warning beacons and thus cheated their village of its prey, for which treason they were condemned to die in a cave flooded by Atlantic rollers at high tide. Anyway, she sent Harry an outline in the autumn of 1902, asking whether he thought it would do. He was inspired. He would write a verse play in French, he said, which would interpret her wild music of the thunders and boomings, the hissings and shriekings of surf against Cornish cliffs, with the high screaming of sea birds superimposed.

There were various reasons why the libretto should be in French. One was that Harry was in a French period as a writer. His latest book, *L'Ame Päienne*, had recently been published and was in that language which he knew as well as English. Ethel had not been too complimentary on the subject, for it set forth a semi-oriental fatalistic system whereby all events and feelings, whether joyful or sorrowful, should be accepted without struggle or agitation of any sort, enabling the quiet mind to progress towards enlightenment. This kind of attitude struck the energetic Ethel as supine and she said so. While she was at it, she accused him also of growling his remarks in an irritating manner; and of vanity in that he never seemed to tire of the adulation of a certain feminine circle in Rome. His philosophy proved equal to the test. He promised not to growl; admitted he might be a little vain, but only of his hair; tried to explain that passivity was as valid an attitude to existence as the activity she prized. Luckily, she had no reservations about his draft libretto. It was as full of fire as anyone could wish.

Another good reason for writing in French was that since Messager had been appointed musical director at Covent Garden, a strong Parisian tide had set in; as, indeed, Ethel had experienced when *Der Wald* had been in danger of postponement in favour of two French works. *The Wreckers* might well stand a better chance disguised as *Les Naufrageurs*.

Neilson, still the stage director, had a low opinion of Messager's practical gifts: 'A brilliant musician who wrote successful comic operas; a man of excellent taste and of great refinement, but the last one in Europe who should have been chosen for such a position. Poor fellow – he was worse than useless!'[1] He had not the slightest doubt, however, of his own infallibility, saying of the genesis of *The Wreckers*: 'It is true Ethel gave me the idea that she wanted to develop, but she did not know how to proceed with it. I promised to write a full scenario, and one night . . . I read it to her and Harry Brewster.'[1]

Whatever polite interest they may have expressed, their reaction was adverse. 'Neilson is phenomenally destitute of dramatic talent,' said Ethel to Harry afterwards. 'Those who have read Ethel's Reminiscences and who have known our very close association in the production of opera,' Neilson later complained, 'have remarked on her silence as to what I did for her . . . I think that gratitude for favours received . . . was not one of her strongest points.'

Brushing aside Neilson, who in any case had decided to leave an insufficiently appreciative Covent Garden for politics, Ethel and Harry pressed on in their own way. It was a strenuous business: 'Alas, the easy and carefree correspondence with my friend – one of the great joys of my life – now degenerated into an endless discussion about *The Wreckers*; in fact our letters were about nothing else'.[2] For she by no means confined herself to the musical side. 'The lines of mine you don't like,' she wrote, 'are just the ones Maurice [Baring] particularly likes. Please don't alter them.' 'You should study French prosody,' he said. 'Your lines don't always bite in French. You see the right place to bite, but the teeth are not always there. The French teeth, I mean.' 'I see now why you object to them,' she admitted, ordering him to remove Maurice Baring's favourites. 'Do try to

[1] *My Life in Two Worlds.*
[2] *What Happened Next.*

avoid melodramatic clichés,' he expostulated at one point. 'I feel awfully full of power,' she returned. 'Deadly sure of what I am doing.'

When the composition was sufficiently advanced, she performed selected excerpts to her friends. The empress's favourite was a dramatic lyric called 'The Dead Rat', sung by a young woman suffering from unrequited love. One day, after a spirited tea-time rendering by Ethel, she ascended the stairs to dress for dinner, her hand under her left breast, 'singing after a fashion too comic to describe: "Ah! mon coeur . . . le rat . . . le rat! Ah! . . . il ne bat plus" '. 'Mais Votre Majesté a exactment le cri de Miss Smyth!' exclaimed one of the attendant ladies.[1] Ethel laughed so much as she was bicycling home that she collided with her dog and they both fell into the ditch.

Eugénie, naturally, did everything she could to advance *The Wreckers*. The Prince of Monaco was her dear friend. Surely the Monte Carlo opera house would take an interest. So it did, until the reigning director left and his successor insisted on other projects. Covent Garden hedged. Leipzig was uncertain, even though a contract was signed, because the man in charge had just been sacked for grossly exceeding his budget. Frankfurt expressed boredom. Prague said it would be too expensive.

But, by good fortune, Ethel had made an important new friend in Paris, the Princesse de Polignac, originally Winnaretta Singer of the sewing machines. Her father, Isaac, had risen from humble beginnings as a strolling player. Winnaretta resembled him in some ways, being ambitious and forceful. 'I have seldom seen a woman sit so firmly,' Harold Nicolson noted in his diary. 'There was determination in every line of her bum.' Her aim in life was not to make money, for she had millions, but to be a leader of society, a patron of the arts, the owner of a salon to which everybody connected with music, literature, painting, the theatre, naturally gravitated. For this she felt it necessary to be married and titled. The only difficulty was her implacable lesbianism. The first impoverished aristocrat she bought didn't keep his side of the bargain and had to be got rid of for persistently making attempts on her bed. The second, Prince Edmond de Polignac, was in every way perfect: elderly, witty, artistic, charming and obedient.

She never looked back. The prince died in 1901 after eight happy years. As widows were acceptable to society, Winnaretta was not put to the trouble of replacing him. She was safely launched. Her

[1] *What Happened Next.*

drawingroom was always full of dukes and duchesses, counts and countesses, lords, ladies and gentlemen come to converse with each other and to view such phenomena as Proust and Verlaine, Sickert, Sargent, Cocteau, Forain, Isadora Duncan, Diaghilev; to listen to the latest works of Chabrier, Debussy, Ravel, Vincent d'Indy and, now, Smyth.

The hostess herself played the piano skilfully and painted in a style so close to Manet that various of her works were later sold as the master's productions by the unscrupulous to the gullible. Some guests, however, regretted that in the redecoration of her house she had abolished the huge bronze rhinoceroses and elephants and other wild animals pouring water down flights of stairs that had given the hall such individuality in the old days.

It was a milieu Ethel found very congenial. Her songs and chamber works were applauded by the assembled notables. Winnaretta nearly got *The Wreckers* taken by Brussels, though not quite. The only complication was that Ethel became madly attracted to her hostess who was unable to respond, much preferring young beauties. Ethel was by this time getting on for fifty.

Harry was quite worried about her. The high emotional pitch at which she was living and the continual frustrations and rushings here and there over *The Wreckers* had reduced her nerves to such a state that, although she tried every day for a fortnight, she was unable to summon up enough courage to go into a shop and ask for a packet of hairpins. He offered advice on the love problem: 'You must not betray your nature. You must love happily . . . The fact is it takes two to make a passion . . . Can you love the particular person who engrosses you now in that spirit? If so, well and good. If not, you have got poison in your blood, and you must not go on swallowing more of it under the pretence that suffering may be good practice for you.' She will, of course, recover in due course. 'Only don't be too long about it.'

After numerous quarrels, Ethel and Winnaretta settled down to a friendship which endured the rest of their lives. In December 1940 Winnaretta, a refugee from France, wrote: 'My heart is full of gratitude for all you put in my life, your music, your incomparable singing, your wit, even your bouts of anger. It will be something I will remember till the last . . . I think of you so much, darling.'

The evolution from storm to calm was due to time, naturally, and also to the fact that they needed each other in a practical sense. Winnaretta believed in Ethel, considered her an ornament to her salon, never tired of promoting her in any way she could. Ethel thought Winnaretta a true judge of music, valued her opinion and, especially, her introductions.

Harry was particularly kind and helpful on the operatic front. Prague had only turned down *The Wreckers* on the grounds of expense, otherwise declaring it 'a beautiful work – powerful and original'.[1] He offered a thousand pounds to cover the costs of production and the thing was fixed for 1906. Almost at the same moment news came from Leipzig that two performances were definitely on the autumn programme. Ethel began to revive. With unusual tact, perhaps partly due to her debilitated condition, she decided that 'the best chance . . . might perhaps be to let the conductor work it upon his own lines and not interfere at all'.[1] The only stipulation was that no cuts were to be made without her express permission.

When she arrived in Leipzig, just before the final rehearsal, and found that the third act had been badly mauled, she blew up, threatened to absent herself, to cancel everything. They soothed her as best they could. The loyal Mary occupied the chief hotel with a party of ten. Celebratory dinners were laid on. But Ethel continued growling and snarling.

In the event, the evening proved a great success. People said they had seldom heard such a volume of applause. There were thirteen curtain calls. The critics seemed ecstatic. Everyone was in euphoric mood, except Ethel who kept on complaining: nonsense had been made of the third act; this must be rectified before the second performance. In order to pacify her, the conductor and director pretended to agree. But the next morning she received a short note from each saying no further changes could or would be made. It precipitated a tantrum, during which she rushed to the opera house, seized all the scores and then took the train to Prague. It did not strike her as unreasonable and ridiculous to demand that a successful production be altered or else scrapped. As for the singers and musicians, cheated of their expectations, why should she bother with them when she was prepared to jeopardize her own future with the conductors and directors of Germany in the name of the sacred right of a composer to have the last word?

One of the reasons she permitted herself so large an indiscretion was that she believed Prague would do things superbly. Who could doubt it? Harry had paid well. But here divine justice caught up with

[1] *What Happened Next.*

her. The director fell down paralyzed by a stroke at the last moment. All was in confusion. There seemed to be a feeling that Harry was made of gold and more could, and should, be prised out of him. The performance was terrible. The press worse. Maurice Baring, come especially from St Petersburg, declared it a disgrace.

Many a lesser woman would have been crushed. But Ethel remembered Gustav Mahler, now in charge of the Viennese opera house. She had been slightly acquainted with him during her young days in Leipzig in 1888 when he was one of the conductors of the orchestra there. He had a reputation with the ladies, for in spite of his ugliness, he had extraordinary charm. One of his victims had been Frau von Weber, married to a descendent of the great composer. The husband averted his eyes as long as he could. A scandal would mean the ruin of his army career. At last, one day on the train to Dresden, he burst into mad laughter, drew his revolver and began shooting.

By 1906 Mahler had had a great number of other adventures and made many enemies, for he was not a conciliatory man. 'It must be admitted,' wrote Bruno Walter, his second-in-command, 'that Mahler's violent actions, his peremptory manner in questions of art, his engagements and dismissals and his fight against tradition and time-honoured customs had helped to swell the ranks of his enemies among the artistic personnel, especially among members of the orchestra, but also among the theatre's officials, the public and the newspapermen.'[1] He had gone so far as to refuse a part to a young lady in whom the Emperor Franz Joseph was interested simply because she couldn't sing. The wonder is that he lasted ten years in the job.

He was on the point of departure when Harry and Ethel arrived in Vienna, *The Wreckers* in hand. Ethel had, by now, a wide reputation as a pest. Though people often liked her, were even totally fascinated, they found her pertinacity a strain. Mahler did not feel inclined for a personal interview. He sent Bruno Walter who, when he saw her, looking gaunt and middle-aged, as he thought, dressed in shapeless tweeds, manuscript at the ready, 'sighed inwardly at what I presumed was in store for me, but she had hardly played ten minutes, singing the vocal parts in an unattractive voice, when I made her stop, rushed over to Mahler's office and implored him to come with me: the Englishwoman was a true composer. Mahler was unfortunately unable to spare the time'.[1]

Walter himself had plenty of leisure. They spent the entire morning

[1] *Themes and Variations*, Bruno Walter, 1947.

89

together, going over *The Wreckers*. 'When we parted, I was wholly
captivated by her work and her personality.'[1] They met constantly
during the rest of her stay in Vienna and remained friends for the
next thirty-eight years. In spite of his good-will, it proved impossible
to stage her opera either in Vienna, or in Munich, where he had
connections. 'He advised me, for reasons he was not at liberty to
divulge, not to press the matter with Mahler just then.'[1] His tact
and persuasiveness were such that she didn't.

Back in England, she set to work with characteristic energy to
compose a number of settings for songs. These were performed, to
the general gratification, in Eugénie's drawing-room, at her sister
Mary's London address and at the house of a new patron, Miss Mary
Dodge, a rich American of somewhat mysterious character, very shy
and reclusive. She paid the musicians, told Ethel to invite whomever
she liked and to preside afterwards over tea and cakes. Meanwhile
she listened from an adjoining room with the door locked. Sometimes
she played croquet, though stiffly on account of arthritis. Never
wavering in her support of Ethel, she was ready to make good the
deficits of public concerts, bought her a house at Woking and gave
her a hundred pounds a year for life.

Nor did her character change. Twenty-five years later, in 1932,
she expressed a sudden ardent wish to meet Vita Sackville-West whose
books had impressed her. 'Do you think she'd lunch with me?' she
burst out. 'If you, Ethel, came too perhaps she wouldn't be bored.'
Another time, after reading *The Waves*, she made a sortie to Virginia
Woolf's home and left a note, escaping before anyone could detain
her. She was fierce-looking, Ethel explained in her letter of introduction
to Vita, 'but capable of great inward glowings . . . odd, abrupt,
extremely happy and the only rich person I know whom riches have
left unspoiled . . . I never admire her front door for if so she'd say,
"I'll have it sent down to Woking". At least, she would if she thought
it would be useful.' All her other friends seemed to Ethel the last word
in dullness.

To return to 1907 and 1908. Ethel was able to arrange quite a
number of private concerts, at one of which Debussy was
complimentary, though there was some suggestion that he had first
been softened by a superb dinner. Winnaretta de Polignac promoted
her in Paris where Fauré was appreciative. There was a performance
at the Wigmore Hall of her songs. The London Symphony Orchestra

[1] *What Happened Next.*

90

included 'On the Cliffs of Cornwall' (taken from *The Wreckers*) in one
of its programmes. The press was, in some cases, quite enthusiastic
and in no case particularly rude. It was true that she couldn't interest
Covent Garden: their finances were such, they said, that the only new
opera they could possibly contemplate would be something by Puccini.
She decided to give a concert performance of the first two acts of *The
Wreckers* in the Queen's Hall. The empress, Miss Dodge and Harry
were all ready to contribute.

There was only one bad omen. Harry began to have mysterious
symptoms, such as temporary deafness, pain in the jaws, liverishness.
At a certain point he seemed to rally, writing from Rome 'that he
now had an attack of worldliness and was enjoying it greatly'.[1] The
remission did not last. He suffered much pain. The doctor spoke of
digestive disturbance and rheumatism. Ethel became more and more
horrified. 'I met you at St James's Palace,' Maurice Baring later
recalled, 'where we lunched with Aunt M'aimee [Lady Ponsonby]
and you took me into the little room near the dining-room and told
me you were afraid HB was dying. This was before anyone dreamt
of it.'[2]

Her premonitions were confirmed when Harry consulted a better
doctor, who diagnosed cancer of the liver. His philosophy did not
fail him in his supreme crisis. He accepted the verdict calmly. 'I am
finished,' he said to Maurice Baring who happened to be passing
through Rome on his perpetual travels. 'I said that nowadays cures
sometimes happened in cases that seemed desperate. Then, quite
lucidly and impersonally but very firmly, he gave me to understand
that for him there was no hope of any such thing.'[2]

He felt his end very near and urged Ethel not to allow her *Wreckers*
concert to be postponed until the autumn of 1908 as the management
of the Queen's Hall had suggested. It was his intention to be present.
He set off from Rome with his son. 'I met them at Victoria,' Ethel
wrote.[1] 'He could walk fairly well and was his usual serene self,
continually saying with a touch of triumph, "Now wasn't I right to
come?" But if after seeing him I had one grain of hope left, it was
because the optimistic cling automatically to hope as the drowning
clutch at the tiniest bits of floating wreckage; for on his face was the
unmistakable look of those who are under orders.' The London doctor
said it was a miracle that he had survived the journey.

By conserving his strength to the utmost, he was able to sit beside

[1] *What Happened Next.*
[2] Letter to Ethel.

her at the concert. His appearance was that of a corpse, dead white, the skin stretched over his features which showed to great advantage 'His head looked like a marble Donatello bust; Sargent told Mary he had never fully realized its beauty before.'[1] In a dreadful way, the evening was a great success. the audience was enthusiastic. The press seemed keen. Harry was filled with delight that this opera on which they had worked so hard together was receiving its due, even though in truncated form. Ethel had not yet revised the third act to her satisfaction. He was dead within a fortnight, his hand in hers.

So she lost the best friend she had in the world. One who loved her truly for twenty-three years; who had stood by her in every crisis, both real and imaginary; who had done his best to calm her turbulent soul with philosophy, wit and common sense. There was an element of the fond father in his treatment of her, his constant indulgence of even the most fantastic behaviour. Yet he never talked down. He never failed her. He provided the stable element in her emotional life.

The best way to recover from the death of a beloved is to find oneself another. Then time assuages grief more rapidly. Present happiness prevents brooding on the past. The vanished love becomes a tender memory, occupying a tranquil corner of the mind, not obtruding into a life in which it now has no concern. Ethel was not able to lay the ghost of Harry. No woman could replace him. She never again met a man she could love in the full sense. So, like many a pious widow, the departed dominated her thoughts to a morbid extent. She was forever quoting his opinions, singing his praises, turning over his letters, guiding herself by what she imagined would have been his advice in difficulty.

Feelings of guilt and remorse troubled her. Had she been worthy of the love of this unique person? Had she not been selfish, so wrapped up in her career and subsidiary affairs as to be unmindful of the pain she must be causing him by her neglect? Thirty-four years later, in 1932, while sorting through their correspondence yet again, she was writing to Virginia Woolf: 'I don't want just now to realize, letter after letter, that no woman was ever so understood, so looked after, had such treasures of help and wisdom and kindness and warmth put at her disposal, as with that realization goes the feeling: Did I give back enough?'

But these prolonged agonies were unnecessary. She had given enough. He had loved her for herself, as she was, fully cognizant of

[1] What Happened Next.

her limitations. She had shown him how to enjoy life after the long hibernation with his wife. She had set him free.

Nine years after he died, as she was beginning to ascend the highest mountain in France, she heard his voice and there he was beside her in a well-remembered country suit, looking at her with quizzical amusement. He vanished before the conversation could continue. 'I have no views on this incident, and certainly needed nothing to bring home to me that he is always close to me, perhaps even closer than when he was alive,' she wrote in 1940. It was his sole appearance as a spirit.

CHAPTER TEN

Resuscitated

Ethel despaired. She couldn't work. She did not care what happened to her. Mary took her off to Venice, to the Palazzo Barbaro which she had borrowed from some rich relations of Sargent's. There were parties and musical occasions and outings in gondolas. Friends were always turning up, passing through. The Palazzo Polignac was further along the Canal Grande. Gradually her courage began to return and with it a feeling that this aimless existence was not the right cure for grief: she owed it to Harry's memory to pick up her life, to resume her musical career. If she immersed herself in work, time perhaps would make her whole again.

She returned to England with the intention of starting on a new opera, but found herself in difficulties over the libretto. She rather fancied one of Gilbert Murray's translations, *Hypolytus*, but as he did not care for the liberties she felt obliged to take with his text, she abandoned the idea. She was also, of course, ceaselessly engaged in trying to get someone to stage *The Wreckers*, for which Miss Dodge was very willing to provide a handsome subsidy.

Her recovery to something like a normal equilibrium was helped by the attachment she now formed with Violet Woodhouse, whose renderings of Bach and Mozart on the harpsichord and clavichord were acclaimed by a wide circle of discerning friends and music critics. She was in some ways very like Ethel. 'Her character, though far from simple,' says Osbert Sitwell,[1] 'held something in it of a child's simplicity and power to be swept by primitive emotions; loving, hating, stubborn, beautiful, impulsive, generous and sometimes perverse, she followed her own way, uninfluenced by opinion and clung to her own ideas with all a child's obstinacy: because she formed and formulated them with her heart and not with her head.' Her voice was distinctive and she was a voluble talker.

She had much charm: 'Her face would lighten directly you entered the room – for she was adept at welcome – and she would rise from her chair and would seize your hand and race you off into another room, to show you some treasure she had been recently given by one

1 *Noble Essences*, 1940.

94

of the many persons who loved and admired her.' Since her husband was rich, she could afford to be 'generous beyond the dreary bounds of common sense'.[1] 'Where is Violet?' some guest asked on a particularly dismal winter's day. 'Oh,' said another, 'she's out buttering the lawns for the birds.'

Her interior, though in perfect taste, was sumptuous, far from the simplicities of Ethel's little cottage. She was altogether feminine, seeming to Osbert Sitwell 'like some velvety dark moth, queen of the summer night'. In contrast to Ethel's eternal tweeds, she dressed in 'smoky garments, mottled, dark but never funereal, satins and silks with many points of light, flecks of scarlet – flashes of flame'. There was also a quality about her that reminded Ethel of Pauline Trevelyan, so greatly loved, dead of consumption in 1897.

Nobody could be a substitute for Harry, naturally, but Violet seemed to have been sent from heaven for her comfort. They went to many concerts together, the one dressed like a bird of paradise, the other a tramp. A particular enjoyment were those conducted by Thomas Beecham early in 1909. This volatile young person had found backers for a series of programmes consisting entirely of modern works. There was an amazing number of extant composers of repute to choose from. The English scene, almost entirely supported by Stanford and Parry at the beginning of Ethel's career, now included Elgar, Holst, Delius, Bridge and Vaughan Williams. Foreign contemporaries were plentiful: Debussy, Ravel, Roussel, Fauré and Saint-Saëns in France; Reger, Mahler, Richard Strauss, Berg and Schoenberg in Germany; the lone Sibelius in Finland; Bartók, Dohnány, Kodály in Hungary; Skryabin, Rachmaninov and the young Stravinsky to represent Russia; Puccini, Leoncavallo, Busoni, Respighi in Italy.

These were only some of the names available to the enterprising Beecham. He himself had no money at the time on account of a nasty passage of arms with his father, whose ample fortune was sustained by the famous pills. He had found it necessary to pursue his parent through the courts in order to find out to which lunatic asylum his mother had been consigned and to rescue her therefrom. The father had not only withdrawn support from his son on this account, but also cut off his allowance. The breach lasted nine years. Since Thomas was charming, witty, very clever and brimming with originality, lack of ready cash by no means impeded him. 'The results of the concerts, attended of course by a mere handful of enthusiasts,

[1] *Noble Essences.*

must have been depressing from a financial point of view, but to some of us they were a revelation. Never in England, indeed only in Vienna under Mahler,' Ethel noted, 'had I heard music rehearsed to such a pitch of perfection.'[1] It seemed to her, and to Violet, that here was the right man for *The Wreckers*. His interest, his enthusiasm, must be roused at once. The coming conductor must be made to support the great composer. They would rise in glory together to the topmost reaches of English music, saving it, in the process, from the mediocrity into which it had irredeemably sunk. 'He is quite a remarkable man and musician,' wrote Delius to Ethel on 17 February 1909, 'and really understands and likes modern music . . . He is wonderfully gifted and destined to play, perhaps, the most important part in the development of modern music in England. My prophecy! Don't forget it! . . . As far as I can judge, the English race is lacking in emotion, the essential part of music . . . Still I believe the coming generation may cast off the spell and express something human.'

No one could suggest that Ethel lacked emotion, whatever else may have been omitted from her make-up. She felt more than ever certain that Beecham was her man. She had seen him here and there at gatherings of various sorts. Now she determined to become his friend. Violet invited him into her drawing-room where she played the harpsichord in such a manner that he professed himself overcome with admiration. Ethel played and sang *The Wreckers* at him, and that seemed also to go down well. 'He, on his side, amazed us not only by the richness of his musical gift, but by his knowledge of classical literature, especially poetry, and his phenomenal memory.'[1]

Miss Dodge was kept informed of these developments and, in a state of excitement, asked whether one thousand pounds would be enough to hire a theatre and tempt Beecham to conduct. He accepted with alacrity. A contract was made with the managers of His Majesty's Theatre for six performances, perhaps to be extended if the opera caught on. Ethel was even able to arrange, through her Ponsonby connection, that Edward VII should attend one of them. She had hopes that this would help to convince Beecham senior that his son was a great genius, which the old man tended to doubt, and destined to a magnificent career, blessed and encouraged by royalty. Her object was to prevent, if possible, the Beecham millions being diverted from music to the foundation of hospitals, or homes for indigent north countrymen.

Full of these happy aspirations, she set to work to recruit the

1 *Beecham and Pharaoh*, Ethel Smyth, 1935.

Christabel and Emmeline Pankhurst in Paris, September 1913 (*The Museum of London*)

Ethel in 1922

singers, a task delegated by Beecham who reserved for himself the formation of the orchestra. It was not long before certain strains became apparent: 'I discovered that in more respects than one my new friend was a disconcerting person to work with.'[1] The least of his misdeeds was that he habitually arrived half an hour late for rehearsals. More fundamental, she came to feel that he was uninterested in singers, much preferring straight orchestral music. He took little trouble with them and had small patience when they made mistakes or happened not to be in their best form. Nor was she able to emulate Delius who, when asked if he approved of the tempo in certain passages, replied: 'Take it just as you think best, my dear fellow.'

'Now in my case it was another story. I could not feel there was much affinity between my music and its conductor, who seemed to me less bent on carrying out my ideas than on seeing what could be made of them by Thomas Beecham.'[1] She did admit 'that I am not one whom conductors can satisfy easily'.[1] And she gave him credit for urbanity and forebearance in that, despite the trouble she caused, he remained perfectly friendly, though elusive as time went on. 'In those days I had not yet learned to pitch my voice on the suave mellifluous note that tempestuous people would do well to acquire as early as possible if they are dependent on the good will of others and desire to tread the musical arena with comfort.'[1]

Beecham, too, felt he had something to complain of: 'Unlike most artists, she was a born fighter and rebel, roused to controversy and reprisal on the slightest provocation . . . This did not make her the easiest of colleagues and her frequent efforts at direct action either in the theatre or concert hall, hindered rather than forwarded the aim which everyone else wanted just as much to attain.'[2] Nevertheless, he felt she was 'without question the most remarkable of her sex that I have been privileged to know. I have been told that here and there in the world there have been observed a few examples of that same fiery energy and unrelenting fixity of purpose, and that almost unscrupulous capacity to accomplish the purpose in hand. It may be, but they have never come my way.'[1]

In spite of all the ups and downs, she was pleased with the result. 'As the week went on the performances got better and better.'[1] She took great trouble that it should be so, coming into the orchestra pit every day to pin amendments to the score on various desks. The

[1] *Beecham and Pharaoh.*
[2] *A Mingled Chime*, Thomas Beecham, 1944.

players found this disconcerting as they never quite knew what they would be expected to play. Nor did Beecham appreciate it much. But Ethel had no doubts. 'On the penultimate evening I remember thinking *The Wreckers* was quite a good opera.'[1]

She had a pint of champagne before the curtain went up. The king was very gracious afterwards, receiving both composer and conductor with practised affability. One would never have guessed from his manner that he had complained of being woken up by the infernal row from the stage at least twice.

The Times was favourable: 'The strong passionate music that gripped the attention from the opening strains of the Revival Hymn, the enthusiasm of the singers, the careful stage management of the crowds all combined to leave a vivid impression on the mind of the audience and must have startled the sceptic in his unshakable belief that English music is still in the cradle and the English temperament incapable of being dramatic.' There were many moments of great beauty, *The Times* considered, one of them being Eugénie's favourite, the 'Song of the Rat'. But poor Harry's libretto was found lacking on occasion: 'O come with me and have a pleasant talk (she said) along the shore, being rather too reminiscent of the Walrus and the Carpenter.' These were small faults. 'Miss Smyth, by the choice of her subject and the strength and sympathy with which she has treated it deserves to take her place with the English writers whose theme has been the tragedy of the sea.'

Ethel assumed her success had been quite enough to ensure that performances would be extended beyond the original six nights agreed in the contract. It was not so. The theatre had been booked for a play. The management held its ground. She could not control her indignation and went about saying such extravagant things that she found herself in the position of having either to answer a case of slander, or else pay a hundred pounds. Miss Dodge paid up.

The next year, 1910, Beecham included *The Wreckers* in his first season at Covent Garden. She had great expectations, she declared, but these were lamentably dashed. The perfidious man had devoted his time and attention exclusively to Strauss's *Elektra* and Delius's *A Village Romeo and Juliet*. She had struggled for years to get her opera on at Covent Garden and now at last when the great day came he had ruined it, she said, pointing to such comments as: 'Miss Booker might remember at the next performance that boys of fifteen, even

---

[1] *Beecham and Pharaoh.*

when they are sprightly, do not generally skip about with their hands on their hips'.[1] The critic also complained that most of the singers were inaudible and, consequently, it was difficult to distinguish duos from solos, let alone follow the story.

She was much consoled by a letter from Durham University enquiring whether she would be so kind as to accept an honorary degree of Doctor of Music, which she did, being afterwards careful to sign herself on all public occasions, Dr Ethel Smyth, or Ethel Smyth, Mus Doc. Titles had always meant a lot to her. She knew their worth as advertisement and was not surprised to receive a communication from Lady Constance Lytton, renowned suffragette, urging her, as a famous woman, to support the militant movement led by Mrs Pankhurst. Although she was all in favour of rights for Ethel, perpetually denouncing the male prejudice she encountered, whether in truth or in imagination, during the course of her profession, she found the plight of other women not so interesting.

By 1910, however, a large number of her friends and acquaintances, including shy Miss Dodge, were concerned with the suffrage question. Votes for women and suffragette exploits were a topic of conversation everywhere she went. Her inclination was to send a rather jocular reply to Lady Constance. But a discussion with an Austrian novelist whose opinions she respected dissuaded her. She even consented to accompany another friend to one of Mrs Pankhurst's meetings, protesting meanwhile that she couldn't take an active part in politics, even for the betterment of womankind, because it would be the death of her as an artist.

First impressions of Emmeline Pankhurst were not very favourable. Some hitch had occurred in the arrangements and there was rather a long pause before the proceedings could begin. This evidently put her in a bad mood. She looked thoroughly discontented and Ethel thought she had a mean expression round her mouth. But when she stood up and opened that mouth in a flood of oratory, Ethel was transported, as many another had been before her. She admired the voice, the figure, short, yet well-proportioned, the gestures, so quick and deft, the beautiful complexion, the flashing eyes, the general air of excellent health. It was more or less love at first sight.

Mrs Pankhurst, on her side, was decidedly chilly when introduced to a well-known composer with so little idea of right thinking as scarcely to have spent five serious minutes on the subject of women's rights

[1] *The Times*, 2 March 1910.

and wrongs. She also considered it showed an unsuitable levity to have been brought to an apprehension of her duty as an eminent woman by an Austrian novelist while the two of them were stretched out on a beach. She had no idea that she was shortly to enter on 'the deepest and closest of friendships'[1] with the new recruit. For Ethel had determined on the spot to join the ranks. Within a fortnight[2] she was writing to Mrs Pankhurst to excuse past negligence and offer her services: 'owing to a very busy and very fighting sort of life, I have never paid much attention to the suffrage question. Lately I have read and thought much about it and want to tell you that no one can be a more profoundly convinced suffragist than I . . . If at any time I could help, other things being equal, I want you to know that no one would be more glad than Yours very truly, Ethel M. Smyth.'

Thus began the most dramatic interlude in this dramatic woman's life.

---

[1] *Female Pipings in Eden*, Ethel Smyth, 1933.
[2] 15 September 1910.

CHAPTER ELEVEN

Militant

Mrs Pankhurst and her Women's Social and Political Union represented the last flamboyancy of an evolution of ideas which had been taking place for more than a hundred years. While abhorrent to many, these developments were inevitable, being part of the general social upheaval connected with the industrial revolution. Men were demanding the franchise for themselves and the reform of electoral abuses. It was the political aspect of their struggle for better wages and conditions of work. Laws would never be passed in their favour unless they had the power of the vote over their local MP. Women were moved by the same considerations, especially in Manchester and the surrounding towns where they formed the majority of the labour force in the mills. The cotton workers' trade unions were run by men, but were almost entirely composed of women.

The main grievance of middle class women was that the unmarried, the wife or widow fallen on hard times, was usually prevented from earning a living except as a governess, or companion to a richer lady whose personality obliged her to hire friends. Much had been done for the education of girls during the nineteenth century by the foundation of schools and colleges. But all the professions were barred to women. Married women had an additional disability in that they were simply the property of their husbands who could take from them whatever money they had, remove children from their care and generally treat them as slaves, should they feel so inclined. It came to be felt by many women, and even men, that this situation was intolerable.

Emmeline Pankhurst was a Mancunian, daughter of a manufacturer, relict of a fiery upholder of women's advancement, workhouse reform, home rule for Ireland, emancipation of American negroes and many another worthy cause, all espoused equally by his wife. She did not concentrate on votes for women, her famous battle cry, until 1903 when she founded the Women's Social and Political Union.

The membership consisted, at first, of the Pankhurst family and two or three friends. But within a few years Emmeline and Christabel, the eldest daughter, had made it notorious throughout Europe and America. They were superb practitioners of the art of public relations. Starting from noisy interruptions of election speeches and the addressing of factory crowds, they swiftly progressed to mass demonstrations and skirmishes with the police which ended in the arrest of many women otherwise the soul of respectability. They flooded Holloway with prisoners who went on hunger strike, were forcibly fed and were able afterwards to write of that barbaric experience, in books and in their weekly newspaper *Votes For Women*.

All these activities were orchestrated by Mrs Pankhurst and Christabel who toured the country in terrific hats and dresses. They flamed with oratory, rousing adherents to what can only be called religious fervour. Not for them the dignified, intellectual and responsible approach of the non-militant women's suffrage societies who believed in the peaceful persuasion of MP's and ministers on a wide range of social reforms in addition to the franchise. What had sixty or seventy years of these tactics achieved in the way of a vote? Only that women could be elected to local councils. It was old-fashioned as well as useless and boring to continue with such plodding gentility. The government must be forced, not begged, to listen, to concede, to bow to the just demands of half the nation.

The suffragettes were by no means the only people to declare war on authority. Apart from the perennial Irish problem, currently centred on the struggle for home rule, the trade unions had discovered the power of organized labour. The years 1910, 1911 and 1912 were marked by an unprecedented series of strikes on the railways, among the boilermakers, firemen, seamen. At Tonypandy the miners rioted and looted for three days before order was restored. In Liverpool the army was obliged to fire on the dockers and two were killed. The London parks were turned into military camps. It seemed as if society were foundering in violence and revolution, as indeed was the case, though few perceived the coming war.

When Ethel's friends learned that she had joined the extremists some congratulated her on at last waking up to her responsibilities as a woman and others were very put out. Strange Miss Dodge, ever generous patron, approved to such an extent that she gave Mrs Pankhurst a car. Lady Ponsonby and the Empress Eugénie were of the opinion that a woman in her position, recently honoured with a doctorate, should know better than to follow a crowd of publicity-seeking hysterics; for who could suppose Emmeline Pankhurst's circus, whatever the heroism of individual members on occasion, improved the image of woman as a responsible person, deserving an adult position in society? She should have chosen the non-militants, whom every rational person could support.

Ethel took no notice of these sage counsels. 'Woman Suffrage is in its essence the cry of idealism buried alive,' she declared in *Votes For Women*. 'It is for this very reason that every soul who once understands, even dimly, what is at stake, gives to this cause as he or she never gave before.' Pausing only to consult the spirit of Harry and finding it in perfect agreement with her intentions, 'I decided that two years should be given to the Women's Social and Political Union after which, reversing engines, I would go back to my job',[1] saying goodbye to politics and the betterment of womanhood. 'The thought of wrongs you are not personally intended to cope with is enervating and dispersing,' she admitted, but the vision of Emmeline carried her forward.

It was, too, a convenient moment for a break. She had just finished her setting of the anonymous seventeenth-century chorus 'Hey Nonny No'. It proved one of her most successful pieces. There was something peculiarly expressive of her own nature and recent bereavement in that defiant shout against mortality:

> Hey nonny no!
> Men are fools that wish to die!
> Is't not fine to dance and sing
> When the bells of death do ring?
> Is't not fine to swim in wine,
> And turn upon the toe,
> And sing hey nonny no!
> When the winds blow and the seas flow?
> Hey nonny no!

'Ethel Smyth was a being only these islands could have produced,' wrote an amazed Sylvia, the second Pankhurst daughter: 'Individualized to the last point she had in middle age little about her that was feminine. Her features were clean cut and well marked, neither manly nor womanly, her thin hair drawn plainly aside, her speech clear in articulation and incisive, rather than melodious. Wearing a small mannish hat, battered and old, plain-cut country clothes hard worn by weather and usage, she would don a tie of the brightest purple, white and green, or some hideous purple cotton

[1] *Female Pipings in Eden*, Ethel Smyth, 1933.

jacket, or other oddity in the WSPU colours she was so proud of, which shone out from her incongruously, like a new gate to old palings.'[1]

She often asked her suffragette friends down to her cottage where they found her ensconced with her piano, her enormous dog and a formidable housekeeper, 'silent . . . with yellow hair and pallid face who might have been trusted to keep the secrets of a Bluebeard's chamber'.[1] Although she talked very readily about herself, her adventures and especially Harry who chiefly inspired her, she said, and whose works constituted her bible, Sylvia sensed a hidden Ethel, sad and vulnerable, 'the spirit of her strange, wild, suffering, striving heart whose secrets none could fathom'.[1] She felt this particularly when listening to the composer's solo performance of 'Hey Nonny No'. 'She had no great singing organ; yet seated at the piano, she could do with her voice and fingers most marvellous things – the work of a full choir and symphony orchestra! Certainly their essentials. Indeed her music never sounded so limitless, so universal, when given by all the voices and instruments for which she wrote them, as by their author alone.'[1] Thus had she captivated Queen Victoria in 1891 with her *Mass in D*, and Bruno Walter with *The Wreckers* in 1906.

Ethel felt warmly towards the young women who comprised the rank and file of the movement, being reminded sometimes of the French Revolution and again of the early Christian martyrs, though they themselves tended to take Joan of Arc for heroine, a person not notably interested in women's rights despite indubitable courage. It was widely thought that Christabel had much in common with her. But Emmeline was Ethel's star. She had offered her two years of a life otherwise devoted to self-promotion and all the connections with prominent people attached to it.

As it turned out, great sacrifice was not required. The best way of serving the cause was to lend it her talents as an artist. She at once composed a 'March of the Women' to replace the Marseillaise with special words they had used before. All suffragettes were obliged to learn the new song, although it was somewhat difficult to master and considered by many not as stirring as the old. Ethel took no notice of the criticism. It was based on a tune she had heard when wandering with Harry in the Abruzzi.

The first performance was on 20 January 1911 at a welcome ceremony for twenty-one released prisoners. 'It is at once a hymn and a call to battle,' wrote the eager reporter for *Votes For Women*.

[1] *The Suffragette Movement.*

'The poem was written after the music was composed,' said Ethel, 'and that is like asking somebody to move gracefully and easily in strait waistcoat and handcuffs.' The words do indeed give this impression. Nevertheless, the applause was terrific. The ex-prisoners then made speeches.

Shortly afterwards, a mixed entertainment was arranged of music, dancing and drama. Lady Ponsonby was persuaded into the audience and Violet Woodhouse took the piano for the 'March'. 'All the music was conducted by the composer . . . who materially increased the effect of the March by some terrific whacks upon cymbals which happened to be lying at her feet.'[1] In the drama section 'the helpless position of the mid-Victorian girl was forcibly shown'.[1]

Mrs Pankhurst was very conscious of how the enthusiastic presence of Dr Ethel Smyth, well-known composer, and her friends, dignified such domestic occasions. She was careful to honour the new recruit, a habit foreign to her general management of her associates. At a mass meeting at the Albert Hall on 23 March 1911, there was a special ceremony, amid the usual inflammatory speeches, consisting of the presentation of a baton with gold bands. 'It was wonderful processing up the centre aisle of the Albert Hall in Mus. Doc. robes at Mrs Pankhurst's side.'[2] The effects were always well ordered.

'The Woman's Suffrage Party are fortunate in possessing as their bard so eminent a musician as Dr Ethel Smyth,' the *Daily Mail* remarked. It was less of a blessing for Ethel's reputation which was by now extremely distinguished. Some critics thought the overture to *The Wreckers* as good as Wagner's to his *Flying Dutchman*. 'There is a virility in her style of expression, a depth in her thought and a resourcefulness in her command of the orchestra that places her music on a higher plane than that attained by any of her contemporaries,' said the *Morning Post* on 7 April 1911. These contemporaries included Elgar and Delius. In Germany they had the impression that ' "Hey Nonny No" is now echoing over England and winning for her the hearts of all who strive and suffer'.[3]

But, as often happens to artists, politics seemed to have a deleterious effect. On 1 April 1911, she gave a concert in the Queen's Hall with a programme of extracts from her operas and other works and, in the second part, new compositions inspired by the suffragette experience. 'There were a good many upholders of the cause present,'

[1] *Votes For Women*
[2] *Female Pipings in Eden*
[3] *Der Merker*, December 1911

The Times reported, 'and a smaller but more discriminating audience drawn from the musical public . . . The politically inclined ladies seemed a good deal puzzled by much of the choral and orchestral music and did not thoroughly enjoy themselves until the end,' at which point the critic was overcome by ennui as he listened to 'Three Songs of Sunrise'. The first, 'Laggard Dawn', represented the cry of women waiting for the sun to rise, that was to say for the new era to be conferred by the vote. It was 'a setting of a melody by the late Prince Edmond de Polignac . . . of singularly small interest'. The second, '1910, a Medley', described a demonstration and contained such lines as:

> Sounds the battle raging round us –
> Up and defy them! Laugh in their faces!

These two items were encored. 'The same honour was happily avoided in "March of the Women" . . . which is written on what we cannot agree with the composer in considering a good tune . . . All three of the political tracts are artistically very far below the level maintained in Miss Smyth's other compositions,' said *The Times* austerely.

Perhaps it was feelings of this sort that caused Beecham to forget his promise to conduct. No message came. He just didn't appear. From the platform Ethel announced her satisfaction at a turn of events a lesser woman would have found upsetting. It gave her a chance, she said, to conduct her work as it should be done. The evening ended boisterously with the audience singing 'March of the Women'.

Why should she care what the critics said about her 'March'? Two months later, on 16 June 1911, an enormous procession of all the suffrage societies took place, led by Mrs Drummond, often called The General, on a horse, followed by a colour-bearer and a young woman, also mounted, dressed as Joan of Arc. Massed bands played the 'March' and the greater part of forty thousand women had been obliged to learn all four verses of it which rang through the streets from the Embankment to the Albert Hall.

In July the concert was repeated at Queen's Hall. 'It would be quite impossible to convey in words the wonderful spirit that pervaded the huge audience,' said the reporter from *Votes For Women*. There were endless encores. 'It was like a big suffrage meeting,' said one contented lady afterwards.

'I often read and re-read every word of each number of *Votes For Women*,' Ethel declared, a feat of endurance that gives the measure of her passion for Mrs Pankhurst, the fount and inspiration of her engagement in politics. Emmeline was not easy to know. Her emotions were entirely centred on Christabel. Anyone who ventured even the faintest dispraise of the daughter was instantly cast into outer darkness by the mother. 'We are two sides of the same medal,' she liked to remark. 'If you uttered one word in criticism of the idol of her life – particularly if it was deserved – you would have to be very dead indeed before she would really forgive you',[1] as Ethel discovered to her cost.

To begin with, all was sunshine. 'I loved and admired Christabel.'[1] Mrs Pankhurst, when in London, lived in a hotel at Lincoln's Inn 'and sometimes I would occupy the second bed in her room'. She couldn't be called a religious woman in the ordinary sense and no more went in for philosophical or metaphysical speculations than did Ethel. But both were liable to elevated moments. There was a memorable night early in 1911, some six or eight months after they first met, 'when she and I, standing in our dressing gowns at the window, watched the dawn rise beyond the river and fight its way through the mist. She was on the eve of some terrible adventure that would end in rough usage and prolonged imprisonment, thinking perhaps of the inevitable hunger strike, while I for my part was tasting the bitter anguish of one fated to look on powerless . . . Gradually we realized that her love for downtrodden women . . . my music, our friendship . . . was part of the mystery that was holding our eyes. And suddenly it came to us that all was well; for a second we were standing on the spot in a madly spinning world where nothing stirs, where there is eternal stillness.'[1]

On lower planes, Ethel found that though Emmeline tended to be easily bored, she loved poetry, scenery and even music, if she could bring herself to sit still and listen. It seems, however, that her ear was not reliable. 'Once, on some strange occasion – it must have been a wedding or a funeral – when we were in church together, she began joining loudly, fervently, even gloatingly in the hymns and sang flatter than I should have thought it possible to sing.'[1] Yet her speaking voice was beautiful: intense and rather low, it reached to the furthermost corners of any hall.

The platform was her métier. There she took fire. 'She used little gesture beyond the rare outstretching of both hands . . . It was all done by the expression of her face and a voice that, like a stringed instrument in the hand of a great artist, put us in possession of every

[1] *Female Pipings in Eden.*

107

movement of her spirit.'[1] She never bothered with notes or appeared to make much preparation beyond eviscerating the newspapers. 'Her pince-nez perched rather crookedly on her nose, an expression of ferocious intentness on her countenance, with lightning speed she would turn over page after page, picking out in half a second every item that interested her . . . Such newspaper technique I never beheld.'[1]

Her life, at this time, besides short imprisonments, hunger strikes and the leading of marches and deputations in London, consisted of a continual round of meetings in the provinces. She would set off in the large Wolseley presented by Miss Dodge, driven by her chauffeuse: 'We were very, very heavily laden with an enormous amount of literature piled on the top which I had to reach by climbing up a little ladder. We would start off at about half past ten in the morning and then we'd have a puncture. Mrs Pankhurst never got out of the car, she never moved from her papers, so I used to jack her up with the car. I took that for granted. She was always absolutely absorbed in working out her speech for the next meeting or reading some book on social welfare'.[2] The struggling girl may sometimes have had Ethel's assistance since, 'on some occasions it was often my privilege to accompany her'.[1] On the other hand, she may have had to jack them both up if they were earnestly engaged in conversation.

Once, as they were driving along Piccadilly through a jeering crowd, a woman was knocked down. The jeering turned to cursings and threats. 'In a twinkling Mrs Pankhurst was on the pavement, her arm round the blowsy victim of suffragette brutality, while with the innate authority that never failed her she ordered a policeman to fetch an ambulance', meanwhile lavishing tender enquiries on the lady and regretting with the most sincere distress that she couldn't accompany her to the hospital because she was due at a meeting. Her 'face, soft with pity, radiant with love, was the face of an angel'. The crowd now began to comfort her, saying the woman was all right and to hurry on to her meeting in case she should be late. A distribution of half crowns ensured that they drove off to cheers. She had conquered another hostile audience. 'But as she settled down somewhat violently in her seat, Mrs Pankhurst might have been heard ejaculating in a furious undertone, "Drunken old beast! I wish we'd run over her!" '[1]

There were times too when the intrepid chauffeuse took her leader down to Ethel's cottage. 'Dr Ethel would improvise and keep Mrs

[1] *Female Pipings in Eden.*

[2] See *The Militant Suffragettes*, Antonia Raeburn, 1973.

Pankhurst perhaps an hour, or an hour and a half, perfectly happy just sitting in her drawing room playing to her.'[1] A mere driver was not invited to join these sessions. 'I used to wait outside on a little bench under an open window and listen with the nightingales literally within a few yards of me in the woods.'[1]

Although so formidable, Mrs Pankhurst was very feminine in some ways. She loved fashionable clothes and never could pass a sale. 'No severer trial to people who loathe gazing into shop windows than to walk down Regent Street with her any day,' Ethel complained. It was no use trying to hurry her. 'With your perpetual *come* on, *come* on, you are as bad as a husband,' she shouted on one occasion.

The suffragette movement had money, thanks to skilful fund raising, but she herself was hard up. Ethel was always urging her to write a few short articles for which American editors, in particular, would pay enormously. Unfortunately Emmeline had a horror of the pen. Even the thought of the lovely dresses she could buy with the money thus earned failed to rouse her. 'It's my duty to look as nice as I can on the platform,' she said wistfully. 'I would do it, dear, if I could, only I really *can't.*'

Ethel was not to be put off. One evening when her friend was comfortably devouring newsprint at Woking, she said, 'About that article.' 'I tell you,' returned Emmeline, 'I can't and won't do it. Please leave me alone.' But by subjecting her to a barrage of questions and ignoring such interjections as, 'I wish, dear, you would leave me in peace', Ethel soon had enough material for a hundred pound article. She spent the rest of the night writing. 'I read it to her in bed next morning; she approved without wasting compliments or gratitude.'[2] It never got posted for she mislaid it in the office. 'I must have thown it away with a lot of old papers,' she said in reply to Ethel's enquiries. 'And I knew her too well – that royal personage – to expect a word of regret whether on the score of a friend's devoted but useless labour or the lost hundred pounds.'[2]

Ethel was also untiring in her efforts to convert acquaintances, friends and relations to the feminist way of thinking. One day early in 1912, she visited the wife of a cabinet minister whom she had met once or twice and found sympathetic. The ministerial staff were terrified by the apparition of Ethel stumping up the stairs, certain that her capacious tweed pockets were full of bombs or other missiles. 'Everyone had tried to dissuade my hostess from receiving me. But

---

[1] See *The Militant Suffragettes*, Antonia Raeburn, 1973
[2] *Female Pipings in Eden.*

she was no funk.'[1] Neither was she inclined to conversion. 'O my dear,' she cried, 'how can *you*, of all people, forsake your beautiful art for politics?'

Ethel replied that this showed what the cause meant to her and demonstrated the depth of her sufferings from male prejudice in the musical world. Yes, but, said the lady, it was surely a pity to step off the ladder just when you were climbing nicely. Ethel assured her that for the sake of her soul and for music, the two were the same, it was necessary to sacrifice herself. Then she harangued her audience on the evils borne by women, such as prostitution, the white slave traffic, venereal diseases, the perpetual denial of the vote. The minister should be informed, she thundered, that militancy would increase month by month to unimaginable heights so long as justice remained undone to half the English nation.

With unfailing politeness, the minister's wife promised to do what she could. 'Now, just for the sake of old times, do sing me something before you go.' Ethel immediately rushed at the piano and gave a spirited performance of 'March of the Women', followed by Brahms, Schubert and other songs in her considerable repertoire. 'O,' cried her hostess, embracing her warmly, 'how can you with your gift touch a thing like politics with a pair of tongs? I can't bear to think of it!' Ethel was unable to disabuse her of an idea that it was some sort of publicity stunt intended to further her career in the concert hall.

Her attempt to enlist the support of Neilson, who had conducted *Der Wald* at Covent Garden in 1902, was even less successful. He had abandoned music for parliament and grown much in self-importance. 'One day when the [woman] question was monopolizing the time of the House, I received a note from Ethel Smyth . . . She wanted to know if I would take lunch with her and Mrs Pankhurst at the Inns of Court Hotel. I consented.'[2] Any hopes they had that he would rise and make an impassioned oration were soon dashed. He gave them to understand that while, privately, he was all in favour of women's rights, he had no intention of damaging his position in the liberal party by publicly espousing a cause disapproved of by his leader and prime minister. Long before the pudding, Mrs Pankhurst was regarding him with silent contempt, while Ethel choked with rage.

[1] *Female Pipings in Eden.*
[2] *My Life in Two Worlds.*

CHAPTER TWELVE

The Holloway Degree

The climax of Ethel's career as a political agitator came in the spring
of 1912. Mrs Pankhurst was newly returned from a triumphal tour
of America during which she had covered ten thousand miles, making
speeches at innumerable suffrage societies, often entering the building
through archways of flowers. Ethel had seen her off at Southampton
the previous winter. Sylvia Pankhurst stood with her on the quay as
the boat sailed. 'She had a passion for ships. At the moment of parting
the siren blew hugely. The adored Mrs Pankhurst, smiling and waving
to us from the deck, was forgotten by the musician who snatched a
notebook from her pocket and scribbled eagerly, exclaiming in her
ecstasy: ''A gorgeous noise!'' '[1]

In February 1912 the two friends were once again at Woking full
of serious purpose. A great window-breaking demonstration was
planned for 1 March to mark their displeasure at Asquith's refusal
to keep his promise to introduce a bill giving votes at least to some
women. 'The argument of the stone, that time-honoured political
weapon . . . is the argument I am going to use,' Emmeline declared.
Ethel was to give her lessons in throwing stones at obstacles, for she
hadn't the least idea how to do it. A heap of stones was placed three
yards from a large fir. 'One has heard of people failing to hit a
haystack; what followed was rather on those lines. I imagine Mrs
Pankhurst had not played ball games in her youth and the first stone
flew backwards out of her hand, narrowly missing my dog.'[2] By dint
of perseverance and concentration Emmeline hit the target at last and
turned a smile of such beatitude and satisfaction on Ethel that it made
her fall into a clump of heather in a paroxysm of laughter. Emmeline
was unable to see the joke.

The demonstration had been announced for 4 March, so the police
were utterly unprepared when, on the evening of the first, scores of
ladies strolling about in Piccadilly, Regent Street, Oxford Street, Bond
Street, the Strand and the Haymarket produced hammers, stones and
sticks and began an attack on the nearest windows.

[1] *The Suffragette Movement*
[2] *Female Pipings in Eden.*

111

'The scenes in the street were remarkable, the women being marched off by the police, in many cases followed by those who were ready to give evidence as to their guilt; the shop assistants hurriedly putting up their shutters, or standing by in shirt sleeves ready to take action at the first sign of any renewed attack, women driving through the streets with their colours freely displayed, encouraging those who were actually doing the damage; and excited knots of people following the arrested women.'[1]

Meanwhile Mrs Pankhurst had taken a taxi to Downing Street with two companions. They got out at number ten, rang the bell and handed in a letter. Then, all at once, they took stones from pockets, bags and muffs and began throwing. As they were standing on the doorstep, it was hardly possible to miss the two adjacent windows. They managed to break four panes between them before being grabbed by the police. As she was being hustled off, *The Times* reported, Mrs Pankhurst wrenched her arm free and hurled another stone in the direction of the Home Office where it luckily found its mark. The practice shoots at Woking had not been waste of time. More stones were discovered on her at the police station.

Three days later, on 4 March, a great demonstration was called for Parliament Square. It was preceded by a meeting in the London Pavilion at which Ethel made an impassioned speech calling on all women to sacrifice themselves for the cause. She herself had refused an invitation to conduct a concert of her works in Berlin, feeling that she could only retain her self-respect by taking part in a militant action. Her place was with her comrades in Holloway. No effort could be too great if it resulted in political liberty.

'By six o'clock, the neighbourhood of the Houses of Parliament was in a state of siege,' the *Daily Telegraph* declared. 'Shopkeepers . . . barricaded their premises, removed goods from the windows and prepared for the worst . . . Everywhere carpenters were busy putting up wooden hoardings or wire screens over the windows.' Thousands of policemen were on the watch, listening for the tinkle of glass and controlling a vast crowd which had come to see the fun. The museums had been closed and also an exhibition of old masters at the Royal Academy. Everybody was disappointed. No demonstration took place. The ladies made for Knightsbridge and Kensington where they did great execution before the law arrived.

With characteristic independence of mind, Ethel did not join the serried ranks of hammerers at Pontings or Harrods, but made her

[1] *Morning Post.*

SIR A. MACKENZIE   DAME ETHEL SMYTHE   SIR HENRY J. WOOD   MR EDWARD GERMAN
"D.B.E."   MR DAN GODFREY "STANDING

At the Bournemouth Festival, 1922

Fête Galante at the Royal College of Music, 1925

way to Berkeley Square, the address of Lewis Harcourt, colonial secretary, widely known as Lulu. He had annoyed her very much by saying in a jocular way to an earnest deputation of suffragettes that he would be happy to give women the vote if all of them were as intelligent and well-behaved as his wife. Ethel thought she had never heard anything so damnably condescending and impertinent and she determined to give him a piece of her mind in the form of a rock through his window. On reaching his front door, therefore, she asked the attendant policeman to direct her to some place in the vicinity. As he turned to point out the way, she launched her missile with the speed and accuracy of one who had spent summers bowling for a ladies' cricket team. She was at once arrested.

'The subsequent trial I thoroughly enjoyed and rather fell in love with our judge'[1] whom she took the opportunity of addressing on the subject of prostitution, the white slave traffic and the raising of the age of consent, mentioning *en passant* Archbishop Benson and quoting a certain MP to the effect that, 'Although not one of us men would like to see a young girl taken advantage of, yet, when it comes to altering a matter like that, well, we think things are very well as they are'.[1] The magistrate listened patiently before sentencing her to two months with hard labour, a stiff penalty for one broken window. It was later reduced by half. Thus she obtained her Holloway Degree, the highest accolade in the movement.

Her courage and disregard for her reputation – her newly completed quartet *1902–1912* had just been performed to critical acclaim – were suitably admired. The Aeolian Ladies' Orchestra announced that it was filled with gratitude for her conduct and proposed to give a reception in her honour on her release. The Actresses' Franchise League, not to be outdone, declared its intention of arranging a welcome breakfast.

It was not a very rigorous imprisonment and there was no hard labour. In an effort to cope with the influx and prevent mass hunger strikes, the authorities relaxed the rules and did everything possible to humour their captives. A special wing was turned over to them where they were allowed to move about freely, at certain hours, and to wear their own clothes.

From the uneatable food and scanty bathwater to the naughty spirits of the inmates, the atmosphere was reminiscent of a girls' boarding school. A dancer sent out for her ballet skirts and gave daily exhibitions of her art. Two gifted sisters modelled animals from

---

[1] *Female Pipings in Eden.*

squeezed bread. Cartoons, stories and jokes were handed round. Prisoners arriving smuggled in letters and tasty titbits. When released prisoners left, their underclothes were laced with outgoing mail.

'The athletic sports in the prison yard, inspired and organized by the younger prisoners to the delight of Mrs Pankhurst, were capital fun. How we got the materials – calico, purple, white and green tissue paper and so on, not to speak of hammer and nails – I cannot remember, but designs and mottoes breathing insult and defiance would embellish the courtyard walls for hours before they were discovered and torn down. Evidently some of the wardresses were afflicted with blindness; also on occasion with deafness.'¹ Ethel's contribution consisted of an enormous pair of convict knickers embroidered with the legend: 'A Mus. Doc.'s notion of small clothes'. Mrs Pankhurst took exception to this *jeu d'esprit* and ordered its immediate destruction. She seldom appreciated even the mildest ribaldry.

There was naturally much singing of 'March of the Women'. 'I arrived in the main courtyard of the prison,' wrote Beecham, who had come to visit his old friend, 'to find the noble company of martyrs marching round it and singing lustily their war-chant while the composer, beaming approbation from an overlooking upper window, beat time in almost Bacchic frenzy with a toothbrush.'²

Those were happy and exciting days, though she never forgot the horribly claustrophobic sensation induced by the slamming of the iron door and the turning of the key. Her cell was adjacent to Emmeline's. They often had tea together as the wardress seemed to forget to lock them up separately. Hunger striking was in abeyance for the time being. The screams and struggles of forcible feeding were not to be heard. Windows and fittings were not smashed. Everyone was instructed simply to complain incessantly to the governor and visiting magistrates of health damaged by cold and damp, disgusting food and primitive sanitary arrangements. It was a great day when they found a boiled cockroach in the milk.

The campaign worked extremely well. Mrs Pankhurst, who had been banished to a basement for a small misdemeanour, was soon elevated to a nice warm cell with a fur rug and hot water bottle. Ethel loyally joined in, though such peevishness went rather against the grain, and was able to promote herself from the floor reserved for consumptives and the feebleminded where she had been placed at

¹ *Female Pipings in Eden.*
² *A Mingled Chime*, Thomas Beecham, 1944.

114

first, and also to obtain the services of a daily masseuse. 'Eventually by dint of whining and grumbling and groaning' about rheumatism mainly, she got out a week early, on 4 April 1912. She had been in prison three weeks, although afterwards she tended to remember it as the original two months.

As soon as the general festivities of release were over, she wrote a propaganda letter to *The Times*, setting out the dreadful sufferings of Mrs Pankhurst's two day sojourn in a punishment cell. It was freezing, damp, without furniture or sanitary arrangements. Offensive graffiti decorated the walls. Crickets infested it to such an extent that one suffragette occupant had had to be removed at two in the morning, screaming mad. No books were allowed, not even the Bible. It was a place 'in which no groom would willingly leave a horse, or even a dog, for an hour'. She ended her broadside on a fine sarcastic note. 'At a performance of Mr Galsworthy's play *Justice*, in which the horrors of solitary confinement are depicted with terrible force, a member of the present government was observed wiping his eyes in the stalls. He could have had the same emotion for the price of a taxi fare to Holloway.'

The next excitement came in May 1912 with the trial of Mrs Pankhurst, Christabel and their two chief adjutants for conspiracy to incite certain women to commit damage to property. The government had decided the best way to solve the suffragette problem was by removing the leaders for a good stretch. They felt the movement would fall into disarray and might even wither completely.

Christabel was tried *in absentia* as she luckily happened to be out when the police called. Being warned, she fled to a friend, disguised as a nurse. 'I did not sleep all that night for thinking. Suddenly in the small hours, I saw what I must do! Escape! The Government should not defeat us. They should not break our movement . . . My law studies had not been in vain. They had impressed indelibly upon my mind the fact that a political offender is not liable to extradition.'[1]

The next day she borrowed a black coat and hat, very different from her usual smart style of dress, and took the boat train from Victoria, sitting inconspicuously in a crowded carriage with her nose in a woman's magazine. She remained in Paris thereafter. Couriers came every week to receive her instructions and her next article for *Votes For Women*. Ethel had introduced her to Winnaretta de Polignac in whose palatial house she was frequently to be found consorting with the rich and the lesbian. She had also a comfortable flat and plenty

[1] *Unshackled*, Dame Christabel Pankhurst, 1959.

of money, from some source or other, for a large and extremely fashionable wardrobe. It was a delicious life.

Meanwhile, her mother in the dock at the Old Bailey called Ethel as a defence witness and asked her to state whether she had at any time been incited to commit unlawful damage. To this she replied that she was much too busy for that kind of thing, but the refusal of the Home Office to allow an enquiry into police brutality in the course of 1911 had so enraged her that she had written in asking to be included in the next protest, whenever that might be. 'If that letter has disappeared,' she said, 'I am rather glad of it because I think it might possibly be cited as a case of inciting my leaders to violence.' She had been duly enrolled for the next procession, but, 'as a matter of fact I was very badly bitten in a dog fight the week before and I was laid up for a month and could not take part. I was very sorry it was so'.

No one had incited her to throw stones on 4 March 1912, she declared. 'I said I had done my bit, that I was sorry I had not had the opportunity of identifying myself with these splendid people, but that I must turn my face the other way and go back to my work.' Then, while resting in a sanatorium in Cardiff where she had gone in the hope of curing her rheumatism, she heard of a certain MP who publicly stated that there was no general demand for women's suffrage: no one had tried to burn down Nottingham Castle, for instance, as had happened during the agitation for reform in 1832. She got straight on the train. 'I did not see how any self-respecting woman could stay at home after that,' she said to loud applause from suffragettes in the public gallery.

These were among the highlights of a trial in other ways somewhat undramatic. Mrs Pankhurst, of course, made a tremendous speech, but much of the evidence came from papers and articles seized by the police in the head office of the movement at Lincoln's Inn. Christabel's repetitive effusions were much quoted. There were quantities of evidence of incitement to violence. The jury found all the defendants guilty and added a plea for leniency, on the grounds that they were sincere believers in their movement. The judge gave them nine months.

There were a lot of suffragettes still in prison after the stone-throwing exercise and more were constantly joining them, having committed sufficient nuisance to enable them to obtain the coveted Holloway Degree. Early in June 1912 a mass hunger strike was ordered and shortly thereafter the prison was filled with the screams and groans and strugglings that accompanied forcible feeding.

Public opinion was beginning to be disturbed. A group of doctors wrote to the *Lancet*: 'It is severe physical and mental torture. Two doctors and four to six wardresses are required to overcome resistance . . . On 26 June 1912 as many as twenty-two had to be released to save their lives.' Abscesses were often caused. Lips, gums and cheeks were lacerated. Pneumonia had resulted from the tube being accidentally pushed into the lungs. The heart was frequently affected. Released prisoners suffered horrible dreams, insomnia, giddy spells and an immense fatigue. Some slept more or less continuously for a week. 'No one whose eyes are not blinded by party passion can deny that the personal violence employed by the government against women is immeasurably greater than the physical violence employed by women against members of the government,' said Christabel in her weekly article for *Votes For Women*. As supreme commander she did not feel it incumbent on her to join the front line. Her place was in the rear, directing strategy.

The government was in a quandary. If feeding was stopped, they were afraid numbers of women would actually starve themselves to death, such was their fanaticism. Yet the process made the prisoners so ill that they invariably had to be let out long before the completion of their sentences. They were defeating justice and also giving it a very bad name. It was not until March 1913 that the answer was found in the Prisoners' Temporary Discharge Act, promptly dubbed the Cat and Mouse Act. Under its provisions, hunger strikers were not fed, but were let out on licence to recuperate and re-arrested when it was judged that their strength had returned sufficiently. Mice who could afford it often followed Christabel's example and headed for the continent.

But as the suffragette movement, true to the character of a revivalist religion, had ossified, the leadership could think of no strategy except militancy and more militancy. Catting and mousing had small effect. Mrs Pankhurst had only to get up at a meeting and say, 'Christabel sends her love,' for screams of joy, fainting in coils and other forms of enthusiasm to arise among the audience in every direction. So that when a programme of arson was announced as the necessary next step in the march to liberation, few questioned its wisdom and those who did were promptly expelled as unworthy to be handmaidens of the revolution.

In the same exalted spirit, a huge demonstration in Hyde Park was arranged for 14 July 1912, Mrs Pankhurst's birthday and, by good fortune, Bastille Day also. Sylvia Pankhurst worked on the design and manufacture of banners and emblems day and night until her legs swelled up to an extraordinary size. There was a brass band a hundred and fifty strong. 'The women in the crowds alone grasped the inner meaning of The March of the Women conducted by Dr Ethel Smyth in her academic robes, hatless in the blazing sun.'[1] Such auditors found 'the swelling music strong and martial, bold with the joy of battle and endeavour, yet with a lasting undertone of sadness characteristic of that rebellious soul'.[2]

Hardly had Ethel recovered from this feat when she was arrested following an attempt to burn down Lulu Harcourt's country mansion, Nuneham House, near Oxford. Two young stalwarts, Miss Helen Craggs and Miss Norah Smyth, a relative, had planned the desperate venture together. First, they went to Abingdon where they hired a canoe in the name of Smith, paddled off to Nuneham and disembarked, taking with them a bag containing a bottle of inflammable spirit, two cans of oil, four tapers, two boxes of matches, twelve firelighters, nine picklocks, two torches, a glass cutter, a hammer in a kid glove, a sticky cloth, a two foot rule, a suffragette flag and manifesto, some chocolate, a pencil and nine pounds nineteen shillings and sixpence. They were discovered, thus burdened, hiding in the ivy on the wall by a policeman something after midnight. They explained, in answer to his questions, that they were camping on the river and, finding it too hot to sleep, had decided to view this fine country house. While the officer was, consequently, arresting Helen Craggs, Norah Smyth took to her heels and was not seen again for dust.

The police then examined the canoe in the hope of establishing the identity of the fugitive. It contained assorted foods and, significantly, a book in which a card bearing the complete words of 'March of the Women' had been inserted as a marker. Only Ethel Smyth could be the owner of that book, they said to each other. The very woman who, only three months before, had lobbed a brick through Mr Harcourt's window in Berkeley Square and made opprobrious remarks about him at the Old Bailey during the trial of the archfiend Pankhurst and her confederates. With the greatest confidence in the world, they descended on her cottage at 8.30 am and arrested her. 'It was judged unnecessary to enquire where I had been on the fateful 13th [of July],' she afterwards fulminated in *The Times*, 'a very easy matter to ascertain, seeing that I left home on the 12th to stay with a sister

[1] *The Suffragette Movement.*
[2] *Votes for Women.*

118

until the 14th and my letters were following me. I was kept in Woking police court all day, although my alibi was established in Oxford before eleven . . . I got home again at 2 a.m. having missed several carefully dovetailed business interviews in London. The facts of my case are, in short, a very perfect example of the methods of the police under the stimulus of a woman-hounding government suffering from nerves . . . There was not one shred of evidence against me, merely some feebleminded guesswork, as of very stupid children playing at being Sherlock Holmes.'

She created a great furore in the magistrate's court 'in spite of attempts to silence me'. She shouted that 'Oxford police had evidently been guilty of incompetence and folly that would disgrace a tyro girl scout'. She threatened an action for wrongful arrest with a huge claim for damages to cover professional loss. The case was, of course, dismissed. Quite apart from her sister's evidence as to where she had been that night, the boatman who hired out the canoe flatly declared she had not the least resemblance to the Miss Smith he had dealt with. 'May I add for the guidance of the force,' she yelled triumphantly in the *Daily Telegraph*, 'that were I disposed to sally forth on a secret and illegal mission, I hope I should refrain from scattering musical or other visiting cards amongst my effects; also that the alteration of one vowel in one's name seeming to me one of the least happy devices to secure anonymity, I might possibly call myself Brown, Jones or Robinson, but certainly not Miss Smith. I fear that if all the Miss Smiths in England are to be arrested, the police will have their work cut out for them.' It's always a great satisfaction to wipe the floor thoroughly with one's opponents.

Life was full of excitement. At about this same time Mrs Pankhurst, newly released from prison after a five-day hunger strike, decided to visit Christabel, whose presence in Paris had not yet been announced to an anxious world. Absolute secrecy was essential as the police were perpetually on the lookout for clues as to where the fugitive from justice might be. Ethel disguised herself in a dark wig, a veil, spectacles and an extremely smart travelling outfit belonging to a rich relative which she obtained by telling the housemaid that she wanted to borrow it for private theatricals. Emmeline was highly delighted with the effect, repeating frequently, 'I do wish, dear, you always looked as you do now.'

They set off after dark, Ethel being picked up on the road in the vicinity of Woking. The car also contained a couple of Emmeline's bodyguard, strong athletic girls with indian clubs concealed amongst

their voluminous skirts. 'It was my agitating lot,' relates Ethel, 'head
out of window to indicate short cuts to the Southampton road across
a bit of country I had often galloped over with hounds in my youth;
but directing an amateur suffragette chauffeur in pitch darkness is
quite another thing.'[1] They felt certain the police were following and
dared not stop to ask the way when lost or draw attention to themselves
by shining torches on signposts. But at last, after many a flurry, they
reached their destination and shortly sailed for Le Havre.

Mrs Pankhurst enjoyed Paris immensely, the shops, the food, the
long talks with her darling Christabel. Ethel could not help feeling
a certain contempt for that young lady who, week by week, urged
others to deeds of heroism and danger while herself remaining
comfortably in the Avenue de la Grande Armée. It was the beginning
of a cloud between Ethel and Emmeline. For the rest, however, she
looked up all her old friends in the Polignac circle and elsewhere, doing
her best to persuade them actively to embrace the cause and also to
promote her music.

[1] *Female Pipings in Eden.*

CHAPTER THIRTEEN

Retirement from Politics

The two years Ethel had promised to dedicate to the movement were now almost passed. Though she never lost interest, and continued on most affectionate terms with Emmeline, the first thrill of involvement and action was over. She did not want to go to prison again. Once was quite enough. It wasted valuable time, gave one unpleasant sensations and was likely to pose the question of hunger striking. If she should be Emmeline's fellow convict and that formidable lady began refusing her food, Ethel might well be expected to follow suit. She might be ordered to. It was a prospect she could not face.

She took no part in the campaign of arson which began in the autumn of 1912 with the burning of letter boxes and continued during 1913 with the destruction of country houses, race course stands, stations and other buildings, damage to golf courses, telegraph wires and so on. Cohorts of girls were consigned to Holloway where many resorted to the hunger strike.

This programme of accelerated violence, advocated by Christabel, caused a serious split in the top ranks. The dissidents were successfully expelled, but they took the newspaper with them. The Pankhursts were obliged to found a new organ, *The Suffragette*, the tone of which became increasingly strident and not simply feminist but against men in general. Christabel ran a series of articles on the Great Scourge (venereal disease). Every female symptom from nervous debility to spots before the eyes was put down to the wicked, licentious life led by husbands on the sly. The sure remedy was votes for women and chastity for men, aided by bromide in the case of the weaker, or perhaps one should say stronger, brethren. These articles were avidly read and discussed by the younger suffragettes who were mostly quite ignorant on all aspects of sex.

October 1912 found Ethel in Stuttgart at Richard Strauss's new opera *Ariadne Auf Naxos*. She did not care for the introduction, 'quite the most tiresome thing ever witnessed', but later on 'all was well, for, to my mind Strauss has never written music more beautiful. . . The opera proper swept me away in parts; the music seemed to me warmer and deeper than nine tenths of the music Strauss generally writes and nonetheless as diabolically clever as usual'. Such advanced musical criticism consorted strangely with Christabel's diatribes on sex in the pages of *The Suffragette*.

Ethel had come to Germany principally for a concert in Vienna conducted by Bruno Walter and consisting of works by Mahler and herself on 5 November 1912. Walter, her devoted admirer since 1906 when she had played and sung *The Wreckers* to him in her inimitable manner, now wrote an enthusiastic article: 'I consider Ethel Smyth a composer of quite special significance . . . I believe also that her work is destined permanently to succeed although its recognition, like the recognition of all true originality, only comes gradually and in the teeth of opposition.' He was of the opinion that sex was irrelevant in matters of art. Ethel disagreed. The sole reason why her music was not frequently performed all over the civilized world, like that of Strauss, Delius, Elgar, was because, unlike them, she happened to be a woman. Experiences as a suffragette only served to confirm her misanthropy. But the reception at the concert left nothing to be desired. Men and women clapped and cheered the overture to *The Wreckers*, a setting of Rossetti for chorus and orchestra, and 'Hey Nonny No'. There were innumerable curtain calls and other compliments. *The Times* was moved to reprint parts of Walter's article.

Her fame as a suffragette had reached Vienna. 'I was asked to address the Women's Club on militancy,' she wrote to Emmeline. 'And as this invitation was followed by three similar ones, I thought it would be a good opportunity to explain that I was devoting myself henceforth entirely to my own job – that being the way, moreover, in which I personally, can best serve the women's cause . . . The room was tiny and held about seventy or eighty people who stood as at an outdoor meeting closely packed together.' 'From her appearance,' they murmured to each other, 'no one would imagine Dr Smyth was a suffragette.'

She harangued them on the evils of prostitution – all men's fault naturally – and the plight of defenceless women driven on to the streets in an effort to supplement monstrously low wages; on the shining valour of the leaders; on the courage of the rank and file who, even when tortured in prison, obtained a moral victory over the enemy man. She explained that militants, far from being the viragoes of legend, were 'particularly sensitive, refined people, braced by heroic self-overcoming to do what is unspeakably hard to be done. And I said every suffragette could emulate these brave ones in some way

122

or other, such as suddenly asking people you never saw before to put their hands in their pockets. They took it very nicely and if the sum is only £3, 6s, well, every little helps.' The assembly then sang 'March of the Women'.

She suggested to Emmeline that some enthusiast with a knowledge of German should be sent to Vienna where the female population appeared lamentably ignorant on matters political. 'Austria is still in the dark ages.' She herself continued indefatigably to address meetings and oblige people to subscribe to *The Suffragette* for which she wrote frequent articles, some abusing men, others reviewing books and concerts. She went to Strauss's *Der Rosenkavalier* and found it superficial. 'I believe the trouble with Strauss is that, superb musician though he be, his main preoccupation is of the *Daily Mail* order. He is not trying to communicate to the outside world a mystery he cannot keep to himself . . . Do we want to be horrified, knocked silly, rolled out flat? He writes *Electra* for us! Or are we frivolity bent? Behold *The Rose Cavalier* . . . We thought we were to learn on our own terms the secret of the sphinx; but no, we are in Selfridges.'[1]

Schönberg she liked even less, though his earlier style had appealed to her. Nor was she alone in her opinion. In Prague they hissed and booed him. 'They say that Strauss who is notoriously appreciative of other men's work has confessed that he can make nothing of this last Schönberg phase and subscribes to the musical insanity theory.'[1]

In addition to these sprightly criticisms, she was writing new songs, turning over ideas for a new opera and arranging further concerts of her works both in London and Vienna. She was also consulting doctors about her rheumatism, now becoming arthritis, and about her ears. For some time she had felt her hearing not so keen as heretofore. She seemed unable to distinguish the various complications of orchestral playing without effort. Her mother had been arthritic and finally so deaf that communication became almost impossible. It was a frightening prospect for one whose life centred on music.

Nineteen thirteen saw her flitting between London and Germany. She was in England in April when Emmeline was sentenced to three years' imprisonment for conspiring to cause an explosion at Lloyd George's country home. Immediately going on a hunger and thirst strike, she was carried out to a nursing home after nine days. As soon as she recuperated, she would be taken back to prison to continue her sentence.

Ethel visited her. 'She was heartrending to look on, her skin yellow

[1] *The Suffragette.*

123

and so tightly drawn over her face that you wondered the bone structure did not come through; her eyes deep sunken and burning and a deep dark flush on her cheeks. With horror I then became acquainted with one physical result of hunger-striking that still haunts me . . . The strange, pervasive, sweetish odour of corruption that hangs about a room in which a hunger-striker is being nursed back to health is unlike any other smell.'[1]

She was much better in a couple of weeks, writing to Ethel, 'Today I had a glass of champagne and fish . . . O kind fate that cast me for this glorious role in the history of women.' It was arranged that she should complete her convalescence at Ethel's cottage. This meant giving the police the slip as she was not supposed to change her address. They soon discovered where she had gone and settled down under a gorse bush outside the gate. Ethel was on the point of handing them a couple of umbrellas, since it was pouring rain, but was prevented by a ferocious yell from the spare bedroom: 'Nothing of the sort! Don't make things pleasant for them!' She was further instructed never to return any salutations they might make. She tried to follow these orders, but her position was fatally undermined by her dog whom the enemy had suborned by means of cheese sandwiches. Every time she went out the depraved animal rushed at the gorse bush and covered the occupants with kisses.

Emmeline slowly began to feel better and reached that irritable stage when one is bored and restless in bed, yet not strong enough for active life. No matter how the devoted Ethel sang and talked, she grew more impatient, finally telephoning to London for a car to be sent down to fetch her. When it arrived, she staggered to the garden gate on Ethel's arm. The detectives sprang from their bush and barred the way. It was their duty to arrest Mrs Pankhurst, they said, since she had obviously recovered her health sufficiently to serve the rest of her sentence.

At this, she appeared more or less to faint. Ethel, who was in a great state of excitement and indignation, held her up. The chauffeuse refused to drive anywhere except on Mrs Pankhurst's orders. The police were obliged to send to Woking for another car. It was a splendid moral victory for Mrs Pankhurst who knew perfectly well what would happen. There she was, dragged off to prison half dead by two huge brutes. On arrival she immediately refused all sustenance and was out in a few days, much enfeebled.

Militancy had now reached tremendous heights. Week after week

[1] *Female Pipings in Eden.*

124

The Suffragette had such headlines as: 'Gigantic fire at Yarmouth
. . . Timber yards a sea of flames . . . Damage estimated at £40,000
. . . Conflagration at Surrey mansion . . . Football stand completely
destroyed by fire.' Golf greens were cut up. Hayricks and letterboxes
blazed. Telephone wires were severed. Bombs went off here and there.
The ancient cannon at Dudley Castle were filled with gunpowder and
fired to devastating effect. 'In the name of common sense give them
the vote and have done with it,' said Bernard Shaw.

The chief manifestation of 1913 occurred on 4 June, Derby Day.
Emily Davison was a glutton for punishment. She had brought forcible
feeding on herself forty-nine times. During those dark hours, she had
come to feel 'that the deliberate giving of a woman's life would create
the atmosphere necessary to win the victory and bring all the suffering
of the militants to an end'.[1] She had therefore thrown herself off a
gangway in prison and head-first down some iron stairs. Epsom was
to be her apotheosis. 'They had just got round the corner and all had
passed but the king's horse, Anmer, when a woman squeezed through
the railings and ran out into the course,' wrote the horrified reporter
of the *Manchester Guardian*. 'She made straight for Anmer and made
a sort of leap for the reins. I think she got hold of them, but it was
impossible to say. Anyway, the horse knocked her over and then they
all came down in a bunch. They were all rolling together on the ground
. . . The horse fell on the woman and kicked out furiously and it was
sickening to see his hooves strike her repeatedly. It all happened in
a flash . . . The horse struggled to its feet . . . but the jockey and
the woman lay on the ground.' The horse was undamaged, the jockey
only stunned. Emily Davison never recovered consciousness.

Her death had none of the political effect she had hoped for, but
the funeral was royal. It was preceded by a repeat of the Woking
drama. Mrs Pankhurst, looking like a ghost from her last hunger strike,
tottered to the door of her apartment, leaning on Ethel, and attempted
to get into a taxi brought by her daughter Sylvia so that she could
join the procession at Victoria. The two plainclothes men on duty
at once arrested her and she was put into another taxi for Holloway.
'It is difficult to write about the arrest of Mrs Pankhurst at which
I happened to be present,' Ethel wrote in *The Suffragette* next day. 'Why
harrow the feelings of others by saying how peculiarly ill she looked,
how after tearing up letters and dressing for the funeral the long wait
told on her?' Ethel also wrote to the Archbishop of Canterbury
accusing him of being morally responsible for Emily Davison's death.

[1] *The Suffragette Movement.*

The actual procession was a great feat of organization and showmanship. Six thousand persons took part, led by a standard bearer carrying a huge cross. The coffin was on an open bier. Thousands wore white and carried madonna lilies. There were two special groups, one in black holding irises and one in purple with peonies. The band played slow marches by Chopin and Beethoven. An empty carriage which should have contained Mrs Pankhurst was immediately behind the coffin. The rear was brought up by representatives of the rival suffrage societies. They marched through dense crowds to King's Cross where the body was put on a train for Northumberland.

It was the last great women's demonstration and the last time Ethel took an active part in politics. She had had enough of them and was longing to write an opera. The Viennese doctors had not been able to do anything for her ears which increasingly troubled her with singing noises and other manifestations of an alarming nature. If she were to become deaf like her mother, how long could her musical career continue? It was small comfort to think of Beethoven. These considerations made her complete retirement from the suffrage scene all the more urgent.

In August 1913, Mrs Pankhurst went to Paris with the intention of leaving for a third fund-raising tour of America in October. She would not be back until the end of the year. Though never conceding that anyone had a right to abandon the cause, and certainly not in order to promote private ambitions, she was obliged to agree that Ethel had more than fulfilled her promise of two years' service. Their friendship was unimpaired by the parting.

The idea that Europe was exactly one year away from conflagration never crossed the political consciousness of either lady. Emmeline's interests were entirely centred on the suffragette campaigns. Foreign women should, naturally, be encouraged to follow the splendid Pankhurst example, but beyond that, international politics did not seem relevant to her purpose. Besides, she had been able to rouse little enthusiasm on the continent, even though Christabel was now permanently in Paris. America had been the principal scene of overseas triumphs. The great tradition of individual liberty had somewhat infected the women there, so that ideas of universal suffrage and entry into the professions appeared right and natural to many.

Ethel's education was much wider than that of her friend. She had sat at the Chancellor von Bülow's dinner-table and listened to his anti-English sentiments with indignation. She had told the kaiser that his views on England and the empire were mistaken in no uncertain terms.

126

The German citizenry had spat on her during the Boer war. An omnivorous reader of books and newspapers, she must have been aware of current anxiety in informed circles over the German armament programme and the effect it had on the precarious balance of power in Europe; of German imperialist ambitions; of the upheavals in Russia and the Balkans which were to prove the first signals of disintegration. Yet her connection with the German musical world was so long and so warm that the idea of such a war as was shortly to follow was inconceivable to her.

CHAPTER FOURTEEN

Irish Interlude

All innocent enthusiasm, therefore, Ethel now addressed herself to the next step in her career. After conducting the overture to *The Wreckers* at the Queen's Hall on 21 August 1913, she was interviewed by the *Pall Mall Gazette* and boasted: 'I am conducting the work again on 20 November in Vienna where they are giving a concert of my works at which they are putting a big orchestra and a magnificent chorus entirely at my disposal. And I have not a penny to pay for it. That is rather interesting, I think . . . I am going abroad next month to work at a new opera . . . I have found a very remarkable libretto by Hofmannsthal[1] and though I have not yet written one note, the première of the opera has already been arranged at the Munich opera house . . . The subject is really comic – comic and fantastic – but that is all I can say about it at present.'

The arrangements seem not to have been as firm as this confident public relations statement suggests. September 1913 found her in the west of Ireland intead of Vienna. She had been bowled over by Synge's *Riders to the Sea*, a poetic but gloomy drama concerning an old woman the last two of whose six sons were drowned within nine days of each other. Such an opera would obviously have to include a great deal of keening, the wild celtic mourning song. She had come with the object of taking lessons in that musical form as well as to absorb the native atmosphere, both in Galway and on the Aran Islands.

There was not a ripple to be observed by the casual visitor to these parts of the rising nationalist temperature. The negotiations for home rule had reached a delicate stage. Dublin wanted a united Ireland. Ulster steadfastly refused to be cut off from Westminster. Sinn Fein had recently been founded. The Irish Republican Brotherhood, forerunner of the Irish Republican Army, was active in the country-side. Sir Edward Carson was making inflammatory speeches to huge gatherings of the newly formed Ulster volunteers. The stage was set for the next seventy years of intermittent and repetitive fight.

On arrival in Galway, full of good cheer, Ethel at once began to enquire where she might find a wake. A genial priest, who highly recommended the beauty of the local girls, directed her to a village

[1] He wrote the libretti for Strauss's *Ariadne Auf Naxos* (1912) and *Der Rosenkavalier* (1911).

Ethel at home with her dog Pan, 1927

At the piano, 1929

five miles off. 'Drove out in the glorious sunset through a flat, desolate, most exciting landscape dotted with splendid Galway peasants – the women with deep crimson petticoats and fawn coloured shawls,' she reported to Emmeline in Paris. There was not a wake in prospect, but an obliging schoolmistress thought she could get up a sort of charade to give some idea. With any luck a real corpse would be available on Ethel's return from the Aran Islands.

When she got back to town after this semi-abortive expedition she 'heard keening! A woman sitting in a doorway (starlight and gas lamps) with one or two sympathizers and three or four children'. Unfortunately they objected to being studied and noted down, and rushed into their cottage, slamming the door. 'Then from within sobbing and sing-song lamentation but the ritual rhythm disappeared . . . It seemed quite in keeping then to hear what I imagined to be a political meeting in the square, carried on under an arc light gas lamp, the speaker standing on a car. It was a black man with a white turban, selling rheumatism cures, toothache cures. He even pulled out (or appeared to) the tooth of (I suppose) an accomplice. The shawled women quite incredulous, but the men: ''I tell you his finger is covered with blood!'' I bought three boxes of toothache cure and gave them to three women . . . O, this darling country!'[1]

The Aran Islands proved even more inspiring. 'Em, O Em,' she wrote on 18 September 1913 from Inishmaan. 'If you could see this place! A place you would be horror-struck at the idea of my getting to. A sheer drop of three hundred feet into the Atlantic . . . I am sitting so that even if I fainted I couldn't roll overboard and sometimes lying on my stomach and peeping over for a second while sea birds are exactly playing their own theme on *The Wreckers* Act II (Prelude).'

She had had some difficulty in arranging keening lessons. The islanders disapproved of foreigners and particularly of their sacred song of the dead being imparted to them. Three women were, however, persuaded to instruct her in spite of the dangers. 'I found the hall in the fishing village full of men and boys. Strange! I peeped in but had on a peasant's shawl etc. and so was not recognized. Presently I am clutched in the dark by one of my women and borne off mysteriously to the school house. We went upstairs. Presently stones began arriving at the wired windows. (Evidently it's a habit here.) We went on and when we had done and lit up again (for we sang in the dark) a crowd outside, curious and inimical.' Her companions advised her to wait. 'Saint of the suffragettes forbid! I went out and

[1] Letter to Mrs Pankhurst.

129

addressed them', in her red petticoat, wrapped in her shawl, speaking vehemently as was her custom, 'and so saying good night I went off and they followed. I was quite excited and pleased and wondering what next.'[1] It was a disappointment when two policemen appeared and her retinue melted away.

A couple of days later, she had crossed to Inishmore, the other main island. 'I was rowed over by three men in a curragh . . . We bruised the canvas on the rocks getting out for the sea was what seemed to me rough and we had to bale out three or four times . . . I expected to be sick, but not at all. It was glorious, like sitting on a butterfly's back . . . Have you ever read Synge's *Aran Islands*? It appears the islanders fiercely resent it and he adored them and made such a picture of them that I could not rest until I had been here.'[1]

Her next port of call was Coole, the country residence of Lady Gregory who attempted there, with considerable success, to create an intellectual and artistic salon in the manner of Paris, with particular emphasis on the encouragement of Irish authors and Irish subjects. Herself a writer, she was a great supporter and friend of W. B. Yeats and had a controlling hand, with him, in the management of the Abbey Theatre in Dublin. One of her originalities was a habit of obliging guests to carve their names on a large tree in the grounds. Ethel duly inscribed hers thereon, remarking, 'Do you really wish that sacred trunk to be defaced by the name of a jailbird?'

Here, at least, Ethel must have heard all the nationalist arguments, the pros and cons of Home Rule, Republicanism, Sinn Fein, Catholic aspirations, the Protestant problem, the Orangemen of Ulster and all the interminable ins and outs of Irish history and grievance. Lady Gregory was an ardent home ruler, not least from a feeling that cultural life, and her theatre in particular, could not fail to benefit if Dublin became a proper capital city, the centre of government and business. They spoke much also of women's immemorial wrongs, but Ethel was unable to convert her hostess to militancy. Lady Gregory remained firmly of the opinion that riot and arson were not a good way of bringing about the millennium.

These two political subjects were curiously connected with Yeats, whom they must have talked of, since he was the star of Coole. In 1895, he had been more or less in love with the beautiful Gore-Booth sisters, Constance and Eva. Though his suit did not get very far, he always remembered them tenderly, dedicating his poem 'The Winding Stair' to their joint memory in 1933. It may be that Constance found

[1] Letter to Mrs Pankhurst.

him insufficiently dashing, for she became the Countess Markievicz and a leading Sinn Feiner, was sentenced to death for her part in the 1916 rebellion against the English government, was reprieved and, after a spell in prison, was the first woman elected to parliament, though refusing on principle to take her seat.

Eva, on the other hand, a poetess, full of charm and goodness, didn't care for men. She settled with her friend Esther Roper in Manchester, where they devoted themselves to the promotion of women's suffrage by peaceful means, and to cultural uplift for working girls through classes on Shakespeare. At a certain point, the ladies met Christabel Pankhurst, then languishing in charge of a knicknack shop set up by her mother in the vain hope of improving the family fortunes. They liberated that young person. In no time she was studying law and making fiery speeches on women's suffrage. Emmeline, who had not suspected these gifts, became frantically jealous and founded the Women's Social and Political Union in 1903 mainly with the object of getting her daughter back from Eva Gore-Booth. Mrs Pankhurst had not been exclusively interested in votes for women before, having concentrated rather on workhouse reform.

In the matter of the arts, Lady Gregory thoroughly approved of Ethel's laudable desire to learn more of Irish singing and promised to produced a really fine keener. She was naturally much in favour of an opera based on *Riders to the Sea* which had first been performed under her aegis in 1904. Thus the days passed in animated discussion. Many years later, Ethel recalled a furious argument she had about women's rights with Yeats on the stairs on the way to bed, and that they had brandished their candlesticks at each other. But her memory was faulty; in this summer of 1913, Yeats was in Sussex with Ezra Pound. The delightful scene must have taken place on a subsequent visit.

Returning to England, she set to work, helped by the Society of Authors, to make an arrangement over the use of copyright with the Synge family about *Riders to the Sea*. As was her habit, she wrote frequently, voluminously and trenchantly. But she was unable to come to terms with them. Perhaps it was for the best in view of her perpetual fear that beloved Em would fatally undermine her constitution, or simply starve herself to death during the next hunger strike. Was it sensible, under these circumstances, to be concentrating one's mind on drownings, dirges, laments, keenings, bereavement? After the high emotional temperature of the last two years, she inclined to the cheerful, the sane and the healthy, and decided to adapt a light story by W. W. Jacobs, *The Boatswain's Mate*. Maurice Baring advised against it, saying she shouldn't waste herself on such banal material. She took no notice. This tale of a female publican pursued by an ex-boatswain and finally, after ridiculous adventures with a blunderbuss, bestowing her hand and fortune on an old soldier, seemed to Ethel exactly right and full of suffragette undertones.

Where to write it? She wanted to get right away from politics. In England she would be continually interrupted with requests for articles and speeches, for concerts in aid of the cause and so on, even though she had declared her retirement from the arena. But the chief obstacle to concentration would be her anxiety about Emmeline's health and the necessity she would be under to visit her in prison and hospital. She was always harrowed by the sight of her dear friend on such occasions, a state of mind which destroyed the equilibrium essential for the composition of an opera. She thought of taking refuge in Vienna, but saw herself jumping on the train every few weeks when news came of Em's arrest and consequent hunger strike. What she really needed was some place so remote that the post was always at least a week old by the time it got there. Mrs Pankhurst would either be dead or recovered before she heard the news.

CHAPTER FIFTEEN

Flight Into Egypt

At this critical juncture, she happened to make a flying visit to Paris where she met a friend of Winnaretta de Polignac, Ronald Storrs, on his way to Cairo where he was oriental secretary to Kitchener, the consul general at the British agency since 1911. Young Storrs had the answer. She should go to Helouan, about eighteen miles from Cairo on the edge of the desert where the palace of the deceased Khedive Tewfik had been turned into a ramshackle hotel inhabited by a collection of English people during the winter. Golf and tennis were provided and desert trips for the more adventurous spirits. For the rest, it was as boring a place as one could possibly wish.

Magnificent. She at once set about the hundred things that have to be settled in order to leave one's affairs more or less tidy. 'I am planning my future life like a mosaic,' she wrote to Emmeline, who had already arrived in the States. 'You have an office. If you have a plan, you wave a hand and people fly to America like St John the Baptist in knickers to prepare for you.' She was not able to leave until the end of November 1913, by which date Emmeline was on the point of return, having caused tremendous excitement among American enthusiasts, who contributed four thousand pounds to the cause. As her ship approached Plymouth, the police came out in a tender and carried her on board, since she refused to walk, and took her to Exeter prison to serve an unexpired sentence under the cat and mouse act.

These events occurred on 4 December 1913 while Ethel was crossing the Mediterranean. She learnt of them on landing at Alexandria on 8 December and was much agitated. 'O my darling Em, I dare hardly think of you, so sorely do I long for news . . . If I could think of you somewhere comfortable.'

Such anxieties were mere background to a busy day. She took the Cairo train at once, arriving in the afternoon at Storrs' address. As she mounted the stairs, the strains of her 'Anacreonatic Ode' became audible, sung by a young army officer and played 'by a splendid girl, medalist of the Naples Academy'.[1] It was their usual Monday musical party, said Storrs with infinite politeness. Within minutes

[1] Letter to Mrs Pankhurst. Unless otherwise stated, all quotations in this chapter are from the Pankhurst/Smyth correspondence.

she had displaced the attractive Neopolitan and was giving her own performance, much enhanced, no doubt, by recent keening lessons, 'but leaped up from the piano on learning that a ghastly Persian religious ceremony that only takes place once a year was to begin at eight o'clock'.[1]

The indefatigable Ethel was soon in the street. 'It is a procession of two tiny drugged boys slashed and smeared with blood on two white horses, followed by torch-bearers and raving maniacs with swords, chanting, streaming with blood and hacking at each other. Armed with a sacred pass, we got through all the police . . . struggling along the outside of the procession to the very top. A big drop of blood flew on to my chin and I never felt more nearly going mad with horror and exultation of blood myself. One felt amazed they didn't accidentally kill this European lady, but they were too drunk with religious frenzy to notice much.' She then caught a train to Helouan, arriving at eleven pm.

There she settled herself in a pavilion in the hotel grounds with her piano, pen and paper. But things didn't go as smoothly as they ought to have done. She found the desert wind 'nervy'. The food brought on bilious attacks. Dreadful nightmares visited her, one being that she was about to be inescapably married. The people in the hotel were maddening. 'The sight of the pyramids – for there are miles of them all down the Nile – is a loathsome one. You hate them, want to spit at them.'

This universal peevishness should no doubt be attributed to a perpetually upset stomach, fretting over Emmeline and an inability to get down to the opera which had been her only reason for casting herself away in such an inauspicious spot. 'I have the awful shrivelling terror of the new work well on me now. Pity I could not begin in England when I was so keen. But this hanging back from the post is absolutely my normal state – nothing to worry over.'

Emmeline's side of the correspondence was by no means calculated to reassure a debilitated friend. She had been temporarily let out of prison after a few days on hunger strike and had fled to Christabel in Paris for recuperation before the next adventure. 'I was taken unexpectedly on my way back from Paris,' she wrote on 19 December 1913. 'The cowardly brutes pushed their way into the reserved compartment at Dover Town. I remained lying on the seat until we reached Victoria.' She would not get out. 'Then they seized me, each by an arm and dragged me headforemost out of the carriage, my legs

[1] *Beecham and Pharaoh.*

134

bumping on the steps and I fell on to the platform. Then a third got hold of my legs and I was flung into a motor car where I lay half conscious all the way to Holloway.'

She refused to use a bed. 'I said to the Doctor, "Two nights I have lain there", pointing to the floor. "From now on I shall not do that but shall walk the floor till I am let go or die." I kept on till 9 pm when the Dr came to tell me I was to be released next morning.' Three days later, she had again escaped to Paris and was lounging pleasantly in Christabel's flat, wearing a very fetching dressing gown sent by the ever-loyal Miss Mary Dodge. 'I have been given an extra sum to spend on my holiday and mean to do it, building up strength to go on with the fight.'

It's a hard thing to be in love with a militant incarnation whose preoccupations are seldom tender. 'I really only want to see the one and only person who is in my thoughts,' Ethel sighs. 'How wise I was to go so far away. Here I shall learn, if anywhere, patience and gain power over myself. In your honour, my darling, if not for my own sake, it must and shall be done.'

She was beginning, nevertheless, to recover her creative energy. Her digestion grew accustomed to the local bugs. The nightmares receded. She became slightly less rough with her enforced companions, to whom she had been preaching militancy night and day, not, she feared, with the elegance and subtlety of Emmeline, but rather after the manner of a Giantess Bloodybones. 'I was driven up to bed away from the writing room by the judge who came up to say he thought he might not be able to play [golf] today (he shall) and was so dreadfully boring and deaf and idiotic and self-satisfied that I said to myself, "This type must perish!" Well, so it will, I hope. He was clasping, however, *Votes For Women* which I had left in the reading room.'

By 20 December 1913 she had started *The Boatswain's Mate*. 'I am getting on slowly but very well with my work. It amuses me greatly and I am bringing in all sorts of little aspects of the male in my couplets which will please C[hristabel] . . . Making the boatswain a typical instance of male fatuousness and, of course, Mrs Waters [the heroine] the reverse.' She declared the story reflected her suffragette experiences and views, but this is true only in the most attenuated and indirect sense. Both the men are ridiculous and the woman is reminiscent of one of Emmeline's personal bodyguard, handy with gun or indian club as the case required. There is nothing of politics, votes for women, the wrongs and injustices suffered by women, or any other serious topic. 'It suits my present mood. I find I can't dabble in passion just now. The passion I feel is not of a lyrical order.'

She became reconciled to Helouan, pyramids and all. 'I am getting devoted to this place and rather expect I shall come back yearly until the vote is won.' In any case, she was not obliged to stay day in day out. Ronald Storrs frequently invited her to Cairo, finding her a welcome addition to his parties, where she tended to cause a sensation. 'Some found her venturous, enquiring spirit too powerful a tonic. I could not and still cannot have enough. She seemed to bring her atmosphere of the hunting field, Johannes Brahms, John Sargent and our friends in Paris with her every time she came into the house – and it was life.'[1] He particularly liked her habit of taking off her knickers when overheated at tennis, putting them under a bush, or into a flowerpot, and then forgetting to retrieve them. Next morning the gardener would politely hand them to his employer.

He took her to see the sphinx by moonlight; and the whirling dervishes by day. She did not think much of them, or, indeed, of any Egyptian, describing them as cretinous, hideous, hopeless, degraded, corrupt, though they seem not to have offered her any particular rudeness. These disagreeable views were almost universal in the English community. She had not held them on her arrival, 'I was rather shocked at the caddiemaster and his whip' with which he ruled the golf course. 'But, after all, the headmaster of Eton wields a cane.' Even the admirable Storrs had a hectoring way with servants. 'O, don't be hard on the poor fellow!' his inexperienced mother said on one occasion. But, he explained, he had merely been saying good morning and enquiring after the man's family. 'It's the tone that astonishes . . . I have however come to see that they not only understand nothing else but, like dogs, they *like* being ordered sharply,' concluded Ethel, whose feeling for justice and equality seldom extended to men, let alone Egyptian men.

She had some hopes that a visit to a royal harem would prove interesting, but they were dashed. Most of the ladies wore 'fifteenth rate European dress with dyed hair' and reminded her of pink and white sugared cakes. The chief attraction was the renowned dancer Serafita, 'about fifty with collops of pink satin fat-bales quivering about as, with the smile of a procuress, she shot her stomach in and out'. She was much incensed also by the cringing attentions paid to two princes, allowed in because under age. It seemed to make the case no better when she was informed that the harem ladies, being deprived, were actually engaged in the seduction of these boys.

[1] *Orientations*, Ronald Storrs, 1943.

Storrs also introduced her to Kitchener's sister, Mrs Parker, an energetic person whose daughter was currently in Glasgow prison for throwing things at Asquith's car. Ethel liked her immensely, 'She's an old ripper. Heaps of fun', and Mrs Parker reciprocated, despite the fact that Ethel badly savaged one of her guests, a woman doctor 'the sort who all the time is giving digs at women, deploring their ignorance, wondering, though "a suffragist", if they were "fit" for a vote. My God. At last I up and fell on her . . . and she smiled and put her head on one side and said she enjoyed my zeal. I have never been ruder to anyone.'

Mrs Parker evidently thought this splendid stuff, for she asked Ethel to come and see her whenever she was in Cairo. Her rooms were self-contained, 'So you won't have to pull out Pharaoh's hair', she said, meaning Kitchener's since he was rather against the women's movement. 'Well, up to now,' Ethel replied, 'the word has not gone forth for action in foreign parts.' 'No,' said Mrs Parker regretfully, 'but it's time.' She had hopes that Ethel might relieve the tedium of official life by some spectacular feat of daring, thus puncturing the cocoon of adulation and complacency in which her brother was enclosed by his circle of admiring young men. Imagine, if she should throw a bag of flour through his car window! Ethel, however, reaffirmed her complete retirement from active politics. So disappointing.

She was far too busy for anything of the sort, having reached a ticklish point in *The Boatswain's Mate*. 'I have got through quite half, I think of my first act,' she reported to Emmeline on 4 January 1914. 'Now comes the very difficult job of writing the little half sentimental scene for Mrs Waters. I want a touch of that. Of something like beauty and languor, not all snap and fun from start to finish . . . But O! How find the right words exactly when you are not a poet, only a person who knows poetry when she sees it.'

She also spent a lot of energy on the conversion of friends and acquaintances. 'I am thrashing poor Maurice B [aring] round into the right road. I think he perceives how much I love him to take such trouble.' Ronald Storrs seems to have put up little resistance. 'He has become, as every intelligent and cant-free soul must, a militant . . . My one righteous man . . . My proudest convert. In addition to these sterling virtues, 'he loves music as a cat loves an armchair'.

Even the judge, formerly so antipathetic, deaf and idiotic had entirely changed his thinking and was now on such cordial terms that 'last night he produced about fifty snapshots of his wonderful child, beginning with its baptism. I wonder what he would say if I produced an album of all my photos of Pan[1] whom I am sure I loved as much as he his child and who was far more handsome.'

She ordered three copies of Christabel's recently published book, *The Great Scourge*, which consisted of collected articles on the perils and prevalence of venereal disease, and distributed them amongst the inmates of the hotel for their further education. Some were not quite so receptive as they ought to have been. There was the party which stood at the sidelines of the tennis court shouting, '*Bravo, les suffragettes!*' Or, alternatively, '*Ah, les pauvres suffragettes!*' when she made a bad shot.

In February 1914 while contemplating Act II of the opera, she joined an expedition to the shores of the Red Sea where an annual camel fair was held at which the coastguard service bought superb thoroughbred animals. 'If you keep them going at a sort of jogtrot it's quite comfortable and anyone could ride a camel . . . The way they kneel down in three jerks for you to get on, grumbling and bubbling and crackling all the time and get up in three more jerks when you are ready is most touching.'

But the chief event was the discovery of a handsome hermaphrodite among the trick riders who were displaying their skill. This individual, Ethel learned with excitement, had been married to a sheik who later repudiated her on the grounds that she wasn't a woman. She herself felt it to be so and took up a man's life as a camel dealer. Ethel was determined to investigate fully. By the promise of a sovereign, she got the young person to agree to be photographed in the nude. 'I seem rather in love with her . . . She likes me, I think, and . . . asked me by gestures which left little to the imagination whether I was a virgin. This when we were by ourselves.' Ethel felt impelled to embrace her at the end of the interview. She smelt terrible.

Unfortunately, she mismanaged the camera. Every single shot was blank. Luckily she had made copious notes of an anatomical nature and regaled a large circle of correspondents with excerpts from them. Some did not appreciate her attitude, thinking it very wrong to take advantage of a poor, ignorant hermaphrodite. One of her sisters reproached her on these lines. 'Poor indeed!' was Ethel's retort. 'Great luck I call it. There's a lot of sentimental bosh talked about sex and I always think even dear old things like Alice should be made to see it has been partly imposed by men in order to have the pleasure of the first comer. Myself, of course, I feel like a pagan on these subjects which is quite compatible with a loathing of prostitution.'

[1] Her dog.

In spite of the highlights, she was quite glad when the trip came to an end on account of the gazelles. 'Though I shall tonight be gloating at dinner over gazelle soup, and at luncheon thoroughly enjoyed saddle of gazelle, I could no more shoot at those exquisite shy little things than at Pan. However, these are the morals of me who is not a good shot and consequently has no passion for slaying.'

She returned contentedly to the Helouan hotel and the next section of *The Boatswain's Mate*. 'I am working splendidly,' she informed Emmeline on 28 February 1914, 'and yesterday finished a little duet. Only takes two minutes, but had to be a little gem.' A week later, she is still 'en veine and working gloriously (have successfully pulled off the most difficult scene of the whole opera).' Nevertheless, she missed the excitement of battle. 'Oh, to be in a crowd with an indian club . . . I think I shall break my heart at not being with your bodyguard.' And there were low moments. 'Oh, how passionately I long for news of you, my dear treasure. Oh, heaven help me to stay here and finish my task.'

Letters came from Emmeline several times a week. 'Do you really know, I wonder, what [they] are to me and how I devour them?' She also scanned the Cairo newspapers for any reported titbit of the English scene, 'but all I read there yesterday was my own arrest'. This was said to have occurred outside Sylvia Pankhurst's house in the east end where her newly formed People's Army was drilling, helped by Miss Smyth on the drums. The police moved in, a scuffle developed with Sylvia leaning from her window shouting encouragement to the troops. Miss Ethel and her drum were arrested, among others. Some time later it transpired that, as in the case of the attempted arson at Lulu Harcourt's country house, the culprit was her young relative, Norah.

Distance and musical preoccupation by no means abated Ethel's fanaticism. 'I am thankful to see a telegram of a valuable church being destroyed. Myself, I think, agonizing as it is, that the time for destroying valuable works of art has come . . . If ever you attack works of art, I will write (as an artist) to all the papers to defend it.' Shortly thereafter, on 10 March 1914, Mary Richardson stole up on Velasquez's famous *Venus*, innocently displaying her nude back view in the National Gallery. Snatching a meat chopper from her muff, Miss Richardson delivered seven ferocious chops before the attendant could restrain her. Traces of the worst, right across Venus's bottom, can still be seen in spite of skilful restoration.

When asked to explain herself, Miss Richardson stated: 'I have

139

tried to destroy the picture of the most beautiful woman in mythological history as a protest against the government destroying Mrs Pankhurst who is the most beautiful character in modern history.' She then retired to Holloway, of which she was a veteran. Nothing better illustrates the emotional and intellectual level of Mrs Pankhurst's movement five months before the most destructive war in English history since 1066.

Ethel was all enthusiasm. 'I am longing to know if you approve of Miss Richardson's action and longing to impress on you that whether you do or don't I do,' she scribbled to Emmeline on 14 March. She wrote to *The Suffragette* on these lines but not, on second thoughts, to the Egyptian papers, having decided it would only mean the descent of crowds of reporters and photographers from Cairo to the detriment of the last part of *The Boatswain's Mate* with which she was struggling, sometimes carried away by euphoria and sometimes despair: 'This morning absolutely stuck in chorus. Felt whole opera ruined.'

It was not her nature to be at a loss for long. Confronted with the problem of the overture in May 1914 and finding 'it won't come nicely so far, perhaps because I'm tired', she had a grand idea. 'I've scrapped all I had written and am writing a quite short very cheerful piece with never a theme from the opera in it, but as chief tune the "March of the Women".' The great task was over at last. She sent the libretto to Vienna to be translated into German, being sure it would be produced in that country during the coming winter. She was also certain that Harry would have enjoyed every moment of it. 'I have had one of my fits of late (they often come with rather relaxed states) of a longing for H, just his smile and the way he used to say "Ethel" when we met after a long parting.' She had at the same time a yearning for her defunct dog for which Harry had professed a particular fondness.

But Emmeline is 'the dear one of now, come to bring fresh love and flame into my life . . . I think it is the crowning achievement of my life to have made you love me.' It was not easy. 'Your ordinary vision embraces the mass, that's why you have always shrunk from personal relations . . . I am the glorious exception for you.' Soon they will meet in Paris and then 'wherever you are, there I shall be too'.

She set off for Vienna on this note at the end of May 1914. It was her firm intention to arrange the simultaneous production of *The Wreckers* and *The Boatswain's Mate* at two different opera houses. That would show what a woman could do. It would teach the English to

neglect her, an international celebrity, acclaimed by top critics of the
most musical nation in the world. 'The composing (successfully) of
The Boatswain's Mate has been the final screw in the lever which lifts
me and *The Wreckers* out of the morass into which the vileness, treachery
and vanity and brutality of the men . . . have pushed us.' She included
Beecham in this category since he had once dared to tamper with her
text. Such were the imbecilities to which she descended when irritated.

Within three weeks she was able to announce the achievement of
her dearest ambition. *The Wreckers* was booked for Munich in February
1915 and *The Boatswain's Mate* for March at Frankfurt. She was mad
with delight. The only trouble seemed to be the article published in
The Suffragette after Mary Richardson's attack on Venus at the National
Gallery. It had been so intemperate that she had been warned to expect
prosecution for incitement to violence if she returned home.

'As I have not the faintest intention of going to prison until both
my operas are settled up,' she wrote just before receiving the final
contract, 'I deeply regret having been so careless.' There was no
necessity, however, for her to appear on English soil until September
when she had arranged to conduct one of her works at the Norwich
festival. By that time everything would be fixed in Germany and 'if
they arrested me then it would be such a grand advertisement for
the cause that it really might be worth it.' She had met no one in
Germany or elsewhere who suggested seriously that time had run out:
not Kitchener, his young men, his sister nor Storrs; not Bruno Walter,
Mahler, not the innumerable doomed courts she visited. But then,
she had been talking to one and all of her private hopes and ambitions
and was not in a mood for political conversation, except in so far as
it concerned votes for women.

Mrs Pankhurst had no premonitions either. During the first months
of 1914 she was in and out of prison like a jack-in-the-box, each time
more emaciated and undermined by hunger and thirst strikes. 'Bless
you, don't worry,' she wrote to the anxious Ethel. 'Try to rejoice
in the sportingness of it all . . . As for our fighting women, they are
in great form and very proud of their exploits, as you can imagine.
The girl who had her head cut open would not have it stitched as
she wanted to keep the scar as big as possible.'

A procession to Buckingham Palace was equally inspired: 'When
we saw the Wellington Gates closing on us as we marched towards
the park, they dashed forward, flinging themselves against them to
prevent their being shut, returning again and again to the charge,
their tender bodies bruised and bleeding. "She told us not to turn

back," said one poor little thing when urged to go away and rest.'

In July 1914, the friends met at St Brieuc in Brittany where there was an excellent golf course. 'Supported by two militants, the ghost of what had been Mrs Pankhurst tottered on the quay.'[1] She was not so frail as she seemed. The blood poisoning was less virulent than usual. She was bathing within days and teaching Ethel how to float on her back.

But almost immediately the world turned upside down. The German waiters at the hotel vanished mysteriously. By midnight on 4 August 1914, the whole of Europe was at war. Ethel returned to England. Emmeline remained in St Brieuc, so that sea air and bathing might restore her health before Ethel rejoined her for a more active holiday. Militancy continued meanwhile. Why not? Women still lacked the vote. But Ethel's mind cleared. 'My dear one,' she wrote just before the battle of the Marne, 'we can't go touring about. It is a physical impossibility and now things are so awfully grim we could not enjoy ourselves . . . The Germans are rushing like hell towards Paris . . . The whole situation has changed in the last 3 days . . . Brittany may become a very impossible spot in no time.' Suddenly the cause, so long and so fervently believed in, had shrunk. 'It is piteous to see those wan white mice[2] still working away at this thing . . . It all reminds me of the old man preaching to a non-existent crowd on the beach . . . If you realized that any moment now disaster may befall the country and that even the man in the street knows it.'

Emmeline saw the light. A few days later she announced that militancy had been suspended during the national emergency. Everyone should support the government. Her orders were obeyed, although a few members had difficulty in adjusting their outlook with the desirable speed. In no time, Mrs Pankhurst was travelling the country making recruiting speeches, handing out white feathers to conscientious objectors, advocating conscription and food rationing. There was one last procession, but it carried banners proclaiming the right of women to work for the war in factory, office and field. The leaders were affably received by Lloyd George.

Never one to do anything by halves, Mrs Pankhurst announced the foundation of a huge home for war babies. Ethel thought it unnecessary 'at such a time to underline the delinquencies of soldiers; besides which, as there is an orphanage on top of every hill in this country, why start another?'[1]. Emmeline was highly annoyed, the

---

[1] *Female Pipings in Eden.*
[2] The hunger strikers temporarily released from gaol.

more so in that she was unable to raise sufficient funds. This surprised her. She who had, without difficulty, collected tens of thousands of pounds for the cause. Her ambitions were therefore reduced to the adoption of four infant girls, to be supported by public subscription. She would bring them up in such a way as to fit them to play a proper part in the new world of women. Ethel objected to this, too, on the grounds of expense and general impracticability. Emmeline replied that her plan would naturally not be of interest to a person who preferred dogs to babies.

The public did not rally to the support of the four little girls. The first battle of Ypres began on 14 October 1914. Wounded men were flowing into the hospitals. People had many other causes to think of which seemed to them more important than Mrs Pankhurst's domestic arrangements. Nevertheless, Emmeline persisted. The scheme was a disaster for all concerned. Mrs Pankhurst seldom had enough time or money to devote to them. Their education proved eccentric. These future leaders of womanhood, Ethel noted with disgust some four years afterwards, 'flitted about like fairies, offered you scones with a curtsey and kissed their hands to you when they left the room'.[1] She spat.

The fact was that she began to be somewhat disillusioned with darling Em. The excitements and ardours of the movement now being a thing of the past, certain aspects of her friend's character tended to get on her nerves. Like many a star, Emmeline found it hard to understand a world where her word was no longer received as a voice straight from heaven to be obeyed without thought or question. Then there was the problem of Christabel, ever more vehemently put forward as a divine genius by her mother. Ethel conceived a fatal dislike of that young woman and her increasingly apocalyptic views which were to culminate in a conversion to Second Adventism. The final parting was precipitated by Ethel's disapproval of Christabel's opinions and conduct.

But the root cause was surely that after five years Ethel's love began to blaze less hotly. It had never been in her nature to submit to the domination of another except when her emotions were deeply roused, and even then hardly enough to notice. Emmeline was, above all, a commander with little use for the equalities of friendship. She, too, began to feel less responsive now that Ethel was no longer a subordinate comrade-in-arms. 'She is the only person I have ever at one time deeply loved and by degrees and because she willed it so, ceased to

[1] *Female Pipings in Eden.*

feel *any* affection for,' Ethel later recalled.[1] The happy reunion in Brittany was not to be a prelude to further rapturous years. The shock of war liberated Ethel from the myopic suffragette vision. Though she never regretted her militant period, she was later ashamed of having supported the destruction of valuable property, of churches and works of art.

[1] Letter to Edith Somerville, 27 December 1925.

144

CHAPTER SIXTEEN

War

The war brought a complete break in Ethel's life in several fundamental ways. 'I could no more work than fly,' she wrote to Emmeline in August 1914. All the elaborate manoeuvres that had culminated in contracts for the grand production of both her operas in Germany had been totally wasted. Even more upsetting, none of the many specialists she consulted in England and Europe could stop the singing noises in her ears, or even arrest the progress of the disease. 'I am . . . finding out how to stop my ears tingling when they begin, but [am] unable to prevent the attacks.'[1] She contemplated the future with dread; also with characteristic courage and energy.

From 1915 to 1918, she was a radiographer in a large hospital near Vichy. It is difficult to imagine this furious ex-militant and eccentric fitting into a disciplined hospital life. Yet with the aid of a simple and fervent patriotism appropriate in a general's daughter, she managed to conform sufficiently. As there was nothing hard or indifferent in her nature, the daily horrors of a war hospital must have been permanent torture. She who had given up hunting and shooting because of a revulsion against killing, was surrounded by blood, agony, death, the extinction of innocent youth. The hospital trains could hardly cope with the numbers of wounded and dying gathered up out of the Flanders mud after having left the shelter of their trenches and advanced on foot into the German fire to be cut down in thousands because the generals could think of no better way of conducting a war. At the end of the day, the survivors usually returned to their previous positions, or to others nearby. Dante never imagined anything like this for his *Inferno*. At the second battle of Ypres in April 1915, gas rolled over the field and many of those lucky enough to reach hospital afterwards were blind, or so damaged in the lungs that they never fully recovered. In 1915 alone 300,000 fell. There cannot have been a spare bed, or free moment for anyone on duty, in Ethel's hospital.

The dreadful years succeeded one another without cessation of the slaughter. The battle of the Somme in 1916 caused 316,073 casualties, nearly 60,000 of them in the first twenty-four hours. On a single day,

[1] Letter to Mrs Pankhurst, 25 December 1914.

145

6 July 1916, 10,112 wounded were landed at Southampton and Dover; these were only the ones strong enough to stand the journey. By 1917, although the western allies had gained a slight upper hand in the carnage with the help of the newly-invented tanks, the French were running out of cannon fodder and there were mutinies. In England scarcely a fit man under forty could be found for the army. But in 1918 the Americans, fresh, vigorous, unbled, began to arrive in force on the western front. The Germans were obliged finally to admit defeat. The hospitals gradually emptied, except those caring for the mad and the permanently crippled.

Solitude and peace of mind are prerequisites for an artist to be able to function. If he cannot keep the world and its distress at a distance, cannot absorb himself in his own dream to the exclusion of all else, his creative powers weaken disastrously. Ethel found she could not concentrate deeply enough for the composition of even a short song, let alone any longer project such as a quartet, a ballet, or another opera. 'Locating bits of shell, telling the doctor exactly how deeply embedded they are, and watching him plunge into a live though anaethetised body the knife that shall prove you either an expert or a bungler, is not a music-inspiring job.'[1]

How to distract her mind until sanity returned and prevent it being overwhelmed by the general dissolution? She solved the problem by writing, for which she had a genuine, though as yet unexplored, gift, as her letters, articles and libretti show. The question of what to write about presented no obstacle. It would be herself, an inexhaustible and, she was certain, supremely interesting subject. The idea had been vaguely floating about in her head for years, certainly since 1892 when she wrote to Mrs Benson, the Archbishop's wife, 'Oh, I wish I were J. J. Rousseau and dared publish my Mémoires! . . . Sometimes I think the day will come when I *shall* dare'. The moment had arrived. Though not so explicit as Rousseau, she came near it. The perceptive reader can pick up many an interesting implication.

She was to write nine books of recollections, but this first venture concerned only her memories of childhood and early life in Germany up to the age of thirty, at which point her mother had just died and she had met Harry again after five years' separation. The recall of the past, a return to a world now vanished for ever in the cataclysm, proved therapeutic. Writing came much more easily to her than composing. She wasted no thought on problems of structure, balance, cohesion, or indeed, technicalities of any sort, but rambled on from

[1] *As Time Went On.*

146

chapter to chapter, reading out each as it was finished to a young connection of the Empress Eugénie's who was in the hospital, desperately wounded. His response was encouraging.

He was quite right. *Impressions That Remained*, as it came to be called, may lack professional polish, but it is imbued with a humour, a vividness, that give it great charm. There is an innocence about it surprising in a sophisticated woman of sixty, yet thoroughly characteristic of that complex being, Ethel. It ran to two volumes in the end and was published in 1919 to an enthusiastic chorus of praise and surprise. *The Times Literary Supplement* considered it 'one of the most remarkable books of memoirs that has appeared in recent times . . . The intensity of the private life which she discloses with something of Rousseau's sensitiveness yet with a mixture of lively humour quite beyond his capacity,' this admirer went on, 'carries the reader away from the outset.' He professed himself 'even a little ashamed at having been admitted to so much intimacy with the soul of one still alive.' The book was evidently strong stuff coming from a lady in 1919, though it reads respectably enough now.

Ethel found herself an instant literary figure, her work being appreciated by such people as Virginia Woolf, who might be supposed to know what she was talking about. It went into various reprints and translations, very useful from the financial point of view. It opened up also, as it were by force of circumstances, a whole new career which could be pursued without detriment to her music and one that would scarcely be affected by deafness, however acute.

She never ran out of things to say about herself, though the chief character might at times appear, superficially, to be Sir Henry Wood, Sir Thomas Beecham, Mrs Pankhurst, or some such worthy. Her pen grew more nimble with practice, subsequent books more neatly constructed. A certain artlessness disappeared without lessening the individuality of her writing. Always a saving sense of fun prevented obsessions from running quite away with her.

At this stage, she had more success as author than composer. Reception of *The Boatswain's Mate* was mixed. Some critics found the orchestration too heavy for a light-hearted story of a lady publican disposing of her suitors. The inclusion of the *March of the Women* in the overture was thought inappropriate. *The Times* declared the style inconsistent, the first act full of jolly folksong variations, the second suffused with Wagnerian gloom. Luckily the audience clapped and cheered to the echo so that she was comfortably able to dismiss these strictures as another blatant example of male chauvinism. It was

147

produced twice, in 1916 and again in 1918 when what people surely wanted was something to make them laugh, which they did uproariously.

After a short spell as interpreter for the Red Cross in Italy at the end of the war, Ethel returned to the promotion of her concerts with full vigour, for she considered literature entirely subordinate, a second string, useful and amusing in its fashion, but in no way equal to her importance as a musician. Nor should her gifts as a conductor be underrated; or perhaps, in this connection, one should say as an actress. She conducted her own works only, in a manner perfectly inimitable, as many a suffragette could testify.

So could Henry Wood, founder and promoter of the promenade concerts. 'She went up to my rostrum, took up my baton and surveyed its length critically. Deciding that it was more than she could manage, she calmly snapped it in two, threw away one half and conducted with the other.' He was less amused by her habit of creeping into the orchestra pit five or ten minutes before a performance was due to begin and pinning alteration slips over the scores. She would not have done this had she not felt as an artist, and as Ethel, that the changes were absolutely necessary. The result was, naturally, some confusion amongst the players who had not been taken into the composer's confidence in time for even the shortest rehearsal. Evidently she felt that a hesitant rendering of her latest thoughts was better than what she now saw as a mistake. Anyway, it was her opinion that if the orchestra were proficient, they would be able to cope with the unexpected.

Henry Wood was a foremost promoter of contemporary music. His promenade concerts were conceived with this end in view. The programme consisted, as it still does, of classics and, for contrast and public education, new works. It was a missionary movement in the arts. Thus, in the twenties, he was airing not only Elgar, Stanford and Parry, already well-established, but also Granville Bantock, Vaughan Williams, Frank Bridge, Holst, Hamilton Harty, Goossens, Bax, as well as Ethel, whom he had first met in 1913 when she had called on him and been mistaken by the maid and himself for a bicycle repairer, on account of her bloomers and general appearance. They became firm friends and Ethel frequently stayed at the Woods' country house, transporting her change of clothes in a battered cardboard box. She tended to arrive at breakfast or dinner with a long list of questions in hand to which she required instant and authoritative answers. When was he next going to include her works in his concerts, for instance?

[1] *My Life of Music*, Henry J. Wood, 1938.

When was a complete programme to be devoted to her? How about her *Mass*, long overdue for revival? She also regaled the assembled family with excerpts from her history, though in this company she thought it better to say that her relationship with Harry had been platonic. For the rest, she played tennis with vigour.

Henry, solid businessman that he was, realizing her potential as light relief, comic turn, or what you will, insisted on her conducting her part of the concert whenever possible. He assured her that people would come from far and near to see her perform, to their mutual advantage. It would pay for the best soloists, he said. 'You have a great following.'

It was good advice and she took it with gusto. The key to success lay in her complete self-confidence and apparent unawareness that she might be regarded as a figure of fun instead of the first great woman composer, the equal, or better, of any man. She generally wore the regalia of Doctor of Music, though she might tear off the headgear, if it chanced to annoy her, and fling it on the ground. 'I conducted the B[oatswain's] Mate Overture at the Proms. Did it very well,' she noted complacently in her diary on 21 August 1921: 'Had an immense reception and four calls and an ovation afterwards. The amusing thing is that whereas last time I conducted, the press elected to say I couldn't conduct, they now praise my conducting! All one has to do is to go straight on and pay no attention.'

Though she never ceased to complain of sexual discrimination and neglect by the establishment, in actual fact her works were often performed in the twenties all over the country and also abroad. Leeds, Hull, Birmingham, Cheltenham, Gloucester, she was constantly on the trot. Salzburg: 'I was one of the only two people (except a singer) who got any applause. The other was Hindemith, a quite young Frankfurter who contributed a splendid string quartet . . . It is a wonderful work and that boy will make his mark'.[1] Generosities and insights such as these mitigate her self-indulgence.

Nineteen twenty-two, indeed, saw her complete acceptance by the man-made world. She was created a Dame Commander of the Order of the British Empire in the new year honours list. It was quite unexpected. Some time before she had tried to get an invitation to a Buckingham Palace garden party, thinking to meet there people who might be of use in the promotion of her career. But Fritz Ponsonby, son of her old friend, had declared it impossible, in view of her disreputable suffragette history and status as an ex-convict.

[1] Diary entry, September 1922.

149

Here, then, was a victory for womanhood and recognition of professional eminence. She who had always loved titles now had one of her own. It came at just the right moment for she was finishing a ballet, *Fête Galante*, which, in due course, would have to be got on to the stage somehow. Perhaps the odds would not be quite so much against a *bona fide* Dame. She fixed it the next year in Birmingham.

This constant round of activity, work, travel was carried on simultaneously with a major love affair, necessitating the dispatch of immensely long letters every day, sometimes several in the twenty-four hours.

CHAPTER SEVENTEEN

With Edith Somerville in Sicily

No one could have provided a greater contrast to Emmeline Pankhurst than Edith Somerville, author, artist, horse coper, farmer, spiritualist, of Castle Townshend in County Cork. The great love of her life had been her cousin, Violet Martin, with whom she had collaborated in a series of books of which *The Real Charlotte* was thought by many to be the masterpiece, though the amusing volumes of stories, originally contributed to magazines and later published as *Some Experiences of an Irish RM*, proved much more popular, bringing the authors fame and even a certain amount of money.

The two women were utterly devoted to each other. Edith never got over Violet's death which occurred in 1915 as the result of a brain tumour. In her despair and loneliness, she turned to spiritualism, a faith that she and Martin, as she always called Violet, had been accustomed to laugh at very heartily in happier days. Now she communed nightly through the medium of automatic writing, firmly believing that all her subsequent books were written by them both and insisting that Martin's name appear with her own on the title page. The publishers were obliged to humour her in this.

The first product of the ghostly partnership was *Irish Memories*, autobiographical to a certain extent, but much more a hymn to the perfections of the dead Martin, the power and poetry of her mind, the sensitivity and refinement of her personality, her lovely hair, skin, feet, hands; the uniqueness of her whole being with which no other was worthy of compare. The book was well received on publication in November 1917. Ethel read it and, as was her pleasant habit in such cases, wrote to Edith appreciatively on 15 July 1918: 'I don't know when anything has moved me more deeply. As I read I was constantly thinking that if the writing of it gave you much pain it must have comforted you too.' They had a mutual friend in Lady Kenmare, Maurice Baring's sister, who lived at Killarney. Ethel was thinking of visiting her soon and wondered whether she might meet Edith there. She had a great desire to make her acquaintance.

Lady Kenmare, however, was not keen on the idea of a house party at that particular juncture. The struggle for Irish independence was in full swing and the country was in an uproar. Armed bands were roving about, murder was frequent, atrocities were committed by both Irish patriots and the British soldiers sent to restore peace. In these circumstances, Lady Kenmare advised Ethel to stay at home.

Perhaps Edith might come to England? They both suffered cruelly from rheumatism, so why should they not, Ethel suggested, meet at Bath, or Droitwich, and inaugurate their future friendship while taking a course of the waters? Edith seems not to have been attracted by the proposal, though she certainly did want to meet her new admirer. 'Come what may,' cried Ethel on 25 October 1918, 'I'm going to Ireland in April.' She enclosed a letter from a French fan of Edith's with this statement. Meanwhile she was reading all Edith and Martin's other books and pressing them on her friends. 'I believe no one gives me more pleasure than you and M. Ross.'[1] *Some Experiences of an Irish RM* had greatly alleviated the weakness caused by a severe attack of 'flu during the notorious 1918 epidemic.

They finally met on 16 September 1919 at a small railway junction where it was necessary to change for Killarney. Ethel was accompanied by Maurice Baring, known to his sister and relatives as Mumble Bumble. She rushed up to Edith and introduced herself. They felt an instant liking for each other and continued the journey in great good humour. The weather being more or less fine and the cloud not too low on the mountains, Lady Kenmare entertained her guests with a drive round the famous lakes. Later, Ethel amused the company with a lively performance of her selected works at the piano. Edith, herself a musician in that she had played the organ in her local church from girlhood, was more and more charmed. 'She played enchantingly.'[2] After a week, Ethel and Edith adjourned to Drishane, the Somerville family house in Castle Townshend, County Cork.

One of Edith's nephews, Nevill Coghill, then a young man of twenty, on the brink of a distinguished Oxford career, retained all his life the most vivid memories of his aunt's new and extraordinary friend. She was sixty-one, short, vigorous and handsome in a napoleonic way, an effect enhanced by her favourite headgear, a three-cornered hat. Her air was commanding, her presence magnetic and, though far from feminine, she seemed to the bemused Nevill adorable. This in spite of the fact that when he partnered her at tennis she would shout, 'Fool!', or, 'Haven't you any legs?', and similar opprobrious

---

[1] Martin Ross was Violet Martin's pen name.
[2] All quotations in this chapter are from the Smyth/Somerville correspondence, unless otherwise stated.

remarks whenever he missed a shot. This was on fine days. On wet afternoons, which are frequent in those parts, she might insist on his playing the violin to her accompaniment. Mozart he could manage without mishap, but when it came to her own violin sonata, a work he had never previously seen or heard, there was trouble. 'Can't you count the bars?' she would exclaim indignantly. 'Come on, count. Again. Again. At last! Of course you can do it if you try.'

Martin was at once informed of the new devolopments and asked whether or not she approved of Ethel. She said she emphatically did, congratulating Edith on having happened on such a fine friend. They had just finished their second posthumous book, *Mount Music*, a novel. Though there could really be no question of its merit, since Martin had presided over every paragraph, Edith gave it to Ethel to read with trepidation.

On 3 October 1919, Martin observed Ethel in bed with the book, totally absorbed, but she forgot to tell Edith the good news. When the poor author asked Ethel for an opinion and was told to wait until the whole had been considered, she was convinced it had been put down as a failure. 'I shall *never* forget,' said Ethel afterwards, 'your sitting on the hearth before dinner, a heap of depression, and I, who claim to be perceptive, but have hitherto not met extreme specimens of lunatic diffidence . . . guessed nothing.' It was one of the great differences of character between them. Ethel never quite got used to it, considering as she did that a woman's first duty was to stand up for herself in a world of men and generally to conduct an unremitting public relations campaign on her own behalf. Modesty was alien to her, except in the most elementary sense.

It was a small matter, mere distant signal at the beginning of an ecstatic friendship. They had much in common: a great sense of fun, for one thing, vitality, courage and a good heart. Both had suffered loss. But whereas Ethel had kept a firm grip on reality, Edith, unable to face the fact of death, retreated into a fantasy world in which Martin lived, changeless, speaking every day on all relevant subjects through the medium of the pen. For a time, Ethel accepted this as possible and normal, if on the morbid side. Had she not seen Harry's ghost on a French mountain? Friends connected with the Society of Psychical Research assured her that communication with the dead was a certainty and cited numerous cases to prove the point. On the strength of this she went so far as to ask Martin to enquire for Harry in heaven and to relay any messages he might like to send or, better still, persuade him to attend the nightly seance and write them himself. The results were vague, yet comforting: 'That you thought she referred to him moved me strangely'.

Then there was literature. Ethel's two volumes of autobiography had very recently been published and Edith promised an enthusiastic review, as did Ethel of *Mount Music* when the moment came. Ethel was surprised, however, by the limited extent of Edith's reading. Many of the classics were unknown to her. Her history was deficient, her poetry scant. Ethel tried to improve her education, but with only temporary success. It did not affect their relationship, the essence of which was mutual attraction and the finding of each other very good company.

When Ethel saw Edith's paintings, she was full of admiration, saying that they must be shown in London where she was certain they would be appreciated. She herself would undertake the job of finding a gallery. Mumble Bumble would advise on which were the best establishments. Her sister Mary would come, bringing rich friends. Sargent was unfortunately in America, but there were others of her acquaintance almost as renowned.

The momentous visit ended on 11 October 1919, by which time they had related their entire personal history, Edith's mundane, in spite of its emotional intensity, since she had lived always at Drishane at the centre of a large family; Ethel's ranging over the countries of Europe and an infinity of cosmopolitan connections. Edith liked her loud voice, her argumentativeness, her trenchant mind. She must have seemed a comet flashing through the misty, ghost-laden damps of Drishane. Her egotism did not disturb Edith; it only made her laugh.

Ethel returned home via Fermoy where her brother was in command of the regiment. She thought of Edith all the way to Dublin in the train, a considerable stretch, especially of her 'large, strong, capable, unutterably delicate and kind hand'. It seemed to sum up its owner and to symbolize their attachment. She was accompanied by a selection of Edith's pictures and no sooner had she reached London than she spread them before the directors of the Goupil, the Leicester and the Grosvenor galleries, all highly recommended by Mumble Bumble, finally coming to an arrangement with the Goupil.

Since Edith was extremely hard up, every penny she could lay hands on being regularly poured into Drishane, Ethel proposed to lend her a hundred pounds to cover the expenses of the exhibition, to be paid back gradually at convenient moments. She was able to make this gesture because *Impressions That Remained* had sold so well. The show was fixed for January 1920. 'You will not make a fool of yourself by

154

exhibiting,' she assured the nervous Edith. In March, they planned a holiday in Sicily, Ethel paying for the tickets, though Edith protested somewhat. 'You *could not* come with me,' said Ethel decisively, 'if you persisted in paying.'

That being settled, Ethel bustled about amongst the editors of magazines and newspapers fixing herself up with articles and recommending that Edith be taken on as a reviewer. She was revising her opera *The Boatswain's Mate*, finishing her ballet, *Fête Galante*, and chasing an elusive Thomas Beecham in order to make him put on her works in a big way at Covent Garden. Nor did she forget to round up an impressive crowd for Edith's private view and arrange a continuous programme of lunches and dinners for her with notables whom she might make use of afterwards, though she was not an apt pupil when it came to self-advertisement. Edith didn't really care for incessant entertainment. She was essentially a countrywoman, missing her dogs and horses, the sea air and the quietude to which Martin was accustomed alive and dead. She would, of course, accompany Edith, but it would be more difficult to communicate with her in London or Woking.

In spite of apprehensions, everything went smoothly. The pictures were appreciated and sold well. The lunches and dinners were enlivened by many compliments and Edith felt quite a lioness, a sensation she had not previously experienced. Ethel was more or less permanently euphoric. Edith had given her a special matchbox that had once belonged to Martin. Ethel regarded it as a talisman, carried always in her pocket, put under her pillow at night. Martin declared herself fonder and fonder of Ethel who enquired whether she might one day be so kind as to autograph, as Edith had already done, all her copies of their works. It is not recorded whether or not the ghost complied.

The two friends had many intimate conversations. 'What you said on the sofa went through and through me, my dearest,' Ethel declared. 'You have all my happiness in your keeping. Don't forget that.' She was certain that Harry would have liked Edith greatly. 'You would hardly believe since I have known you how often I have seen his face with a certain smile on it which was amusement and affection and delight.' In due course, they would all four meet in heaven and what a magnificent party that would be. Martin and Harry were already improving their acquaintance.

On the subject of Sicily, however, they had a passage of arms which showed that Edith had a different view of their relationship from Ethel.

Much as she had adored, and been adored by, Martin, there had never been anything overtly sexual between them. Ethel had had many sentimental affairs, but when she was really in love, as with Edith, she wanted something more than a friendly handclasp and peck on the cheek. Her object in suggesting the Sicily trip was to overcome the barrier she felt was between them, caused by Edith's shyness and reticence in emotional matters.

Edith was not expecting such developments and it seemed to her perfectly natural that her sister Hildegarde and brother-in-law Egerton should be invited to join them on their trip which was to last three months. Might not Ethel be glad of somebody else to talk to during that time? Hildegarde liked chatting about music. Why shouldn't Ethel ask her brother to come along too? Ethel's reaction was prompt and definite: 'A monstrous comedy . . . You must be raving mad'. She was certain Martin would say the same, if consulted.

Edith persisted for some while, perhaps from a feeling that three months facing up to Ethel, much as she admired and loved her, would require supporting forces. She couldn't help thinking it would be comfortable to bring a little of Castle Townshend with her. Martin would accompany them, naturally, but there were, unfortunately, limits to the amount of diversion she could provide. A number of acrimonious exchanges took place before Ethel got her way. 'I want you and me to settle our affairs in peace and quiet.' They set off early in February 1920 via Paris where they were to stay a few days so that Edith could be introduced to Winnaretta de Polignac who not only put on concerts but also exhibitions of artists of every grade of distinction.

Leaving Winnaretta, they proceeded through Italy, a somewhat tedious journey since the railways were in disarray. Trains went when they went. Delays occurred because coal had run out and wayside trees had to be chopped down as a substitute; or else for no ascertainable reason. Thieves abounded. Luggage strayed. At last they reached Taormina in triumph. The weather was warm, the scenery exquisite, the flowers in full bloom and their delight in each other's company unfailing. Ethel had been on a memorable tour of Sicily with Harry and she associated its beauties with love and happiness and 'lots of painters squatting about', poets and 'colonies of Oscar Wilde-men' to give a cosmopolitan accent. Edith painted enthusiastically and Ethel leaned against an adjacent rock, smoking and reading. She was fluent in the local dialect, a great help in their daily struggles with inefficiency and dirt. They hired a young beggar

156

to carry their effects and keep off other beggars and pertinacious children.

Next they made a tour of the island. Ethel was perpetually rushing round ruined amphitheatres, temples and other Roman and medieval remains in the history of which she was thoroughly versed. Edith was not so keen on this aspect. 'An undisciplined desire to prowl in the narrow, mysterious streets, and to investigate the hidden wares of the rat-holes that serve as shops in Siracusa'[1] had to be suppressed as Ethel engaged a carriage and took her to the Greek theatre, lecturing the while. 'Nothing more dead could be imagined. It looked more forlorn and cast-away than the bones of an old ship rotting on a mud bank.'[1] There were times when Edith thought longingly of Hildegarde and the dogs, and above all of Martin who had none of her usual volubility in these strange climes. 'I wish I were psychic . . . I might perhaps give occasional legs-up to your writing with V. M.,' sighed Ethel as her friend unsuccessfully struggled with the pencil.

Nevertheless, she would allow no subversive talk of perhaps cutting the holiday a little short, in view of lumbago which made the traversing of rough country painful; the necessity of seeing how things were getting on at home under the management of Edith's sister and brothers. Let all that wait. How could the damps of Drishane be better for lumbago than the superb climate of Sicily? No. They must press onward and upward. Never mind the way the men stared at two unchaperoned ladies of uncertain age; or the procession of small boys that followed wherever they went; or the amazing squalor of the so-called hotels where fluted columns and marble staircases led to verminous beds.

These rigours were varied by a visit to the Duke of Bronte. He was a descendent of Nelson's sister and had inherited the title and estates conferred on his ancestor by a grateful King of Naples. His magnificent castle was full of Nelson relics and he himself, Edith informed Hildegarde, 'is quite a pet, like a little bandbox duke on the stage. He and his old sister in a gorgeous chestnut wig and pearls as big as eggs pay me a formal visit each morning.' Ethel was already acquainted with this striking pair who made prodigious efforts to entertain their guests by means of picnics, parties, receptions and outings of all sorts accompanied by armed retainers as the country roundabout was infested with bandits.

The garden had many paintable corners and Edith availed herself of them. It was a halcyon interlude and one day as they contemplated

[1] *Happy Days*, E.OE. Somerville and Martin Ross, 1946.

the superb vista spread beneath the castle on all sides, a feeling of ineffable mystery seemed to tremble in the golden air and they both felt certain that it was a manifestation of Martin.

The middle of May 1920 found them in Rome on their way home. Here Ethel went down with 'flu and Edith nursed her tenderly, though troubled with sciatica herself. The next step was to obtain the necessary exit permit from the authorities which involved a scene of high drama, worthy of the best traditions of Italian opera. They went to the main police station where 'it was discovered and brought home to us, that with a carelessness, a forgetfulness, and a stupidity amounting to turpitude, we had omitted to register ourselves with the police in Sicily. Permission to leave Italy was out of the question . . . We must return to Taormina to have our papers put in order . . . I have often had occasion to admire my esteemed friend, Doctor Ethel, but never more than when she found herself confronted with this catastrophe. Continuing uninterruptedly in voluble and violent explanation and discussion, she held the official with a blazing blue eye, while she pushed a ten-lire note, across the counter, towards him. The official with an equally blazing brown eye, reiterating his adverse decision, covered the note with a quiet hand, versed in rapacity; and imperceptibly, in artistic diminuendo, the difficulty vanished; permission to depart was granted'.[1]

And so they left in triumph for their respective homes.

---

[1] *Happy Days.*

CHAPTER EIGHTEEN

Arguments

Ethel returned more in love than ever. Although she had not been able to seduce Edith, she had by no means given up hope of doing so. Her state of mind is reflected in the letters she constantly wrote. Edith's replies seem to have been almost as ardent, except on the subject of sex. They have not survived because, at a certain point, feeling they were too passionate and fearing Ethel might show them to some friend, she asked for them back and put them on the fire. But their general drift can be deduced from Ethel's.

They missed each other dreadfully. On 22 May 1920 Ethel wrote, 'I wish I could make you understand what a difference it makes to me to express some part at least of unsayable things. It takes half the dull ache, or the fierce ache as the case may be, out of the present moment when I have lost you and haven't yet found myself'. By 30 May Edith had begged her to come over to Drishane. She was obliged to refuse, at great cost to her peace of mind, because of the press of work and business which had accumulated during her three months' absence.

On 7 June 1920, she was in a state of 'unutterable happiness' after a letter from Edith saying she meant more to her than she knew. She also said she felt she had her hand in Ethel's. On reading this 'time and space disappeared and there remained only the dizziness you must have known often in your life'. She was reminded of the occasion in the train on the way to Syracuse when Edith had absently taken her hand and 'I sat quite still for a long time, lost, wondering if you knew.' Then there was the day when it seemed the impediment between them had vanished 'and I suddenly felt that if I kissed you, unritually, it would *not* be a false note.'

Edith went even further writing that the thought of Ethel made her pulse beat faster. 'So after all, you do care, not only for my love . . . but for me.' Ethel was mad with joy, having more or less resigned herself to becoming 'a comrade you could ill spare because you have no one of your own size in great intimacy'. On 14 June Edith again asked her to come to Ireland. She was still too busy revising 'Hey Nonny No' which was to be performed at Sheffield and working on

159

her ballet *Fête Galante*, but suggested that Edith might come over to Woking soon, at her expense.

Ethel was now encouraged to hope that she might gradually educate the totally inexperienced and ignorant Edith in matters of sex, and perhaps wean her slightly from her obsession with Martin. 'You do not, how often have I said it,' she began on 11 June, 'love a person because you deify them. It is because something in them combines chemically, if you like, with something in you and results in love.' Edith seems to have taken it pretty well, for by 19 June she has declared that Ethel's letters make the day for her. 'I leant back on the sofa and coped with a sharp pang of happiness,' said Ethel on reading this.

But Edith had still not grasped the lesson properly. 'If there's not complete honesty between us where should we be?' cries Ethel on 26 June 1920, in despair at her friend's lack of comprehension. 'You are one of those who don't wish to go deep into hearts on principle, because hearts are not your field of exploration.' Edith and Martin (who was, of course, taking a full part in the discussion via automatic writing) had always shrunk from sex being 'fastidious and rather virginal . . . But don't you see that I am *not* all this, that your law is not my law, that I can do and risk things you *could not.*' There was a small matter of refraining from bawdy stories, for instance. 'Why make you uncomfortable? I have others I can talk this foreign language with.' And 'it does not follow,' as Edith and Martin seem inclined to think, 'that I run about Hook Heath with no clothes on. No. To do that I should have to be very innocent or very thick-skinned and I am neither . . . What is fitting and right and even charming for you,' she continues next day, 'would be a sham for me. And a tragic mistake. And I want you to realize this is my feeling about it.'

Although Edith was not persuaded to wider views, she wrote an 'unutterably dear letter' protesting her love for Ethel who assured her, 'I *do* know I mean something to you, much if you like.' The discussion proceeded briskly. One should not 'as one gets older, forget how one felt in one's youth,' said Ethel on 11 July 1920. 'One never gets quite old, and then the principle is always the same.' She cannot agree with Edith and Martin 'that, well, non-spiritual emotions must necessarily be base . . . If I thought that, I would have become a nun long ago . . . Of course I allow that these impulses can and often do end in loss of quality all round, but so I think can spiritual and moral excess, only this fact is less generally recognized.'

Sometimes the argument took an acrimonious turn. By 20 July 1920, it appears that Martin has said that Harry's morals, greatly

Ethel conducting the police band at the unveiling of the memorial to Mrs Pankhurst in the Victoria Tower Gardens, London, March 1930

Dame Ethel Smyth by Neville Lytton, Earl of Lytton, 1936

to be deplored in their earthly form were definitely improving under heavenly tuition. 'The soul must drive, not the body. Tell her that,' was the message to Ethel. 'I wish I could talk to her.' Ethel was furious with the impertinent ghost. Harry had been perfectly pure in his own way. His morals required no mending. There had been nothing wicked in the physical expression of their love. She was provoked into pages of scorn on the subject of Edith's prudishness and gentility.

In the end, Ethel was obliged to make do with a purely emotional friendship. It did not lessen her affection. Three years later, after Edith had stayed with her, in October 1923, she was writing: 'I have a sick longing for you back again. All the love of you and your ways and every one of them (except towards your lap dogs) that has been held back by a barrier of work and preoccupation all these months, comes down like a flood now.'

The fact was that Edith could not change. She had been brought up to believe that sex was a doubtful proposition, especially for women. Even worse, that it was of itself an evil only redeemed, and that not much, when practised within the bonds of holy matrimony. It was also entirely connected with men in her mind, of whom she had a horror in the physical sense, being no bisexual. Although she had loved Martin heart and soul, she regarded that love as elevated and purified, rather than diminished, by the absence of sexual expression and Ethel could not persuade her otherwise. She was now sixty-two, in daily communion with a spirit from the past which repudiated Ethel's shocking ideas and disreputable behaviour in this respect. She would have betrayed her beloved Martin, still so alive though unfortunately invisible, had she listened to Ethel's temptations. Nevertheless, Ethel meant a very great deal to her. No one else had been able to alleviate the terrible loneliness and despair consequent on Martin's abrupt departure for the next world.

During this crisis of friendship, Ethel was enduring another, and far worse, trial. Loves come and go, however intensely one may feel at the moment. It's another matter with ears. She had always hoped that the doctors would find a cure, as they generally assured her would be the case. But now her good ear began booming and singing in the same way as the other. Some days it seemed even worse.

Edith was very concerned and wanted to come over immediately and accompany Ethel to Paris where she was shortly to have an operation. Not that she trusted much to that, feeling only, 'It may recover, but somehow or other I don't think it will.' She refused Edith's offer, saying; 'There are black bits of life that are best faced in solitude.

They must be stared at in the very eyes and one must give oneself time . . . Thank God that I'm a voracious reader.' She was finding conversation difficult to follow: 'I feel a sort of felt wad between me and the voices of this earth . . . I suppose I . . . shall get accustomed to being, as it were, encased in a diver's helmet under the sea.' But who could say whether it would stop at that? 'I asked myself, "Do I wish to go on living now?" If you were here, my arms round you, my head pressed against you . . . Or if we sat on that sofa behind me and my lips were against your cheek, I should perhaps say, "Yes, I want to live." And when I think that you would be lonelier without me, I say decidedly, "Yes, I *do* want to live", for I believe I love you more than myself and that is saying a very great deal, let me tell you. But for you, I can imagine no greater blessing than if a voice should say to me, "You won't be asked to face this; so you needn't worry." '

Yet still she would not allow Edith to come. It may be that the *cri de coeur* was enough to restore her courage; or she thought that such open emotions would be too much for her reticent friend to sustain. In order to relieve her own anxiety, Edith was obliged, therefore, to send Martin on a quick trip to Paris with orders to report. Soothing messages were brought back, though the operation eventually proved unsuccessful. But, like a true daughter of the Indian army, Ethel rallied her spirits. The outlook for music was black, but there was writing. She was even able while in Paris to hold melancholy at bay with the composition of a funny story about a woman from Shoreditch met in a train in 1902. She included it in her collection of essays, *Streaks of Life*, published the next year, 1921, and the influence of Somerville and Ross is plain. It was her only venture into the pure comic genre.

On returning from Paris, she went over to Drishane and stayed for more than two months during which time she polished up her new book. The chief item in it was her recollections of the Empress Eugénie who had recently died aged ninety-five, vigorous to the last. The miscellaneous contents also embraced memories of Queen Victoria, struggles to get her operas performed, the position of women in the musical world and a review of Edith's novel *Mount Music*, very laudatory and originally written in Taormina during their magical spring in Sicily. By the time Ethel left for Woking in early October, they had spent the best part of six months of 1920 together. They never saw so much of each other again.

The subject of sex had been settled once and for all. Their letters thereafter are those of dear friends and contain no passionate reproaches or lovers' complaints. If they fight, it is over the ordinary irritations of life likely to arise between two such different characters. Lightness, laughter and sympathy are the main impressions conveyed by the correspondence with only an occasional excursion into the deeper feelings; or, in Ethel's case, longing for a more complete relationship.

Edith summed it up best perhaps. 'I believe we both feel very much the same in the comfort we get out of one another. We both wanted it, but only for you, we shouldn't have found each other.' Again: 'I can say (and do) things to you that I couldn't to anyone else and you understand but others wouldn't. Goodbye Dearest (for example!) ever your loving Edith.'

She depended a great deal on hearing from Ethel. 'I do miss your letters sickeningly,' she exclaimed on 9 January 1921, not having received one for three whole days. She always read them to Martin, who pronounced, 'I delight in her letters. She makes me laugh something in the way your mother does – a peculiar trenchant directness and humour tempered by extreme common sense. I still maintain that she is mad, but I think all nice people are.' 'You talk straight at the paper and it sticks. I don't believe you write it at all,' Edith added. This is an apt description of her own letters.

Ethel always had plenty of interesting news as her activity was, as ever, incessant. On 19 January 1921 she had just come back from Hull where one of her works was performed. At a certain point, unable to bear the conductor's lack of skill, she snatched the baton from him. Both Martin and Edith enjoyed the scene. On hearing, a week later, that Ethel had had another relapse in the ears, the solicitous Edith got Martin to send the best doctor she knew in heaven over to Germany, there to consult a reliable specialist: 'I was sent to Dresden to find him,' the spirit faithfully reported, 'and spoke to him of Ethel. He said to tell her not to give up hope, but she must mind what he says about ears and weather. He would like her to go to a warmer climate and dry.' Under further questioning, the doctor urged her to carry on with her music, not to play golf in the rain and to look after herself.

Although Ethel only took as much of this advice as suited her, the attack passed off, which she very likely put down to celestial intervention, having no doubts about the reality of communion with the dead as yet, an opinion reinforced by meeting on the local golf course Radcliffe Hall, later famous as the author of *The Well of Loneliness*. She was an ardent worker for the Society for Psychical Research and communicated most successfully with a departed woman friend well known to Ethel in former days. Miss Hall was accompanied by her lover Lady Troubridge who, they informed Ethel in the course of conversation, was suffering from an unmentionable disease given her by the beast of a husband she had fled from. She also did a little sculpture to help pass the time. In addition to editing the psychical journal, they both bred dogs, a number of which died, though others won prizes. 'They told me thrilling things and are simply dying to meet you,' Ethel assured Edith, for whose expected visit she prepared by hanging her pictures outside the bedroom and, over the writing table, 'I have put a Giorgione tea party where the ladies have nothing on and the gentlemen are dressed to the nines . . . These are the friendly thoughts of one who truly loves you'.

Among new acquaintances she made at this time was Laurence Housman, brother to the poet. 'I very nearly like him quite much, but when he smiles he flashes his teeth at you as if each individual fang had an electric light in it. And I can't make out if they are or are not real rooted teeth. I so nearly asked him when for the eleventh time he touched the switch and I felt quite faint . . . I feared I should catch hold of them, anything to have certainty.'

Her forthcoming *Streaks of Life*, replied Edith, should be advertised as a 'companion volume to Mr Laurence Housman's "Flashes of Fangs", really a very nice name, or "Flashing Fangs" with foreword by Messrs Tug, Holdon and Wrenchitt'.

Nor had Ethel lost sight of Emmeline Pankhurst, though taking small pleasure in her company nowadays, a fact which it seems must have escaped that lady's attention, for she invited her to come on a proposed visit to New Zealand where the political situation as regards women was said to be interesting. Poor Emmeline had fallen on hard times. The valiant Mary Dodge had been obliged by income tax troubles to cut down on the allowance which, at Ethel's suggestion, she had been making her.

Lady Rhondda, a fierce supporter of the cause in its great days and owner of *Time and Tide* magazine, offered some sort of public relations job with the paper, but Emmeline did not see herself as the humble employee of a past follower. In fact, there wasn't a job she could do with dignity, especially as she had no talent for working in the sort of partnership an ordinary career demands, whether or not political.

There were other difficulties, too. Dr Flora Murray, an old campaigner, 'succeeded in raising £2,600 for Christabel and her mother (and I think it was a great mistake including Christabel who should work for herself). The silly woman who lives with and ministers to Christabel's vanity had actually persuaded her to take a hall in London in order to denounce the givers for giving so little! A list of names was to have been a feature. I don't know who nipped this elegant enterprise in the bud.' Ethel tried to get Lady Rhondda to take on Christabel as a reviewer, in the hope of alleviating her mother's financial position at least partially.

But Emmeline was not in the habit of taking advice. Occasionally it was to her credit, as in the case of the four little girls she had adopted in 1914 in the certainty that public subscriptions could be raised for their support. They had long become a burden. 'Of course she was *mad* to adopt those children and ought to have seen it ages ago. I told her so and that she ought to put them into institutions, but she said fiercely that she had taught them to call her Mother and she'd stick to them.'

The last years were sad. This romantic revolutionary, gifted with oratory, never was elected to parliament, nor was her adored Christabel. Neither of them could fit into the workaday world after the adventures they had had, the power they had wielded over their adherents, a number of whom, like Lady Constance Lytton, had ruined their health in a fanatical desire to serve the cause, as embodied in the two leaders. Mrs Pankhurst did lecture tours. Christabel, forgetting politics, preached Second Adventism. Who can say what her mother thought of that? She must have excused it, however, for they proposed to set up a tea shop together in the south of France and, indeed, did so for a short while until it crashed, inevitably.

Mrs Pankhurst had repudiated her second daughter, Sylvia, who was very left wing, working in the east end slums and voicing opinions her now conservative mother found unacceptable. Worse than that, Sylvia took a lover, had a son and refused on principle to marry. Mrs Pankhurst felt the slur on the family profoundly. Ethel considered it the main cause of her death in 1928. 'Mrs Pankhurst died of chagrin – of pain and horror at the disgrace brought on her name by that disgusting Bolshie daughter of hers,' she wrote to Edith. 'There was nothing wrong with her and by ill luck she was alone when the blow fell. And she *could not* stand solitude, brooded, got blood poisoning and was, alas, in the hands of Christabel who, in my opinion, is . . . dotty, just the last person to help . . . Mrs Pankhurst dreaded being twitted about it on the platform.'

What memorial should be raised to this most flamboyant woman of the age? Some thought a portrait for the National Gallery; some a hospital bed, 'a good though rather dank idea'. Christabel declared for a statue, 'and I think, for once, she is right'. It was duly erected in the gardens beside parliament. Ethel conducted the police band in 'March of the Women' at the unveiling ceremony.

CHAPTER NINETEEN

Ghosts

To return to 1921/22: The political situation continued very disturbed in Ireland. Ethel and Edith had many an acrimonious passage on the subject, the one being an Irish nationalist at heart and the other expressing the right wing British reaction. 'Your unspeakable countrymen.' In particular, Ethel refused to believe that English soldiers could have committed the atrocities imputed to them. 'They . . . have done more mischief and spread more hatred of England than anything since the time of Cromwell,' Edith reiterated. Those rebels caught were generally 'the press-ganged boys . . . wretched lads dragged out by force and then captured and – often – shot. They say the authorities offer them the alleviation of being doped before sentence is carried out.'

Things had been fairly calm in Castle Townshend until 1921, but now Edith was in the thick of it. While Ethel was dashing hither and thither conducting the overture to the *Boatswain's Mate* at a promenade concert, trying to get Winnaretta de Polignac to fix a performance of the same in Paris, running from Bath to Bournemouth, to the Queen's Hall, to Guildford, coaching a negro in one of her songs, pressing her new ballet, *Fête Galante*, on various producers, Edith was struggling, by means of diplomacy and guile, to prevent her cattle and horses being stolen, her house looted and burnt down. All the bridges along the one road out of Castle Townshend had been blown. It was impossible to get to the station, or the shops of the nearest town – not that there was anything in them. The farm produce could not be sent to market. No one was buying livestock.

What to do for money? Perhaps she could paint some portraits and send them by boat to Cork and thence to Ethel for exhibition. It didn't work. She might write a play, Ethel giving advice from her extensive experience of the opera. She tried it. Mrs Bernard Shaw, who originated in Castle Townshend, thought it wonderful, but Shaw was crushing. Ethel's connections seemed unable to help in the matter of literature and art. With horses she was surprisingly successful, managing to place two hunters sent over during a lull in hostilities. She also offered asylum at Woking. But Edith preferred to stay and defend her property.

There were certain encouraging aspects. A farmer said: ' "They'll do nothing to you, Miss. You're greatly thought of through the country". So my spendthrift keeping of hounds has stood to us after all! And you needn't abuse me for extravagance any more, it only amounted to fire insurance.' Then, luckily, her naval brother, Hugh, happening to be in command at the base at Queenstown, was able to order a destroyer to anchor in Castle Townshend harbour with fifty marines at the ready to scale the cliffs the minute his sister let off a flare or waved a red lamp. Last, but by no means least, there were the ghosts.

The more military of these had been organized into a squad by her deceased Uncle Kendal, late of the cavalry and always very brave and dashing. They were on perpetual guard, sometimes repelling attack by loud footsteps, sometimes by penetrating the minds of the marauders and causing them to change their plans. Since the country people believed in ghosts just as much as Edith and knew that she communed with them nightly, this line of defence was probably as good as the other.

'Martin says there has been an unwearied cordon of spiritual help round us . . . Absolutely there is no other reason why we have escaped so easily,' she wrote on 13 August 1922. 'In comparison with other places, *nothing* has happened to us, although we have had some horrible people up here.'

These had to be dealt with carefully. 'We are learning patience in a hateful school that has taught us many other virtues compulsorily – such as being lowly and reverent to all one's inferiors and when you are asked for your cloak giving also your coat and skirt and silver-backed hairbrushes.' The strain was great. 'Ethel, I am *tired* of all this. It isn't "on the nerves" in the least, it is only that I am sick of it all and am begining for the first time in my life to wish I were "a happy English child". Everything is so troublesome and humiliating and dangerous and so *maddeningly* inconvenient.'

Yet, she could not possibly leave. Everyone depended on her. It was true she had her brother Cameron in the house, but her opinion of him was small, though affectionate. 'For the last week I went to bed prepared to be called out at any moment and to find the house in flames. You may say I know nothing of history, but if I haven't read it, I have lived it and I can assure you it is very unpleasant.' She tried to keep going by painting and writing a new novel which she often despaired of, too, in spite of Martin's reassurance.

Ethel was much excited by these letters, the more detailed of which were sent via the destroyer as the rebels were liable to open the post, should that be functioning. They gave such a vivid picture, far better than anything to be gleaned from the newspapers. She wanted go to Drishane, join in the fray and support the weary Edith, who agreed. 'You would make £100's if you came over and investigated and wrote it up. And then we should never fight again, as you would find *I was right!*'

But it was never possible to get there when things were actually happening. So that although she made one or two trips, the excitements were few. She missed, for instance, the great day when the catholic priest, Father Lamb, routed twelve armed men single-handed, chasing them up the hill, yelling curses, pursuing two into a public house where they had taken refuge, seizing their rifles and smashing them on the road.

She was not at hand on the night Edith was awakened by 'bubblings from the puppies, then a sort of dull thump. I arose, got my hunting crop (sole available weapon) and crept forth up the passage in the dark, listened at C[ameron]'s door – silence – then at top of stairs. Then a sound as of sideboard drawer being pulled open. "They're here!" I thought, but before going to light the red flare I thought I had better rouse the Chimp [Cameron]. Went softly into his room. Called him. No response – groped to bed, pawed it cautiously and found only heated emptiness. I thought, "They've got him!" and was going downstairs, when, in darkness, heard step on stairs. It was C[ameron]'. It turned out to be a false alarm. 'Dearest,' she wrote to Ethel, 'it is such a comfort having you to howl to.' And again, 'I never, *never* would have believed Ireland would have come to this, if I hadn't lived through it.'

Sometimes the letters were partly in schoolgirl French for greater security. Even so, Ethel seemed not to realize the extreme dangers to which her friend was exposed. She used them in a newspaper article without consulting Edith, though it is true she disguised the names slightly. 'That was unprofessional, Ethel,' Edith reproved when she heard of it. 'Apart from other reasons, prominence of this kind is not healthy. I still have horses to lose and houses to burn.' It was an anxious and dreary existence with no coal, no hot water and precious little light. 'I often marvel at the way we all sit calmly on the lid of a very seething pot and play croquet and make hay as if we were in Kent or Surrey. I suppose they did the same in Russia and in the Cities of the Plain . . . Martin keeps on saying that there is hope at last but (as I have often said to her) their notion of time is not ours.'

Ethel's burdens were of a less sensational nature. The brilliant career she had so longed for had materialized. She was a Dame. And yet: 'I am now begining to understand why, when success comes at last, one doesn't find it as nice as one had hoped. Every soul in England writes to ask me to conduct, or to dine, or to lecture, or to join a club or something and my life is spent in writing letters and sending parcels.' It was absolute hell.

'Don't talk to us about "hell" because you are so famous and sought after that you are run off your legs,' said Edith. 'I wish we had half your complaint. When we're run off our legs it is because 200 Mexican toughs are after us with jack-knives.' De Valera was believed to have imported them in order to ginger up his forces. Ethel had no good reply to this.

But in 1922 she made a momentous trip to Germany. The object was, naturally, to promote her works and try to discover a cure for her ears. Things were almost as dramatic as in Castle Townshend. Murderous bands were not roving about, nor houses looted and burnt, yet the situation was even more sinister. The whole economy had collapsed. Inflation was such that anyone without a job, and there were many, starved. Old friends of the prosperous middle class were living on soup, having sold everything which could be turned into money. 'I have been through such heart-rending experiences,' she wrote in August 1922. 'What chaos! I feel that any moment a revolution may break out.' She longed for the reassurance of Edith's brave presence in the midst of these terrors. 'If you knew what I have suffered being cut off from you thus . . . Dear, don't let go of me.'

Yet they were on the brink of letting go. It was not only the Irish sea which separated them. Edith summarized the position on 7 April 1923: 'You are absolutely free of family ties. Your family and you love each other, I know, probably as much as we and ours do, but you . . . need only to consider yourself, your work, your artistic engagements. You are not tied up with your people in a hundred little ways (which you may not believe in, but which nonetheless exist, and are far more intricately binding than the big ones). You have a house of your own and are beholden in no way to anyone. It is a splendid position and I often wish it were mine. But it never was, nor ever will be, so there's no use talking about it. And I'm inured now to my limitations and don't often feel they are hampering. But they are.'

She could no more change than Ethel and the obstacle was fundamental. They were both now sixty-five. How could they change?

How could two such histories coalesce? Their love had been true and good while it lasted. It could not go on for ever. They had different objects in life. Edith was nothing like as ambitious as Ethel. She was the head of a clan, 'a stone in a tribal necklace' as Ethel called it. The position suited her perfectly.

After the Troubles died down, time turned back. Crowds of relatives came to enjoy tea, croquet, boating, tennis. It was the 1900's all over again. It was heaven, as Martin could testify from her experience of higher spheres where exactly the same amusements enlivened the celestial day. Edith had no desire to change it for the excitements of metropolitan life, of rushing from city to city, cultivating the local influences, obliging them to work in one's interest. She did not wish to make new friends every twenty-four hours, or look forward to a succession of love affairs. The shade of Martin lay too darkly on her spirit for it ever to be free. In 1922, having sold a horse, she purchased a cupboard, more or less resembling an altar, and placed it in St Barrahane's church where she had played the organ since girlhood, and decorated it with flowers and other memorials of Martin. In 1924, she instituted a week of remembrance with special prayers at the altar. Martin had been a saint on earth, why not in heaven?

Although Ethel continually spoke of Harry and had elevated him to the rank of universal guru, an accolade not bestowed on him in life, she was far too vigorous a character, too interested in the world about her to withdraw into the twilight realm of ghostly memories. She lived in the present, as she said, savouring each moment to the full as it came. Perhaps she was incapable of such deep love as Edith had given Martin. Perhaps it is not a good thing to love as much as that.

They did not exactly quarrel as a result of these fundamental divergencies, but small matters which before had been passed off with a laugh became considerable irritations. There was the way Edith would definitely arrange to come to England and then put it off at the last minute. 'You are, it seems to me, incapable of making a plan and sticking to it and give excuses one after the other!' Ethel exclaimed with pardonable annoyance on 19 February 1923. 'It's a sort of *senile decay*,' she continued on 1 April. 'Though if you live in the midst of a country (and a family) that are similarly invertebrate it doesn't much matter, I tell you it is disastrous if you have to do with someone of a highly organized life, like ME. But as well fight a feather bed as try to make an impression on an utterly fluid character.'

She found the dirt of Drishane increasingly difficult to stomach.

'I'm glad I can't see your studio or smell it,' she said on 20 December 1922, 'for *I* remember what Drishane smelt like the last time I was there. If Pan's head smells, I can wash it, and him. But you can't purify a room polluted for months by little dogs except by burning it down.' The dogs were ill-mannered as well as unclean. 'If I were back at Drishane,' she wrote on 12 September 1924, 'though the bedclothes are what they must be, I should not care as long as I could lie there and talk as of old. That is, if allowed to by the outraged occupant. Then I felt, "No use, I *can't* get over that shrinking and it would come out." . . . I wondered if, down in the depths, I had alienated you because of my scolding about the dog-mania and its results?'

Worst of all, she lost her belief in direct communication with the dead. The whole paraphernalia of spiritualism and automatic writing began to bore her. She concealed it from Edith as long as possible, but on 28 February 1926 was obliged to say, 'I wish, because of you, that these things were in my line. But you see I have too many things that *are* – love of reading per se, interest in various themes treated in books . . . not to know the difference between being really interested or not . . . That world only has interest for me through you'.

Thus the zest gradually evaporated from their relationship. They saw each other seldom. The eight or ten letters a week shrank to so many in the year by 1925. But there was no open breach. They continued to congratulate each other as their successive books appeared. Edith was particularly thrilled by a performance of Ethel's *Mass* in Birmingham on 7 February 1924, conducted by Adrian Boult. It had been preceded by a dress rehearsal in heaven on 28 December 1923. 'She would have been proud to hear it,' declared Martin, whose favourite section was the *Credo*. The conductor was some German spirit. She had not been able to catch his name. The Empress Eugénie and her son the Prince Imperial had attended, amongst many others, including Harry, of course. The concert was held 'in a beautiful building like a cathedral' that reminded Martin of Notre Dame, 'the music swelling out of the shadows . . . The whole effect was magnificent.' The ghosts were so excited at the séance that they kept snatching at the automatic pencil, 'just like a group at a telephone trying to grab the receiver from each other'. These were the sort of revelations that Ethel was begining to find tiresome.

It was the first performance in the next world and only the second here below. Thirty years had elapsed since Bernard Shaw had jocularly reviewed it under the pen name of Corno di Bassetto. Now he wrote an appreciative letter, saying soothing things, such as, 'Your music is more masculine than Handel's'; and, 'You booted Elgar contemptuously out of your way as an old woman'; and, 'But for you I might not have been able to tackle St Joan, who has floored every previous playwright.'

Ethel's own immediate feeling was more muted: 'On the whole satisfactory, but you know how hard I am to please . . . Audience warm (for stodgy Birmingham). Chorus fine. Boult *first rate*. Orchestra putrid,' she informed Edith. All the trombones were played by policemen.'

Press of business notwithstanding, she had exerted herself over an exhibition of Edith's pictures which opened at the same time. The painter was prevented, either by circumstance, muddle, or rheumatism, from attending as she had planned. The ghosts, who had been getting up their art criticism, turned out in force. The unanimous opinion was, said Martin, that 'you had greatly improved, your colour was so well put on.' Earthly critics echoed them and sales were such that Edith actually made some money.

In 1925 Ethel went on a holiday in Greece with a young relative and wrote amusing letters to Edith of her progress over trackless mountains to abominable lodgings, sustained by frightful food. It was reminiscent of their famous adventures in Sicily. 'I am so reminded of 3 years ago when on this momentous date of April 23rd we were together at Maniace! Well, this has been another wonderful tour.' Sometimes they walked for six hours in rain and wind. 'My rotten muscles get suppler and stronger every day. Ditto digestion and general well-being.' In 1927, she published an entertaining account of her trials and tribulations, *A Three Legged Tour in Greece*.

In spite of the happy memories, Ethel was unable to revive the old cameraderie with Edith, whose letters became much less interesting once the Troubles were over and whose personality seemed to fade. Her final judgement comes in a letter to Virginia Woolf some years later: 'The real inwardness of that connection has worn itself out owing to automatic writing, though I ask myself if that is not merely a symptom of arrested growth that was pre-ordained. I suppose some people do come to the downward slope sooner than you would have expected and that the germ of downhillishness must always have been there. I often think how her real bent was painting and how she took to writing because of her cousin, who was the real writer. But Edith is so competent that she could not help becoming a good writer too, carried, no doubt, by the cousin. And the impetus lasted after M. Ross's death.'

CHAPTER TWENTY

Mothering Virginia Woolf

It was inevitable that Ethel should again fall passionately in love. Her nature required it. In 1927 it seemed that Vita Sackville-West was to be Edith's successor. Ethel had met her long before, in 1912 or 1913, in her sister Mary's drawing-room, 'when she was engaged to Harold Nicolson, also a guest. But I did not know this and distinguished myself by asking . . . in her presence, "Who is the little man exactly like a pretty Dutch doll?" '[1]

Their acquaintance languished for the next fifteen years, although they were interested to read each other's books. Ethel particularly enjoyed *The Land*, an extended poem which received the Hawthornden prize in 1927. She wrote an appreciative letter that resulted in a lunch party. It was a great success. 'Vita is a *dear*,' Edith was at once told. 'Of the chocolate box type of beauty, an appearance that belies a rather warm reputation.' She found Harold Nicolson most agreeable (he arrived with a cage of canaries) and admired their mutual devotion 'in spite of her passion for selected specimens of her own sex'. She was 'a keen mother', yet, 'one feels it is absurd her having a family – as silly as if Athena or Cleopatra travelled with a nursery'.

The friendship prospered. They wrote frequently, visited each other, discussed all manner of books. Unlike many husbands in Ethel's experience, Harold Nicolson had no objection to his wife's new acquaintance and seemed always to be happy to find her installed for the weekend when he arrived from London. He was thoroughly amused by her conversation, her self-confidence, her mannerisms. He didn't mind the way she shouted because all deaf people did that. In the event, their cameraderie lasted until her death. Sometimes he encountered her on railway platforms, slightly tiddly; or at foreign dinner tables conducting furious arguments in German, French, Italian. There were occasions when he was able to assist her hearing by courteously adjusting her aid so that the amplifier was turned outwards instead if being pressed against her bosom. She was also liable to plank the contrivance, which resembled a wooden box, on the table and then, jumping up in the excitement of her discourse, march about, oblivious of the machine clattering after her on the floor.

[1] Letter to Edith Somerville, 20 May 1927.

Ethel was immensely taken not only with Vita's looks, but her intelligence and a certain strangeness about her, the withdrawn secret spirit of the natural solitary, as it seemed, in spite of a tempestuous and varied emotional life. But Vita was not physically attracted to Ethel, more than thirty years her senior, and in any case was currently much in love with Virginia Woolf. Ethel, on her side, did not feel the true passion that she had for Edith, or Emmeline Pankhurst. The void in her life remained, despite professional success both as writer and composer.

The more Ethel heard about Virginia Woolf, the more she longed to know her. For some reason, the introduction did not come through Vita and they met only on 20 February 1930. In January Ethel was asked by the BBC to chair a programme called *Point of View*. This was the moment. She decided to approach Virginia and persuade her to take part. She had published her long essay on women's wrongs, *A Room of One's Own*, in October 1929 and Ethel had read it with approbation, especially such sentences as, 'The woman composer stands where the actress stood in the time of Shakespeare'. And, with pleasurable indignation, the quotation from a book on modern music: 'One can only repeat Dr Johnson's dictum concerning a woman preacher, transposed into terms of music, "Sir, a woman's composing is like a dog's walking on its hind legs. It is not well done, but you are surprised to find it done at all." '

On 28 January 1930, therefore, she addressed her first letter to Virginia, saying amongst other compliments, 'I have often suppressed a wish to write and tell you part of what I feel about *A Room of One's Own*'. Could she drop in one afternoon to discuss the programme and any other matters that might arise? 'I want to see you, if you do not detest the idea too much? You *might* (who knows?) quite like me if we were to meet.'

Two days later, Virginia replied: 'If you only knew how often I have wanted to write to you – and only didn't for fear of boring you – to thank you for your books and articles . . . There is nothing I should like better than to see you – and you might like me. Who knows?'

The occasion was not arranged without difficulty. First, the Woolfs were off on a country visit. Then they got 'flu. Letters flew backwards and forwards. Ethel feared she was being put off with false excuses. Virginia swore it was not so, asked for the loan of volume one of *Impressions That Remained* which she had mislaid. 'What a fascinating book! How did you learn to write like that?' Ethel, wholly placated,

175

immediately sent both volumes as a present, stating in the same letter that Virginia would have to excuse her appearance when they finally saw each other. She had no smart clothes fit to interview fame and beauty, nor any intention of getting them. 'I needn't mend the hole in my solitary dress, as I had fully intended,' the polite Virginia responded.

The long postponed day came. Ethel arrived at tea time with her latest book, *A Three Legged Tour in Greece*. Virginia, by no means recovered, received her in a dressing gown. 'I heard the bell ring,' she noted in her diary next day, 'then a brisk tramp up the stairs; and then behold a bluff military old woman (older than I expected), bounced into the room, a little glazed flyaway and abrupt, in a three cornered hat and tailor made suit.'

'Let me look at you!' Ethel cried in her loud voice. She had been thinking of nothing else for the last ten days, during which time she had drawn up a list of subjects to be discussed and clarified.

The first concerned Virginia's great grandfather James Pattle, whose extraordinary adventures as a corpse in India General Smyth had been accustomed to recount at the dinner table to good effect. 'As big a scamp as ever you saw,' the old gentleman would say, 'and as bad a fellow in every way . . . Well at last he drank himself to death and they found to their astonishment he had left directions that he should be embalmed and buried next his old mother in the family vault at Marylebone church.' The grieving widow – often abominably deceived by him in life – insisted on his being put into a barrel of rum in the spare bedroom until a boat arrived to carry him to England. 'Well, in the middle of the night,' the general would continue, 'there was a loud explosion; she rushed into the room and found the cask had burst and there was her husband half out of it! The shock sent her off her head then and there, poor thing, and she died raving.' His friends did not give up, however. They put him in another cask and shipped it down the Ganges. 'The sailors hadn't the most distant idea what they'd got on board, and thinking the cask was full of rum, which was the case, they tapped it and got drunk, and, by Jove, the rum ran out and got alight and set the ship on fire! While they were trying to extinguish the flames she ran on a rock, blew up and drifted ashore.' The conclusion of the story, always a tremendous success, was: 'A letter came from the rector of Marylebone saying the Pattles had never had a vault in the church at all.'

This was just the sort of conversation to lighten the depressing miasmas of 'flu. Ethel informed her new friend also of her entire life

Ethel Smyth by Powys Evans

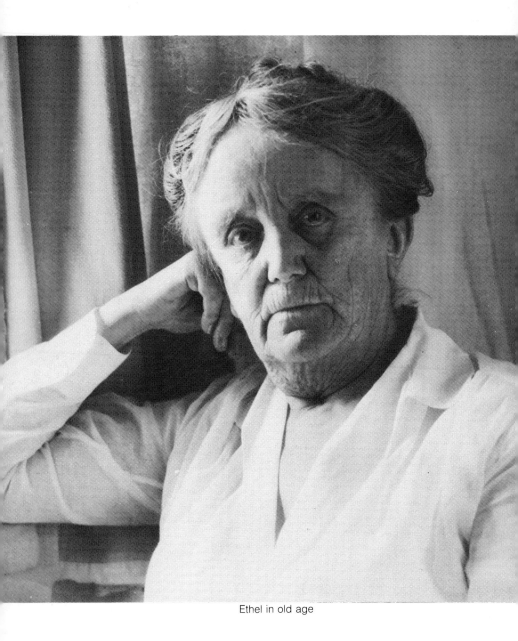
Ethel in old age

history, in particular giving a full account of Harry, part of whose book *The Prison* she was engaged in setting to music in the form of an oratorio. She declared her intention of reading all Virginia's works, though the latter had some doubts as to whether they would entirely agree with her. They spoke of *The Waves* which Virginia was in the middle of writing; and of composing, which Ethel declared to be essentially similar to the creation of novels. They considered the nature of love.

Virginia observed her visitor closely as she talked. At animated moments, 'her cheeks redden. Her faded eyes flash. She has a broad rounded forehead' where a vein 'like a large worm'[1] sometimes swelled. This happened, one supposes, as she described a recent fight with the director of the Royal College of Music. She was certain their friendship would endure. Virginia felt it really might. 'So sincere and abrupt is she, and discriminating withal – judging Vita and her secondrate women friends shrewdly – that perhaps something gritty and not the usual expansive fluff may come of it . . . There is something fine and tried and experienced about her besides the rant and the riot and egotism – and I'm not sure that she is the egotist that people make out.'[1]

'I am very strong,' she shouted, and proved it by 'then eating a biscuit and drinking a glass of vermouth and going off to eat a supper of macaroni when she got to Woking at 9.'[1]

Virginia was fascinated, but being uncertain of her real stature as a composer, and feeling incompetent to judge, wrote a week later to Saxon Sidney-Turner, a treasury official she had known for many years: 'What is your opinion of Ethel Smyth? – her music I mean? She has descended upon me like a wolf on the fold in purple and gold, terrifically strident and enthusiastic – I like her – she is as shabby as a washerwoman and shouts and sings – but the question of her music crops up – I don't mean that she cares what I think, being apparently indomitable in her own view, but one day you must tell me the truth about it. Anyhow as a writer she is astonishingly efficient – takes every fence.' The message she received in answer to her enquiries was: 'They say she writes music like an old dryasdust German music master.'

Ethel had few second thoughts. On reaching home she sent first an extravagantly worded telegram. Next, a copy of *The Prison*. Thirdly a letter, followed by another. 'I felt bitterly that I might have known you years ago if life had given me a chance,' she exclaimed.

[1] *The Diary of Virginia Woolf*, ed. Anne Olivier Bell, vol. 3. 1980.

'Can I see you again soon?' Since Virginia had had a relapse, however, she promised moderation. '1. I will not stay more than a certain time – nor pay any attention to "Don't go yets". 2. I will bring my green baize cover, my mute, *anything*. 3. I swear I wouldn't tire you.' She was sure they were at the beginning of a momentous relationship. 'I wish I could explain what meeting certain people has always meant to me. It's like a bit of the vital principle itself put into one's hand, like seeing Paestum was (and is). But such people aren't met every minute on the later laps of one's career through this astonishing, incredibly rich world.' She set to work on those of Virginia's books with which she was unfamiliar. 'I *must* read them.' The more so in that she had 'laughed inwardly to see how exactly you and your written self resemble each other.'

Virginia replied the next day, 27 February 1930. 'Well, if I did what I want, I should ring up whatever your number is and ask you to come tomorrow.' But she dared not. Absolute quiet and rest had been prescribed. Leonard Woolf was always terrified that any indisposition might lead on to depression and mental collapse, as had frequently happened before. She hoped to be better in a week. 'I'm taking prodigious care. You're at the bottom of all the spoonfuls of codliver oil and malt that I gulp down . . . I want to talk and talk and talk – about music; about love.' She, too, regretted that they had not encountered each other sooner. 'Years ago, 3 or 4 at least, when I first met Maurice Baring, he made my heart jump by saying "You must come and meet Ethel Smyth", but nothing came of it . . . What a fool one is.' She ought to have taken advantage of the moment when 'I saw you . . . coming bustling down the gangway at the Wigmore Hall, in tweeds and spats, a little cock's feather in your felt, and a general look of angry energy . . . You reminded me of a ptarmigan – those speckled birds with fetlocks.'

Yet her feelings were ambivalent. On 4 March 1930 she was writing to Vita Sackville-West, 'Let me know when you'll come, or every instant will be ravaged by the rapacity of Ethel Smyth.' On 10 March, she wrote to Ethel: 'I am, soberly and truly, again in robust health . . . Will you suggest a time? Will you really come and begin again? – for I feel that we were torn asunder, just as we were opening our mouths to say something of the greatest importance.'

'Where can I begin all the things that might be said?' she cries on 15 March. Let Ethel regale her meanwhile with 'letters to me brim full of amusement and excitement'. Sometimes she lay awake at night trying to imagine what sort of rooms Ethel inhabited, what regime she followed from the moment the housekeeper served up her breakfast.

They met several times a month, such was their enthusiasm for each other's company. But Ethel's vehemence could be tiring for one of delicate constitution, subject to nervous headaches, perpetually overworked by the daily stint at the Hogarth Press, which she and Leonard ran practically singlehanded, let alone the struggle to finish *The Waves*. 'There is no doubt but that Ethel Smyth is mad,' she informed her sister Vanessa Bell on 11 April 1930, 'and determined to know you also. I sat with her for 2 hours at the BBC the other night – hearing her life history in a loud voice.' 'You can't bore me; if thats what you were thinking,' she wrote to Ethel in changed mood on 22 April, '. . . I have 15 letters to write and at least 3 foot of MS to read and two worrying, tiresome authors whose fate, they say, depends on me, to knock on the head. Naturally, therefore, I warble on unnecessarily to Dame Ethel Smyth; who won't read all this, being in a hurricane today, putting in trumpets, cellos and a trombone or two in the bass. She thumps it out on her piano; and is only roused to life by her dog; does she ever eat her dinner, or is it always cold?'

The whole tone of this letter, quite a long one, is friendly and teasing. But Ethel was dreadfully upset by it, especially the last paragraph which reminded her irresistibly of *Dodo*, a best-selling novel by E. F. Benson published in 1893. One of the chief characters in the book was Edith Staines, a composer who shouted and sang and thumped on the piano for hours, demanding that her meals be brought to her there. Archbishop Benson had been so shocked by his son's wicked caricature of Ethel that he had asked his wife to invite her to dinner, even though she was his pet aversion, and had struggled to be charming to her for a whole evening.

Now, thirty-seven years later, the ghost of *Dodo* rose. It seemed certain that Virginia, whom she so profoundly adored, regarded her as a ridiculous freak and nothing more. All her illusions were shattered, all her hopes of a marvellous friendship with the genius of the age. She immediately wrote several letters of violent reproach which irritated Virginia, very naturally. 'I am sure you are perfectly right to be angry with what I said in my letter,' she wrote on 28 April. 'I don't remember exactly what it was but I expect it was the sort of banter . . . I always scribble in letters . . . I am . . . glad that you should be disillusioned – I hate illusions. So no more.'

But there was much more. Ethel, horrified to have put a foot wrong,

179

replied by return of post on 29 April 1930, 'It never occurred to me that that was banter . . . The thought that you seriously adopted the Dodo view terrified me. I shall never misunderstand again when you chaff.' Virginia is so difficult to know, she protests, a baffling character, now hot, now cold, forthcoming, inacessible, fond of company, needing solitude. She will make no more demands, expect nothing. 'My instinct and fixed creed about you is to be glad you are in the world and see you when we both can.'

Two days later, on 1 May, she arrived in person, in order to make sure her apologies and love were accepted, the breach healed. 'My head spins: ears ache: Ethel just gone,' Virginia sighed to Vita.

'O Virginia what a fool I was,' Ethel cried on 2 May, 'but you must and shall understand, for you see I really do love you, no more and no less than I shall five years hence, and thought you were about to wring the neck of an abortion . . . I care so much about you, am as incapable of imagining the world without you as I was in 1892 when I first met Lady Ponsonby, a woman old enough to be my mother and felt in one hour that I loved her . . . by the way that she handled the sealing wax and red ink etc on her writing table . . . a shatteringly conclusive proof that love, for me, lies in the region of the imagination.' She who had so needed a mother in youth, had now become one in age. The beautiful and fastidious Virginia aroused strangely tender, protective, motherly sensations, quite different from anything she had felt for Edith Somerville.

Virginia could not help mocking Ethel. Perhaps she feared being laughed at herself by her other friends. 'Ethel has made me a decration of violent but platonic love,' she informed Vita on 5 May 1930, spelling collapsed under haste and excitement. 'An old woman of seventy one has fallen in love with me,' she told her nephew Quentin Bell. 'It is at once hideous and horrid and melancholy-sad. It is like being caught by a giant crab.'

But it was not an intolerable fate. 'I heard a ring,' she wrote in her diary on 16 June, 'went up and saw an old char in her white alpaca coat; sat her down; disburdened her of cardboard boxes full of white pinks; and looked at her rather monumental old colonel's face (girt round with an inappropriate necklace, for she was going to lunch with Beecham). I get, generally, two letters daily. I daresay the old fires of Sapphism are blazing, for the last time. In her heyday she must have been formidable.' After lunch, they went to Kenwood for a picnic with Vanessa Bell and Duncan Grant, a successful excursion which ended with a ten pm supper of sandwiches and strawberries 'in the highest glee' in Bloomsbury.

Moreover, Virginia was attending performances of Ethel's works and writing appreciative, even flattering, letters afterwards. She was telling Ethel of her marriage and her illness. 'As an experience, madness is terrific, I can assure you, and not to be sniffed at; and in its lava I still find most of the things I write about.' 'You must be one of the bravest people that has ever lived,' said Ethel. Virginia confided her doubts and difficulties about *The Waves*: 'Things are going so badly . . . The truth is I don't know how to write this book – I might, given another 10 years of trying. No it is an impossible book . . . And it will end in failure, the worst failure of them all.'

With Leonard, she visited Ethel in the first week of July 1930: 'She has more beauty and even comfort about than I expected from her alpaca coat. The red and pink roses were thick on the walls. The flowers were lush in the beds. All was glowing and bright. She has white roughcast walls; and no furniture that has cost more than a pound or two . . . I got the impression of a very genuine breeze-blown mind, a free entirely energized character – no impediments no inhibitions . . . I can't give the sense of her largeness and space and ease and good breeding and character. She is, oddly, much more expert as a hostess than as a guest; doesn't talk too much; is penetrating and quick.'[1]

'Lord! how I liked you! How I rejoiced in your existence!' she wrote on reaching home, protesting her enjoyment of the game of golf which was part of the entertainment, her appreciation of Ethel's local acquaintances. She went again, alone, spending the day talking and talking. 'You are, I believe, one of the kindest of women, one of the best balanced, with that maternal quality which of all others I need and adore – what was I saying? – for that reason I chatter faster and freer to you than to other people . . . I like writing to you, who are so good to me, and let me sit chattering, and keep so immensely wise and good all the time.' This was evidently not one of the occasions when her head spun and her ears ached. A remarkably different picture emerges.

Ethel sent her presents of flowers, going to considerable trouble picking them in her garden and loading them on to the train. The sound of Virginia's voice gave her exquisite pleasure, she said, even on the telephone. There was also something very special about her nose. The recollection of it sometimes overwhelmed her at night. She thought of Virginia constantly, the lovely image pervading her mind

---

[1] *Diary*, 6 July 1930.

whenever she paused in her multitudinous activities. 'If there is one thing that goes deeper in me than others it is fear for delicate things that matter to me and I think it is quite true to say that if I have a chance of looking after you, of mothering you as you put it, it is the best thing that could happen to me.' But Virginia was already fully mothered by Leonard.

Ethel could not help feeling jealous of Vita, especially when the wicked Virginia wrote such passages as: 'Well, here I am lying in Vita's adulterous sheets . . . Vita is putting bath salts in my bath and talking agreeably.' 'Why have *I* not a lovely house run on castors, with damask sheets, servants to do this and that, wherewith to entice Virginia?' she mourned, contemplating this picture of an attentive Vita with distaste. But she continues, 'I should hate it really. The authentic Ethel Smyth likes sordidity, shabbiness.' All the same, 'I . . . shall always long, I think, to be able to do, or give, or be, anything that could please you, damask sheets (I myself *prefer* cotton, warmer) or anything else.' At times she felt like Prometheus, she said, whose liver was daily torn out by a vulture.

She was not, however, without a sense of the idol's defects. Perhaps a few of the remarks made behind her back had come round to her. 'I think you may have qualities I should stumble badly at in someone else.' These included 'lack of generosity, jealousy, treachery, instability and so on'. She found her childish, too, 'I expect it must often be so with people of genius, though not perhaps in such startling style as in your case.' What troubled her most was the uncertainty as to whether Virginia was capable of sustained affection: she had once airily wondered if she actually cared much for anybody. Could she be 'merely a good starter, has she any use for a late comer? She went off with me at a good pace, but is that simply because of my own dragging capacity?' A vulture of a question.

Virginia tried to reassure her, protesting that 'if I were ill I should be quite as ready to come to you as to Vita'. She loved luxury, admittedly, but 'sanity is what I want. A robust sense of fact'. The extraordinary Ethel can provide it. 'I'm naturally vain but almost equally naturally fastidious: I mean, I adore being liked; but when I see how generous and free and fierce you are, I feel (I think this is true) but I'm not worth it.'

Ethel was mollified. The sun shone again. Virginia asked if she might read some of the letters and diaries of which she had heard. She invited her to spend a night at the Woolfs' country house in Sussex.

Ethel went at the end of August 1930, but found the atmosphere somewhat strained, although Virginia said she enjoyed the occasion immensely, felt 'revived and fertilized' after it. Leonard, on the other hand, was not much in favour of Ethel, considering her an unrestful influence. He objected to her monologues, one of which, he complained, had lasted a full twenty minutes, and thought *The Prison*, which she was trying to get republished to coincide with the production of her oratorio, based on the same, utter rubbish.

Virginia was not sure. 'Do you think it can be all nonsense? – *The Prison*?' she asked Vita. 'If so, isn't nature odd, keeping an old woman in a state of positive frenzy for weeks, if it's all nonsense what she writes.' But then, she reflected, was she not in the same case? Suppose *The Waves* turned out to be nonsense? 'I wander over the downs, declaiming and making up and altogether working myself into a frenzy too: and what's the good of it?'

On 29 August 1930, she suddenly fainted in the garden and it was some while before she came round fully. On hearing this, Ethel sent a telegram, to which Virginia replied: 'How I shd like to see you! What a pleasure if you walked in!' Ethel jumped on the train. The most Leonard could do was to restrict her to two hours. Virginia's evident debility alarmed her and she wondered, on reaching home, whether she ought to have gone, knowing her reputation for taking it out of people. 'You did me nothing but good,' Virginia reassured her, although far from recovered and with a headache that alarmed Leonard considerably. 'How invigorating, oh and more, it is to me to see you I cant tell you Ethel, how I adored you for that dash here . . . How it kindled and enraptured me to have you by me,' she wrote on 3 September.

She was obliged to miss the treat promised her by Ethel for 4 September at the promenade concert. 'You must come,' she had written as far back as 11 August, 'as I think it will be your only chance for months and months of seeing a superb sight – me conducting an orchestra.' They were to play her *Anacreonatic Ode*, composed in 1908, heard to such effect as she arrived in Ronald Storrs' house in Cairo in 1913, and various of her songs.

Virginia and Leonard sat attentively in front of their wireless. 'How like she is to her music,' Leonard said. 'How robust and at the same time piercing,' said Virginia who was of the opinion that the other modern composer in the programme, Lord Berners, had been knocked flat; or so she wrote to Ethel next day, gently dissuading her from another visit. Leonard thought it out of the question for her to see anyone. All day he carried her from garden to bedroom and rushed about with chamber pots, trays and medicine.

Ethel was evidently upset by the prohibition, for Virginia found it necessary to write on 11 September 1930: 'Please Ethel, don't think you ought, for reasons of the highest morality, never to see me or write to me again. I should miss you. Oh, yes I should', together with many another affectionate message. 'This friendship,' she continues on 15 September after reading a good portion of Ethel's diaries, 'is one of the strangest aesthetic experiences I have ever had . . . since we were so ill advised as to live many years without contact.'

'I could hardly keep myself from cursing Leonard for being so positive against you,' she writes on 19 September. 'If Ethel were here, then, instead of dangling my hand in all these books and papers, I said, I should hold her white cuff . . . and she, who knows exactly how to settle the race and excitability of my mind, would tell me – oh, what sort of wardrobe she has in her bedroom . . . Then at a certain moment Ethel would open her eyes which are (here I was visited by an extremely vivid picture of your almost childish smile) so blue and laugh: and I should feel so set up, that I should lose whatever the pain happened to be . . . and toss life like a pancake . . . I can't conceive that you would ever tire me; no; nor agitate me; or harass me; but only make me feel like a good child, nestling its head into a perfectly fresh pillow.'

Ethel was at this time in Bath desperately trying to alleviate her arthritis with the waters and her ears by means of a specialist to whom she had been recommended. She returned little better, if at all, though her spirits remained unimpaired.

Virginia recovered perfectly, writing letters full of gaiety and wit to 'that old sea-monster encrusted with barnacles' of whom Vita had become delightfully jealous. The Woolf in-laws were described in all their stifling bourgeois horror, compounded by an impenetrable Jewishness. She went with Ethel to hear a Viennese quartet at the Austrian embassy, not from love of music, but in the sure hope that the sea monster would 'almost certainly commit some rape'.

So she did. On arrival she 'unpeeled herself of sweater, jersey and mothy moleskin before all the flunkeys, knocking her pasteboard hat to right and left and finally producing from a cardboard box fastened at the edge by paper fasteners a pair of black leather shoes' with which she replaced her boots, saying: 'The truth is I'm a damned snob and like to be smart'. They settled to the quartet. At a certain point, Ethel's remarkable voice was plainly heard: 'Isn't this slow movement sublime

– natural and heavy and irresistible like the movement of one's own bowels'.[1] The surrounding diplomats blushed. It was an enjoyable evening.

Meanwhile, Ethel was writing a memoir of Harry to preface the new edition of *The Prison* she proposed to bring out. Virginia's firm, the Hogarth Press, would have been a natural choice of publisher, but this was not a possible arrangement since Leonard had such a contempt for Brewster and all his works. Virginia ventured to disagree with him. 'A perfect little memoir,' she enthused on receiving the first version from Ethel with a request for an opinion and advice on improvements. She appended various critical suggestions, some of which Ethel followed, adding that Heinemann would be sure to take the book, which they did.

Always one to do a job thoroughly, Ethel subsequently arrived in her friend's drawing-room with a quarto sheet whereon were inscribed twenty separate questions requiring definite answers. Some concerned Harry and his memoir; others required Virginia's real thoughts as to the propriety of suicide and related subjects. She was very earnest and determined. The veins swelled up in her forehead with the effort. Not an attractive sight to fastidious eyes. Nevertheless, Vita was informed, 'she is a game old Bird and I respect her to the point of idolatry'. Ethel's idolatry was such that she felt if Virginia threw her over, or otherwise failed, 'I don't think I could live'.

Virginia's fascination even led her to say on 22 October 1930, 'Would you like me to write something about you?' Ethel was delighted. She would give Virginia her huge collection of letters. 'So I am to some extent Ethel's literary executor, a post I have always vaguely desired.'[2] She studied her friend sitting opposite in a triangular hat mended with pins by the manageress of a hotel in Bath. 'One would have to bring out her enormous eagerness. She was telling me how she reads Travel books; and her eyes – her blue rather prominent eyes, positively glitter. And this is not talk about herself, or her music – simply about how people climb – their adventures . . . But she looks now and then aged.'[2]

The question of Harry perplexed her, 'that looming imponderable figure'.[2] At a certain point, he had hovered in artistic and intellectual circles in England, during the early days of Lady Ottoline Morrell's career as a hostess. So she enquired of Ottoline and of Logan Pearsall Smith and they said, 'Oh a petit maître; a drawing-room

[1] Letter to Vanessa Bell.
[2] *Diary.*

185

philosopher; to which Logan adds the son of a dentist, and Ottoline adds, he made love to me and I found him intolerable.'

The idea was only a passing fancy on Virginia's part. That she should have entertained it at all shows the fascination Ethel exerted. They continued very affectionate during the early months of 1931. On 21 January they both spoke at a meeting of the London National Society for Women's Service on professions for women. *The Prison* was published and received some enthusiastic notices. Ethel had also finished the oratorio of the same name and had been able to secure a production in Edinburgh to be conducted by herself, followed by another in London under Adrian Boult.

On 2 February 1931, Ethel was rehearsing in Portland Place. Virginia was present. The house was vast and not very attractive, she thought. The room where they were looked into other people's windows and over a tangle of fire escapes, chimneys and roofs. The hostess resembled a shapeless sausage, and Ethel's sister Mary a swathed satin sausage. These sausages sat side by side on a sofa. 'Ethel stood at the piano in the window in her battered felt, in her jersey and short skirt conducting with a pencil. There was a drop at the end of her nose . . . She sang now and then; and once, taking the bass, made a cat squalling sound . . . She knocks her hat from side to side. Strides rhythmically down the room . . . strides back. Now the furniture moving begins, she said, referring to some supernatural gambols connected with the prisoner's escape, or defiance, or death.'[1]

The extraordinary thing was, Virginia reflected, that 'everything she does with such forthrightness, directness that there is nothing ridiculous'.[1] But the music? Virginia didn't care for it much. Yet 'what if she should be a great composer?' Ethel herself had no doubt of it. 'As she conducts she hears music like Beethoven's . . . She thinks this is about the most important event now taking place in London. And perhaps it is.'[1]

The performance in Edinburgh was a tremendous success. Calls for the composer were innumerable, the press as flattering as any artist could wish. Ethel felt terrific on coming back to London where a smart party had been arranged in her honour by Lady Rosebery, one of her patrons. At last she had defeated the conspiracy of men against her. They had been obliged to acknowledge her as the genius of the age. She thought of *The Prison* as her masterpiece, a true collaboration between herself and Harry, as *The Wreckers* had been before. It never

[1] *Diary.*

entered her mind that the London performance might be differently judged. No. It would become a standard item in the concert hall and on the BBC which she had already persuaded to revive her *Mass*.

In this euphoric mood, therefore, she took Virginia to the celebratory party at Lady Rosebery's house in Berkeley Square on 24 February 1931. Unfortunately Virginia's nerves were in a very bad state. She had just finished *The Waves*. Exhaustion and over-strain brought on depression, the smallest upset caused an hysterical reaction. Her sense of humour deserted her. Instead of the good laugh she should have enjoyed at what she considered Ethel's preposterous society connections, she felt sensations of humiliation, disillusion, madness as she viewed elderly butlers, peers, champagne, sugared cakes and listened to inane chit-chat. She had been dragged there against her will. Ethel had betrayed her to wolves and vultures. 'If you weren't here I should kill myself – so much do I suffer,' she exclaimed to her devoted husband on reaching home. She took a sleeping mixture and remained in a perturbed state for several days. It was a fortnight before she forgave Ethel who, all unconscious of transgression, had thought it a jolly fine party. To seal their reconciliation, Virginia bought her a new wig.

But Ethel's dreams of a future where *The Prison, The Wreckers* and all her other works would be continually performed by the best talents the musical world had to offer suffered a setback. It was damned and blasted in London, the *New Statesman* being particularly withering: 'Both Ethel Smyth and Henry Brewster have made brave attempts at mediocrity, but both have failed without attaining that bottomness which is completely diverting.' Ethel immediately engaged the critics in battle through the columns of the *New Statesman* and *Time and Tide*. Virginia urged her not to, pointing out that it was undignified and did her position no good: 'Any answer, any explanation, any refutation weakens one's case . . . any acknowledgement of what you despise seems a tribute to the despicable.' Ethel was far too upset to heed this wise advice.

She also tried to get Adrian Boult to put *The Prison* into a BBC programme, badgering him to such an extent on inappropriate occasions that he turned against her, though he had been quite well disposed before. They had once even made a joint expedition to Mary's country mansion. Ethel was suffering from a roaring cold at the time and produced a roll of lavatory paper on the train, explaining to the startled Boult that it was far more hygienic than a lot of damp handkerchiefs loaded with germs. For the rest of the journey she trumpeted regularly and threw the discarded bits of paper out of the window. This was highly unconventional behaviour for a lady of that date.

'Old Ethel . . . came yesterday,' Virginia reported to her sister on 14 May 1931, 'and was melancholy beyond words; old, battered, depressed . . . She says she has seldom found life harder, and wakes at 3am when she has to wet, in such despair that she cries aloud Courage, courage! and prays to God who has deserted her. I've promised her a champagne dinner at Boulestin's, but even that is not of much avail.'

However, she rallied, writing to Virginia on 17 May: 'When I saw you long, long ago it seems for I rather lost count of time, the ship was leaking and generally unseaworthy and I doubted whether it could be repaired. Since then I have been on the repairing job.' But it was not well done. Considering herself 'quite fit for human consumption again' she appeared in Virginia's drawing-room on 20 May, 'stamping like a dragoon with a wallet full of documents. For 3 hours she nailed me to my chair while she rehearsed the story of her iniquitous treatment by Adrian Boult . . . She then went through, with the minuteness and ingenuity of a maniac, the whole history of her persecution for the past 50 years; brought out old letters and documents and read them aloud, beat on my chair with her fists; made me listen, and answer, and agree at every moment; and finally I had to shout that I had such a headache that unless she stopped talking I should burst into flames and be combusted.'[1] She felt like 'a stoat nailed to a barn door', an image ready in her mind, used in *The Waves* which she was still revising.

'You've got to listen to me – You've got to listen,' Ethel kept shouting. 'And it's all fabricated, contorted, twisted with red hot egotism; and now she's launched on a campaign which means bullying every conductor and worrying every publisher, and rich man or woman, as well as unfortunate friends, until she gets that hopeless farrago of birds and last posts played and all HB's rubbish printed again,'[1] the disgusted Virginia complained, on rising from the bed to which she had been obliged to retire for two days in order to regain her strength. 'I don't feel I can even face her unless 2 keepers are present with red hot pokers . . . Undoubtedly sex and egotism have brewed some bitter insanity.'[1]

Mad or not, Ethel's methods produced results. She was able to procure a performance of *The Wreckers* in September 1931, though there was much trouble during rehearsals, owing to the neglectful

[1] Letter to Vanessa Bell.

behaviour of the leading lady who seemed too much of a favourite with the director. 'Dirty little bitch and he is simply a disgrace to director-humanity.' *The Prison* also was fixed for November in the Queen's Hall, herself conducting. In this case, however, she was obliged to contribute to the costs.

CHAPTER TWENTY ONE

Game Old Bird

It says much for the strength of Virginia's feeling for the old dragoon that it took only three weeks and some bunches of flowers to restore harmony. Leonard's hopes of expunging Ethel were disappointed. They were on excellent terms again, Virginia overflowing with compliments on *The Prison*, Ethel expressing love, reformation and admiration by turns. He did somehow manage to reduce the number of her visitations, whereupon she became a sort of circulating thunder storm, growling down the telephone and through the post to the detriment of his nervous system.

It was of no consequence that Virginia complained to Vita of Ethel having 'dragged me to the top of the downs in a hurricane talking about God and the Wreckers', smelling, the while, 'of old lust'. Or that Ethel, with pathological suspicions rampant, enquired whether Vita had not attended the first night of *The Wreckers* as she had promised because Virginia had on purpose chosen that evening to descend on her, leaving Leonard to listen to the broadcast and report. 'With her all things are possible.' She requested an immediate telegram from Vita on the subject: had there been a plot, or not? The offending ladies felt they hadn't behaved well. Both went to a later performance and treated her to dinner afterwards.

These incidents were scattered events. Their correspondence in general continued with regularity and an irrepressible gaiety. The painful story of Ethel's sister Mary became a form of light relief. Having recklessly spent her fortune, Mary was obliged to sell her house and all its contents. Gone for ever were the days of glittering parties, full of celebrities, given to honour Ethel's concerts. She now existed on what contributions her impecunious family could make. Yet she seemed in no way cast down. 'All she does,' Ethel wrote to Virginia, 'is to comment on a . . . neighbour as a "perfect fool" because the woman said she couldn't afford a second bathroom! She was very smart but can hardly walk: not because of "her knee", not because of "her heart" but simply because from vanity she has her toes bound up like bunches of asparagus and crams them into shoes the size of a runner bean pod, to achieve which end a chiropodist has to attend her twice a week.' A very incarnation of Harold Skimpole, Ethel thought.

'Ah my dear Ethel, how you would have laughed yesterday,' wrote Virginia on 3 October 1931, and proceeded to relate, in superbly funny style, an unsolicited visit by 'an old apelike man' and 'two young women with shiny noses'. The ape's sister, it transpired, now a boarding-house keeper, had once owned a school wherein Edmund Blunden, since so eminent in literature, had endeavoured to acquire the rudiments of education. The old man 'then made a much impeded speech to the effect that he is an elementary school teacher in Kent, but directly descended from the author of Ralph Roister Doister, the first English comedy . . . And therefore with this blood in our veins, he said, we tend to try as a family not very successfully, far from it, to write. My daughter here, she writes, stories for children, as yet unpublished . . . And this young lady, Mademoiselle – she lets me call her Susanne – . . . who's at the Sorbonne has been studying – which book? – oh, Mrs Dalloway – and wants to ask you – now Susanne, what are the questions you want to ask Mrs Woolf? I've forgotten, Madame, said Susanne, wringing her red bald hands . . . That is could I ask you to explain as Mr Blunden has so kindly introduced us what, why that is, you have written your books?' The letter continues thus for several uproarious pages.

The next excitement was the publication of *The Waves*, on 8 October 1931. Ethel wired immediately: 'Book astounding so far. Agitatingly increases value of life', and, two days later, 'Final paragraph almost smashes the machine of life with its terrible duty.' Yet she had reservations. 'The book is profoundly disquieting, sadder than any book I ever read.' She thought also that the characters lacked humanity and with it the capacity for true feeling. *To The Lighthouse* was more to her taste.

Her own immediate interest was the performance at the Queen's Hall on 11 November 1931 of *The Prison*, to which her old supporter Mary Dodge had contributed financially. Virginia promised to attend, 'and if I fail through sheer devilry, not of my own seeking, don't blame me'. Leonard definitely refused, wouldn't even put in an appearance at the supper afterwards. 'Lord, no.'

The occasion was melancholy in spite of the ebullient spirit in which Ethel conducted her part of the programme. Though Elsie Suddaby sang superbly, the press, that bastion of male chauvinism, remained obdurately cool. 'Her use of the Last Post must be set down as an inexplicable aberration,' *The Times* remarked.

To this disappointment in a matter so near her heart was added another, more fundamental. 'O, Vita,' she wrote, 'it *was* a good performance and the agonizing thing is that it will be the last time I shall conduct in a big work, for I do not hear finely enough now to please myself.' She suffered not only from increasing deafness, but what hearing remained was distorted, a deathly condition for a musician. None of the dozens of doctors consulted had been able to arrest the progress of the disease. Her courage in the face of the inevitable was one of the things that made Virginia call her 'a game old Bird'.

Nevertheless, Virginia did not enjoy the concert, it seems. 'Last night, sweating with horror, I listened to the Prison, set to music – if cat calls, early birds and last posts can be called music – and Lord the defunct butlers and ladies maids who sang – by Ethel Smyth. When Maurice Baring emerged, bald as a coot, and leering for all the world like George 4th – and asked me to sup, I vomited there and then on the red carpet.'[1]

No wonder Ethel found her changeable. But she did try Virginia's patience. Thoroughly dissatisfied at the reception of *The Prison*, she bored everyone with long complaints and diatribes. In spite of all, the friendship of these two remarkable women was now so firmly established that it lasted until Virginia's suicide in March 1941. Quarrels were always followed by reconciliation, either immediately or after a short interval. Ethel usually accused Virginia of being cold-hearted, easily taken in by flattery, wasting her time on people who never could be useful, deliberately misunderstanding harmless remarks and refusing to listen to explanations. 'Since thy servant may not speak and live, let it be left at that.'

Virginia had an even better line in abuse: 'I think Ethel Smyth's the most attitudinizing unreal woman I've ever known – living in a mid-Victorian dentist's waiting-room of emotional falsity – likes beating up quarrels for the sake of dramatizing herself, enjoys publicity and titles from universities and Kings, surrounded by flatterers, a swallower of falsehoods, why should I stand this manhandling, this brawling, this bullying, this malusage?'

There might be dreadful sessions when Ethel called in order to clear things up, as she said, intending no doubt, to calm the situation, once her point of view had been accepted. 'The memory of that discussion is one of such horror,' Virginia wrote after one of these visits, 'it makes me feel so degraded, so humiliated . . . that – well, I dont see how I'm to see anyone easily, or write, or speak freely to anyone who may insist upon a scene like that again.'

[1] Letter to George Rylands, poet, old friend and one time assistant at the Hogarth Press.

But it was impossible not to be mollified in the end by Ethel's passionate repentance. 'I went home ill with despair at what, so utterly without meaning it, I had brought about . . . If I cannot steer my boat beside you without running into you, though with you the light will go out of life for me, I shall know what to do – go,' she declared on 30 July 1932. Virginia was quite wrong 'in thinking that I don't realize how shattering, how odious, how loathsome a scene is to you . . . All the time it was as if a knife were being plunged in my heart . . . Will you give your blessing on this creative effort of mine to be on my best behaviour?' Virginia did. They were soon on the friendliest terms.

Nineteen thirty-three was their year of crisis. After that things became easier as they grew to accept each other's defects without rancour, though scenes did sometimes occur, and Virginia continued to make cutting remarks. 'The reason why Ethel Smyth is so repulsive,' she required her nephew to inform his mother, 'is her table manners. She oozes; she chortles; and she half blew her rather red nose in her table napkin. Then she poured the cream . . . into her beer; I had rather dine with a dog.'

Ethel was more generous. On 13 August 1933 she felt she had 'spoken rather critically, frigidly about V.' to Lady Ottoline Morrell, 'whereas the truth is that . . . I do deeply *love* her'. In the beginning, she had expected 'something more human, less mood-ridden, less disconnected'. It was impossible to get really close to her. 'Consequently . . . if something cut deeply into my life it would not strike me to share it with her, or talk to her about it.' This mysterious sense of distance was the chief thing she had to bear with as much grace as she could muster, passing it off with nick-names such as Frozen Falcon, or Snow Goddess, though it was expedient not to mention them to Virginia unless she happened to be in an exceptionally good frame of mind.

Relations with Leonard were quite straightforward. 'I do think a certain husband called L a little drier than is comfortable in one you don't see often,' she said to Lady Ottoline on 18 July 1934, 'but I do like him once he has been stewed up, like dried Australian apricots.' She considered him unmalicious, yet he seemed '*selfish* about Virginia and would like her sitting there, either alone or next door, or à deux with him always'. She remained on reasonably good terms with him, however. When, unable to endure her voice another minute, he put his hand over her mouth, she did not protest at the liberty and even was silent for several seconds. He had a marmoset permanently sitting on his shoulder.

She was now equipped with a small ear trumpet. This made for 'a screaming howling party', when she was present. 'We discussed religion, sex, literature and other problems . . . in a roar.' A successful occasion. 'Oh do tell me all about your suffrage life,' Virginia begged at one point. It was difficult to satisfy her curiosity. 'The worst of it is,' Ethel remarked, 'I live so intensely in the present that until I turn up old letters and diaries I forget whole chunks of essentials in the past.'

During the first half of 1933, they were able to have many interesting conversations on the subject as Ethel was writing a short memoir of Mrs Pankhurst which she incorporated in her book *Female Pipings in Eden*, brought out in December of the same year. Virginia thought the title silly, but Ethel insisted. 'In strict confidence,' she was able to inform her nephew, 'Ethel used to love Emmeline – they shared a bed.' Virginia exaggerated.

The book was more discreet. She sent Virginia the manuscript for criticisms and suggestions saying: 'I've tried to avoid any hint that she really loved me as few people have. I hope it's not perceptible. And anyhow she cut the cable, with my connivance it is true, but really Christabel was (and probably is) mad.' A friend had seen her recently and reported that 'she looks horrid and dirty in bed'. That might be due to her conversion to second adventism, Ethel surmised. 'Not worth while washing.'

Virginia, who had received and criticised the other essays as they were written, considered the Pankhurst chapter the best in the book, 'I like it very much indeed . . . by far the most convincing suffrage argument there can be'. It was also less egocentric than some previous sections where Ethel's grievances and sense of persecution had run away with her. On second thoughts, she advised cutting it down. 'I think there is still vapour adhering – things that could be sat upon and pressed tight.' And she made another attempt to get Ethel to change the title. Her final view was extremely complimentary: 'I wish, vainly, you'd write more biographies . . . I assure you, you have a thousand natural gifts in that way which we hacks have long lost.'

Unfortunately Ethel's enthusiasm was not roused by Virginia's current publication, *Flush*, the autobiography of Elizabeth Barrett Browning's dog. 'I didn't tell the following to V,' she confided to Vanessa Bell, 'but Flush is the sort of book that gives me the kick-screams to think of, indeed I only read two chapters and could no more.' She had said enough, however, to cause a temporary coolness, though Virginia pretended, 'No of course I don't mind your not being able to cope with Flush'. It's one thing to refer to your own book as 'a silly little joke' and another to have that opinion confirmed by a friend.

The first excitement of their friendship past, Virginia came really to prefer an affectionate and lively correspondence to much actual meeting. 'Please write. I think your letters the best I get.' But whatever the ups and downs, the tiffs and misunderstandings, she could say in 1935, after five years of Ethel's attentions. 'One of these days our moons shall shine broad in each other's faces – when I come to Woking . . . So I kiss the top of your head and farewell. What a comfort to think that nothing I could say or do would make you think better or worse of me.'

CHAPTER TWENTY-TWO

Death

In January 1933, Hitler came to power, and though some were alarmed by his nazis, especially in Germany, few, if any, foresaw the extent of the suffering and ruin he was to bring upon the world. There is an element of the supernatural, and consequently of the unreal, in such concentrated evil which inclines people to disbelieve in, or avert their eyes from, the danger inexorably advancing until it is too late to escape. Had not the last war, won at so desperate a cost only fifteen years ago, been the war to end all wars? Was England not supposed to have become a land fit to be inhabited by a race of heroes? The severe economic depression of the early thirties had dented these ideal dreams. The new young writers, surveying the unemployed masses, developed a social conscience. Wishing to identify with the proletariat, always tricky for the comfortably brought up middle class intellectual, they were driven to such effusions as, in the case of Auden:

> One, two, three, four,
> The last war was a bosses' war,
> Five, six, seven, eight,
> Rise and make a workers' state.

Or, on the part of Spender: 'A writer who wishes to produce the best work that he is capable of producing, must first of all become socialist in his practical life, must go over to the progressive side of the class conflict . . . Unless he joins it his writing will become increasingly false, worthless as literature.'

These were common themes among writers of the thirties and they were ready to put them to the test by joining the republicans in the Spanish civil war and getting killed. One of Virginia's nephews, Julian Bell, a promising poet, was of their number. It was a strange episode in the history of English literature, romanticism driven to an extreme which isolated them from the common man with whom they so desired to conform. Nor were they the only ones to be seduced by Marx and Lenin, as the sinister confessions and revelations of Anthony Blunt and other highly placed public servants have shown in recent years.

The unregenerate Ethel, now seventy-five, though perfectly aware of current events, especially in view of her many German connections, had given up active politics for good in 1913. They seemed to have nothing to do with the artistic life as she conceived it. Time was short and it was necessary to make the most of it. Few modern composers were more often heard than the grand Dame from Woking, male prejudice notwithstanding. 'I wiped the floor with Elgar,' she wrote on the train from Torquay to Bath. 'Lord how I loathe that surly, arrogant bear.'[1] He had to wait while she took an encore. Such a satisfaction.

'Last night was really rather wonderful,' she announced from another part of the country, while eating brown bread and butter; 'Beecham who presided instead of that inflated fool Elgar (who fortunately was taken with a bad stomach-ache at his Gloucester seat and couldn't come) is an enchanting speaker.' Bruno Walter and other influential friends were also present.

August 1933 found her in the Hebrides, on the Isle of Barra. Compton MacKenzie, 'a dear, so childlike and wild flowerish', had arranged a demonstration of a traditional tweed-shrinking song. 'Picture to yourself a sort of long trestle table . . . six old women on one side and six on the other and a long bit of damp tweed which they rhythmically punch and pat, singing immemorial songs, working up quicker and quicker and occasionally offered a sip of whisky, (I provided one of the two bottles), . . . till at the end of a ballad of some forty verses they hurl themselves about like maniacs.' She then made a speech with many gestures signifying admiration which the audience, Gaelic speakers to a woman, with the utmost politeness pretended to understand.

The winds on Barra were so strong that she gave up her bicycle and walked the beaches and cliffs, enchanted by the beauty of it all. One day, accompanied by two young friends, she watched seals at play. The girls sang to them the ancient seal melody with its haunting refrain. 'They can't hear that against this wind, too low,' Ethel shouted and she yelled the tune 'as if it were an express train between Waterloo and Southampton . . . The seals were thrilled . . . I spied a quite gigantic black seal as big as a very big cow and I think he was copulating . . . He *may* have been scrubbing his stomach on a rock and saying to the others that that was what he was doing.'

This sort of thing led to a conversation with her companions in the course of which she was informed that 'lots of girls have themselves

[1] All quotations in this chapter are from the Smyth/Woolf correspondence unless otherwise stated.

197

operated on nowadays so as not to endure tortures on marriage nights. What a pity you, let alone me, were not thus treated. But principally you. Why not try it now? It's never too late to rend.' 'Shall we go and be done together?' Virginia giggled. 'Side by side in Bond Street?'

Ethel next proceeded to North Uist, where the storms obliged her to linger. Harris was superb, not only for the scenery but for 'an hotel fit for a Christian', the first encountered in those parts. It was full of fishermen, one of whom kissed her goodbye without have asked permission. He resembled an orang-utang.

Invigorated by all these adventures, she returned to the fray. Her chief occupation was the promotion of an Ethel festival to mark her seventy fifth birthday on the stage, in the concert hall and at the BBC. She tried also to arrange a revival of her ballet *Fête Galante* for which Vanessa Bell had been persuaded to paint a new set. 'I think your decor one of the loveliest things I ever saw.' Determined to have Dolin as leading male dancer, she interviewed him backstage where his mother, looking like an old charwoman, 'scrapes the paint and grease with a curry comb from under his armpits between the turns and with the other hand gropes and produces from a suitcase the Bourrée in E sharp peremptorily demanded by her genial blackguard of a son, and with her elbow pushes meshes of grey hair out of her eyes.' He professed himself keen on the idea. But it was too late for it to be included in the festival.

She was now on excellent terms with Beecham, Henry Wood being temporarily out of favour, and he promised to conduct the *Mass* at the Albert Hall, where Queen Mary was persuaded to attend. Adrian Boult, in charge of the BBC orchestras, was disinclined to have anything to do with Ethel or her music, on account of unfortunate past experiences, but he was overborne. Friends, including the invaluable Mary Dodge, got up an Ethel fund for certain necessary expenses.

The whole operation was a great success and showed in what esteem Ethel was held by the musical establishment. The proceedings opened with the Queen's Hall concert on 3 January 1934. 'Many congratulations on terrific ovation,' Virginia scribbled next day, though her private opinion of *The Prison* remained vitriolic. Chamber music and songs poured out of the radio. 'Ethel Smyth . . . has been deafening us every evening on the wireless with her caterwauling,' she complained to her nephew on 10 January. 'At last she burst into one flame and had a gigantic party to eat sausages at midnight.'

On 18 January, a lunch was held in her honour at Grosvenor House.

Virginia sat next to her. Three hundred people came. Beecham made a speech and brought the house down by saying he had visited her in her confinement. Roars of laughter. He was referring to her Holloway days, he said. More yells of merriment. Ethel replied in similar light vein. Unfortunately Virginia could never sufficiently relax at such jollifications which require a certain simple-heartedness. 'That appalling cheap tawdry lunch that Ethel enjoyed so,' she sniffed to Ottoline Morrell. 'Really she is like a child with a sugar mouse.'

Festivities ended on 3 March 1934 with a grand performance of the *Mass in D* at the Albert Hall, Beecham conducting. Queen Mary sat bolt upright in the royal box. Ethel was beside her. They made a striking tableau. The fact that she could hardly hear a note in no way diminished Ethel's high spirits. When the royal farewells had been said, she led the way to the nearest Lyons 'where half the aristocracy in England', according to Virginia's computation, 'sat on hard chairs, drank tea like vinegar and ate rancid butter . . . "I hate religion" I roared into her deaf ears.' It was the culmination of her life as a composer. She had written nothing substantial after *The Prison*. Within a few years, she had given up going to concerts: the effort to hear was futile.

Books became her refuge. Her energy had by no means evaporated and she had always found writing easier than composing. Words came fluently to that indefatigable talker. 'I believe you have secretly invented some sort of machine that you think into and it foams out on to the paper like the best café au lait, versé by an expert,' Edith Somerville said. It sums up the charm and vitality of her prose which is never convoluted or self-consciously literary. She did not torment herself with problems of construction or nuances of poetic expression. Humour was her forte. She might be called an inspired amateur.

Thomas Beecham's labours during the Ethel festival had earned him a cordial place in her affections. Such was her enthusiasm, indeed, that she wrote a laudatory biographical essay which was published in 1935 under the title of *Beecham and Pharaoh*. The Pharaoh part refers to another, longer, essay about her own adventures in Ireland in 1913 when she took lessons in keening, and in Egypt where she retired to the desert to write her opera *The Boatswain's Mate*.

She also began a new volume of autobiography, *As Time Went On*, a task to which she had often been urged by numerous friends and admirers of *Impressions That Remained*. 'Virginia has made me dedicate my book to her because it was she who went on about the book *having* to be written. I hope it will be worthy of the honour,' she wrote to

Vanessa Bell on 7 February 1936. It was not so easy to find the appropriate phrase. 'How do you know the present verbal preferences in high intellectual circles? You never know. Suddenly a word gets tabooed. And I don't want to give her a painful prod by using such a word.'

All went more than well. First Virginia sent a telegram and then a letter: 'I think it's a triumph, and if I go half way down the road to immortality, it will be because my name is on your title page. How you do it God knows – I mean I can't see *how* it's done – how face after face emerges when there is apparently so little preparation, no humming and hawing, all so inconsecutive and unpremeditated . . . I think it's far the best thing you've done since the first immortal volumes . . . What you must do is to *continue*', putting her present friends into the next instalment. 'To tell you the truth I'm obsessed with the desire that you should paint me.' But she changed her mind on that point almost immediately.

Ethel's pleasure at these wonderful compliments (the press also behaved well) was marred by the incurable wasting illness her dog contracted, dying practically on the day of publication in May 1936. 'I now know I loved him better than anything on earth,' she wrote to Ottoline Morrell on 17 May. 'Still soberer truth to say I have not the very slightest wish to live.' Practical woman that she was, however, she had learned from experience that a new puppy and a fully occupied mind were the sovereign cures for grief. 'I am trying to analyse the love you can have for a dog, in some ways far transcending anything you can feel for a human being, in the shape of an article,' she told Vita Sackville-West. The article became a short illustrated book, *Inordinate(?)Affection*, published later that year. 'I feel sure you won't need telling that you need not fear to encounter nauseating whiffs of sentimentality,' she assured Eddie Marsh[1] on presenting him with a copy. It is her statement on the nature of dogs and their place in human life and fully explains her attack of the kick-screams on reading the coy anthropomorphisms of Virginia's *Flush*.

Her next venture, brought out in 1937, was a biography of her old friend Maurice Baring. She had for some time been saying that it should be done and suggesting various authors, but no one had felt inclined to pursue the idea. Perhaps they thought Baring insufficently interesting in life and letters. Or that he would be difficult to work with. But Ethel had known him since his boyhood. As the nephew of Lady Ponsonby, he was connected with some of her most

---

[1] Sir Edward Marsh, civil servant and patron of the arts.

passionate memories. He had fallen on sad times and might not long survive. 'I'm utterly miserable about Maurice,' she wrote to Eddie Marsh in 1937. 'He's now almost entirely bedridden, can't even read as it fatigues him too much and can converse but little for the same reason. In fact his life is a martyrdom . . . The only thing he likes is being read to.' He lingered eight more years.

While Ethel knew him well enough to realize that he was likely to be fractious, particularly in his debilitated condition, she was encouraged by the recollection of his delighted reception of her article on him in the *Quarterly* in 1924. The project certainly revived him up to a point. He became energetic enough to be quite troublesome, objecting to the use of his letters and to photographs not altogether flattering; wanting to polish up her prose so that it became more like his own. 'You know how granite he can be,' she sighed to Eddie Marsh.

Any mention of his private life was out of the question which was a pity as she knew a great deal about it. 'No,' she told the curious Virginia who wondered if they had ever been lovers. 'The relations between me and Maurice were always a family affair minus incest, besides which I, averse to society, to clothes and all that, was the last person to attract him in that way. He wanted sheen. His men friends were of any class. His women always of the one.' She admired his writing, the width of his culture, the sensitivity that seemed so at odds with a pronounced grovelling before the wealthy and the pursuit of society women. 'Maurice's loves were always amazing to me. Of the two requisite ingredients in his passions, I don't know which was stronger, ''smartness'' or (to be fair to him), intelligence . . . I feel certain he can never have had one happy affair.'

He was a nuisance to the last, insisting that the proofs be read by Eddie Marsh to obviate the misspellings and other mistakes he was sure Ethel would pass over. If he were well, she exploded, 'I should simply tell him to go to blazes.' Instead, out of the kindness of her heart, she had a special copy of the book made for him in three small volumes, of a size easy for an invalid to manage. Each was inscribed, 'Love and trepidation from Ethel' because she had avoided showing him the complete text, fearing endless correction and delay.

Luckily he was pleased and flattered, sending a long congratulatory telegram signed, 'Your grateful, devoted and overwhelmed Maurice'. Others of her friends, and much of the press, were equally soothing. Virginia, however, thought it her worst book, an opinion with which it is impossible to quarrel. The long chapters summarizing his works are heavy going and hardly counterbalanced by those details of his personal adventures she was permitted to recount.

In 1938 Ethel was eighty and rather fancied the idea of another festival, but it did not come to pass, though some of her works were played. She was put out, feeling it could do nothing but good to have plenty of jollifications in these anxious days. Every thinking person realized that war was practically certain. Hitler had annexed Austria in the spring. Ethel's old friend and supporter, Bruno Walter, was obliged to leave Vienna where he had long been principal conductor of the Philharmonic Orchestra. In the autumn, Chamberlain flew back from Munich clutching the ridiculous piece of paper which he thought guaranteed 'peace with honour' and even, 'peace for our time'.

Ethel's ears now entirely prevented her from enjoying music, including her own. When she tried to listen to a couple of records made especially by Adrian Boult, the only impression she got was of 'poisoned rats behind the wainscote'. There were melancholy moments when her legendary courage almost failed her. 'All books connected with music and specially dealing with my own time (and memories) give me pain because I then feel so bitterly that I am utterly shut off from that world . . . I shun even the musical columns in the press.'[1] Nevertheless, she interested herself in the affairs of the British Women's Symphony Orchestra, a hopeless concern which finally collapsed from inefficiency, despite everything she could do in the way of propping it up with Henry Wood and other notabilities.

Although she was begining to feel her age, as inevitably happens in the ninth decade, she followed Virginia's advice and wrote, more slowly than heretofore, another volume of autobiography, *What Happened Next*, published in June 1940. She visited Virginia towards the end of that month and their old affection flowered over the tea cups. 'Oh you never looked back as you turned the corner of Meck[lenburg] Sqre the other night – so you never saw me waving,' Virginia wrote, 'It was thus that I endeavoured to thank you for coming all that way in the heat. My gratitude, and indeed love, was lost upon your grey coat and straw hat.'

Virginia had a high opinion of *What Happened Next*. The richness and variety of Ethel's life, the vitality of it, the humour and shrewdness with which she viewed the world, made her feel humble, she said. 'Can't think how Ethel ever liked me, such a new moon slip of a life compared with her full orange harvest glow.' The book ends in 1908

---

[1] Letter to Sir Henry Wood.

with the death of Harry. Virginia found it profoundly moving, 'as if the lights lowered and yet one saw everything'. Ethel must press on with another volume. Thirty-two years' worth of adventures and observations lay in her head waiting to be turned into words.

'My book has had a famous press,' Ethel wrote jubilantly to Henry Wood, 'and is selling well'. But time was running out for the old warrior. In the summer of 1940, she developed diabetes, 'Lord how rotten it makes you feel'.[1] She who had hunted and bicycled and tramped over mountains sometimes now wondered 'whether the hundred yards that yet separated me from my homestead could possibly be tackled. Would my legs do it?' She had started a further volume of memoirs and found she could not go on. 'I could no more write, seriously write, I mean, than climb the Matterhorn . . . I do feel that pro tem my brain force, such as it is, has deteriorated,' she told Virginia. 'I just jot down what I am doing, what reading, anything noteworthy in the war, or in my useless, purposeless life of today, such as: "Oct 1. Having finished The Claverings, I am beginning it again to see if I underrated it. (Can mental debility go further than that?) Oct 4. Yes, I think I did underrate The Claverings." '

It much distressed her that she was not able to take up some form of war work. 'I can't do any mortal useful thing in this awful time to help.' Physical weakness sapped her courage. Bombs fell nearby. 'When I really thought this nine inch wall house could but come down, I was secretly terrified.' The housekeeper, however, was in such an abject state of fright, that Ethel rallied and resumed command.

December 1940 found her somewhat recovered, thanks to careful diet and insulin treatment. She took up the new book again, though it was a struggle. 'While I am actually writing it's not so bad, but when I've got to a point at which one can decently stop, disinclination come rushing over one and with a weak sigh of relief one takes up the book of the moment and sinks into an armchair, toes on fender, and as likely as not goes to sleep.' Also, she was by no means certain that the effort was worthwhile. Could she still write? After re-reading a recent article on *The Effect of War on Music Production*, 'I think I never wrote such pointless twaddle'. But she had regained enough spirit to fall in love with a widow, partly Belgian, living some miles off. 'I can understand less than half she says and oh! I do like her so!'

Time is inexorable. On 2 March 1941, 'I suddenly felt I could not go on just now with the autobiography . . . At least I could, but it darkens my days trying to'. She thought she might summon the energy

[1] Letter to Lady Wood.

203

to organize a meeting in Woking to discuss the idea of a United States of Europe after the war. It would be so nice if Harold Nicolson would be guest speaker. He declined the offer.

Although Virginia and Ethel corresponded regularly, they had not met for a long time. It was said that Leonard objected to his wife spending a night away from home and that the day trip to Woking in wartime conditions would be too difficult. But on 5 March 1941, these problems suddenly evaporated. 'O, my dear V, how splendid that you can come "any Wednesday".' Ethel has heard of a chicken which she can get hold of and there's half a bottle of champagne left over from Christmas. 'I think I *may* bore you, am not sure, but it's all part of life. I've been very down of late. The constant rain did it and pain. It rained, I think, essence of rheumatism, but you must try and remember the days when I was a bright young thing, two years under 80.' The great occasion was fixed for April.

Nothing in all this prepared Ethel for the fact that it was Virginia who was down, Virginia who was in torment. On 28 March 1941, realizing she was going mad, fearing she would not recover this time, or at least be unable to write again, she drowned herself. No one, except Leonard, imagined it might happen. 'I had no idea only a week before when I saw her that there was any such probability,' wrote Vanessa Bell on 8 April. Even if I had I can't see even now what one could have done, for any attempt to watch over her would have made things worse at once. There always had to be these dangerous moments – as often before – when she was ill enough to do such a thing but not collapsed enough to be really controlled.'

'She was the centre of the one horse life I have led since music left me in the lurch,' Ethel exclaimed to Henry Wood on 25 April. 'Her wonderful estimate of me as a writer . . . her wonderful affection such as only a genius can give made up my life . . . I am glad I never knew that she occasionally felt that past malady might return, and anything more terrible than that I cannot imagine.' For eleven years Virginia had reigned supreme in Ethel's heart. None of the innumerable minor attractions and passions she had experienced since 1930 had affected this relationship, so strongly maternal and therefore so essentially different from previous loves.

The shades were fast descending on Ethel too. Her head remained clear, but her bodily health gave way. The diabetes was permanent and, on top of that, she was continually attacked by bronchitis, pneumonia, blood pressure, rheumatism and all the multitude of ailments which accompany extreme age when the organism is losing the fight to stay alive. Her refusal to give in to weakness resulted in a series of falls. 'Don't expect to find even the ghost of the old Ethel unless in the joy your appearance will give her,' she wrote to Henry Wood in a shaky hand on 28 February 1942. '*I am done for* . . . But after all, I've had a good life.' 'Don't come, dear friends,' she continues on 5 June, 'to see what remains of your Ethel.'

She was now stone deaf. Conversation had to be carried on by means of pencil and paper. Memories sustained her. 'I have hardly let an hour pass that I do not find myself plunged in recollections of our Sicily tour,' she wrote to the equally aged Edith Somerville on 22 July 1943. 'I live a good deal in bed and people are very kind to me . . . I find it impossible to read a book except those I almost know by heart (like Dickens) . . . I am really fairly well, but the 17 or 18 little concussions I have behind me make me feel (and no doubt *it is so*) very, very stupid.'

In April 1944 she fell in the night during an encounter with the bucket she used as a chamber pot and was not discovered until morning. She seemed to rally and looked forward to a visit from Henry Wood, busying herself with questions of food and drink, no simple matter in those rationed times. There were guests on 5 May also, who were reminded of Wagner as she lay on her uncomfortable old iron bedstead. On 8 May 1944, she lost the last battle. As she ascended to heaven, Martin informed Edith Somerville later that week, her *Mass* was played by the best deceased musicians, Cameron Somerville conducting. She was reported unimpressed with his performance.

So died one of the most vivid characters in the musical and literary circle, one whose adult life had spanned the 1880's to the 1940's, several wars, a great revolution in ideas and manners; whose experience of the world had bred a profound humanity; whose titanic energy had worn out many a lesser soul; whose wit and warmth had delighted legions of faithful friends; whose love had been returned by some of the most eminent and the most diverse women of the day.

People remembered in particular her honesty, her downrightness, the careless way she dressed which was so appropriate to her character. They recalled tremendous fights and shouting matches that ended in roars of laughter; how frightening she could be and yet how fundamentally kind; how interesting and full of gaiety was her conversation, provided she could be kept off the alleged conspiracy of men against her music. No amount of pointing to the public honours she had received and the number of times her works had been performed up and down the country and on the continent could bring her to reason on this subject.

Then there was her singing. It seemed to express another Ethel, lonely, unworldly, ecstatic. 'The whole performance was so complete and so poignantly perfect,' wrote Maurice Baring.[1] 'The rare and exquisite quality and delicacy of her voice: the strange thrill and wail . . . the whirlwind of passion and feeling.' And the ancient Edith Somerville never forgot that far off first meeting during which she had been 'transported to a place of beauty more wonderful even than the beauty of Killarney'.[2]

Some declared she wrote better than she composed. Did not her music tend to the Germanic, the old-fashioned, whereas her books were remarkable for their unselfconscious style and a modern outlook on life and morals? With all the fury of a dedicated artist, Ethel repudiated this view as a stupidity, an heresy, an abomination; and she was right. Though lively and sufficiently out of the ordinary to arouse the enthusiasm of many critics besides Virginia Woolf, her books cannot be said to have added to the stock of English literature. The case is otherwise with her music. There she has a definitive place. It has been remarked[3] that *The Wreckers* would have ensured her musical future in any country but the England of 1906 where operas, almost all foreign, were only performed for a short summer season at Covent Garden. No survey of English music is complete without a reference to *The Wreckers* and to her *Mass in D. The Boatswain's Mate* comes high on her list of achievements, as does her *Concerto for Violin, Horn and Orchestra.* Her work 'remains an important part of that new seriousness of purpose that characterized the renaissance of English music'[4] from the late nineteenth century onwards.

Her failing, if such it should be called, was not lack of power or sincerity, but rather of purpose which led to uneven quality. Bold harmonic experiments are often not carried through. Original themes peter out. The influences of the great masters Beethoven, Brahms, Wagner were strangely entangled in this divided soul with those of a lighter kind, such as Sullivan and the composers for the military bands with which she had been familiar since childhood. This dichotomy prevented the expression of a truly personal style, supreme individualist as she was in all other aspects of life. Yet, at her best

[1] *The Puppet Show of Memory.*

[2] *The Times* 31 May 1944.

[3] See Martin Cooper in *The New Oxford History of Music*, 1974.

[4] See *The New Grove Dictionary of Music and Musicians* 1980.

she could produce an impression of grandeur on the one hand and, on the other, effects of surpassing tenderness and beauty. She has been unjustly neglected these past forty years.

Appendix

Ethel Smyth's chief compositions are listed here.
Operas:
Fantasio, 1894.
Der Wald, 1901.
The Wreckers, 1904.
The Boatswain's Mate, 1914.
Fête Galante (opera-ballet), 1923.
Entente Cordiale, 1925.
Orchestral works:
Overture Antony and Cleopatra, 1890.
Serenade in D, 1890.
Concerto for Violin, Horn and Orchestra, 1927.
Soli, Chorus and Orchestra:
Mass in D, 1891.
The Prison, 1930.
Chorus and Orchestra:
Hey Nonny No! 1911.
Sleepless Dreams, 1912.
A Spring Canticle, 1926.
Unaccompanied Chorus:
Songs of Sunrise, (1) Laggard Dawn, (2) 1910, (3) March of the
Women, 1911.
Dreamings, 1920.
Soul's Joy, 1923.
Chamber Music:
String Quintet Op. 1, 1884.
Sonata for 'Cello and Piano Op. 5, 1887.
Sonata for Violin and Piano Op. 7, 1887.
String Quartet, 1902–12.
Two trios for Violin, Oboe and Piano, 1927.
Organ:
Five short Chorale Preludes, 1913.
Prelude on a traditional Irish melody, 1939.
Songs:
With piano accompaniment: Lieder und Balladen Op. 3, c. 1886.
Lieder Op. 4, c. 1886.

Appendix

With chamber music accompaniment: Four Songs, 1908.
With orchestral accompaniment: Three songs, 1913.

Three Moods of the Sea, 1913.

There is also a certain amount of unpublished chamber and piano music of lesser interest, some unfinished.

Sources

MANUSCRIPT SOURCES

Collections of Ethel Smyth's unpublished letters are to be found in this country at: the British Library; King's College Library, Cambridge; Queen's University, Belfast. And in America at: the Walter Clinton Jackson Library, University of North Carolina, Greensboro; the Berg Collection, New York Public Library; the Humanities Research Center, Austin, Texas.

Edith Somerville's letters are at Queen's University, Belfast.

BIBLIOGRAPHY

A complete bibliography covering so long and varied a life as Ethel Smyth's would run to hundreds of volumes. I have therefore listed here only those works appearing in the footnotes, together with a few absolute essentials.

Baring, Maurice, *The Puppet Show of Memory*, Heinemann 1922.

Beecham, Thomas, *A Mingled Chime*, Hutchinson, 1979.

Bell, Anne Olivier (ed.), *The Diary of Virginia Woolf*, vol 3, Hogarth Press, 1980.

Bell, Quentin, *Virginia Woolf*, Chatto and Windus, 1972.

Benson, E. F., *Mother*, Hodder and Stoughton, 1925.

Collis, Maurice, *Somerville and Ross*, Faber, 1968.

Henschel, Sir George, *Musings and Memories of a Musician*, Macmillan, 1918.

Neilson, Francis, *My Life in Two Worlds*, C. C. Nelson, Wisconsin, 1952.

Newmarch, Rosa, *Tchaikovsky*, Wm Reeves, 1908.

Nicolson, Nigel (ed.), *The Letters of Virginia Woolf*, vols 4, 5, 6, Hogarth Press, 1978–80.

Pankhurst, Christabel, *Unshackled*, Hutchinson 1959.

Pankhurst, Sylvia, *The Suffragette Movement*, Virago, 1977.

Ponsonby, Magdalen, *Mary Ponsonby, a Memoir*, Murray, 1927.

Raeburn, Antonia, *The Militant Suffragettes*, Michael Joseph, 1973.

Sitwell, Osbert, *Left Hand, Right Hand*, Macmillan 1945–50.

Smyth, Ethel, *Impressions That Remained*, Longmans Green 1919.

        Streaks of Life,, Longmans Green 1921.

        A Three Legged Tour in Greece, Heinemann, 1927.

Sources

A Final Burning of Boats, Longmans Green, 1928.

Female Pipings in Eden, Peter Davies, 1933.

Beecham and Pharaoh, Chapman and Hall, 1935.

As Time Went On, Longmans Green, 1936.

Inordinate(?) Affection, Cresset, 1936.

Maurice Baring, Heinemann, 1938.

What Happened Next, Longmans Green, 1940.

Somerville, E.OE, and Ross, Martin, *Happy Days*, Longmans Green, 1946.

St John, Christopher, *Ethel Smyth*, Longmans Green 1959.

Storrs, Ronald, *Orientations*, Nicholson and Watson, 1943.

Walter, Bruno, *Theme and Variations*, Hamish Hamilton, 1947.

Wood, Henry J., *My Life of Music*, Gollancz, 1938.

Woolf, Virginia, *A Writer's Diary* (ed. Leonard Woolf), Hogarth Press, 1953.

Index

Index

215